973.925   Greene, John Robert,
GRE   1955-

           The presidency of
           Gerald R. Ford.

$15.95

DATE			

6/95

BAKER & TAYLOR

AMERICAN PRESIDENCY SERIES

George Washington, Forrest McDonald
John Adams, Ralph Adams Brown
Thomas Jefferson, Forrest McDonald
James Madison, Robert Allen Rutland
John Quincy Adams, Mary W. M. Hargreaves
Andrew Jackson, Donald B. Cole
Martin Van Buren, Major L. Wilson
William Henry Harrison & John Tyler, Norma Lois Peterson
James K. Polk, Paul H. Bergeron
Zachary Taylor & Millard Fillmore, Elbert B. Smith
Franklin Pierce, Larry Gara
James Buchanan, Elbert B. Smith
Abraham Lincoln, Phillip Shaw Paludan
Andrew Johnson, Albert Castel
Rutherford B. Hayes, Ari Hoogenboom
James A. Garfield & Chester A. Arthur, Justus D. Doenecke
Grover Cleveland, Richard E. Welch, Jr.
Benjamin Harrison, Homer E. Socolofsky & Allan B. Spetter
William McKinley, Lewis L. Gould
Theodore Roosevelt, Lewis L. Gould
William Howard Taft, Paolo E. Coletta
Woodrow Wilson, Kendrick A. Clements
Warren G. Harding, Eugene P. Trani & David L. Wilson
Herbert C. Hoover, Martin L. Fausold
Harry S. Truman, Donald R. McCoy
Dwight D. Eisenhower, Chester J. Pach, Jr., & Elmo Richardson
John F. Kennedy, James N. Giglio
Lyndon B. Johnson, Vaughn Davis Bornet
Gerald R. Ford, John Robert Greene
James Earl Carter, Jr., Burton I. Kaufman

The Presidency of

GERALD R.
FORD

John Robert Greene

UNIVERSITY PRESS OF KANSAS

Published by the University Press of Kansas (Lawrence, Kansas
66049), which was organized by the Kansas Board of Regents and is
operated and funded by Emporia State University, Fort Hays State
University, Kansas State University, Pittsburg State University,
the University of Kansas, and Wichita State University

Library of Congress Cataloging-in-Publication Data

Greene, John Robert, 1955–
The presidency of Gerald R. Ford / John Robert Greene.
p.   cm. — (American presidency series)
Includes bibliographical references (p.) and index.
ISBN 0-7006-0638-6 (cloth : alk. paper).
ISBN 0-7006-0639-4 (paper : alk. paper)
1. United States—Politics and government—1974–1977.   2. Ford,
Gerald R., 1913–   I. Title.   II. Series.
E865.G74   1995
973.925′092—dc20   94-20037

British Library Cataloguing in Publication Data is available.

Printed in the United States of America
10 9 8 7 6 5 4 3 2 1

For Patty, T. J., and Christopher

CONTENTS

FOREWORD

The aim of the American Presidency Series is to present historians and the general reading public with interesting, scholarly assessments of the various presidential administrations. These interpretive surveys are intended to cover the broad ground between biographies, specialized monographs, and journalistic accounts. As such, each will be a comprehensive work that will draw upon original sources and pertinent secondary literature yet leave room for the author's own analysis and interpretation.

Volumes in the series will present the data essential to understanding the administration under consideration. Particularly, each book will treat the then current problems facing the United States and its people and how the president and his associates felt about, thought about, and worked to cope with these problems. Attention will be given to how the office developed and operated during the president's tenure. Equally important will be consideration of the vital relationships between the president, his staff, the executive officers, Congress, foreign representatives, the judiciary, state officials, the public, political parties, the press, and influential private citizens. The series will also be concerned with how this unique American institution—the presidency—was viewed by the presidents, and with what results.

All this will be set, insofar as possible, in the context not only of contemporary politics but also of economics, international relations, law, morals, public administration, religion, and thought. Such a broad approach is necessary to understanding, for a presidential administration is more than the elected and appointed officers composing it since its work so often reflects the major problems, anxieties, and glories of the nation. In short, the authors in this series will strive to recount and evaluate the record of each administration and to identify its distinctiveness and relationships to the past, its own time, and the future.

The General Editors

PREFACE

In early April 1989 several hundred students of the American presidency converged upon New York's Hofstra University to discuss a presidency which, to that point, had been generally ignored by scholars—that of Gerald R. Ford. Throughout the three days of the conference, "Restoring the Presidency," scholarly panels analyzed the minutiae of the Ford years with the help of over seventy alumni of the administration, Congress, and the press. Ford, then seventy-five years old and looking trim and fit, was also in attendance. Joking with an afternoon audience of conference participants, Ford claimed to be "very, very glad, that still today, anybody wants to talk about [me] for three whole days."

Yet there were many people who questioned the need for such a detailed discussion. Most of the reporters who covered the conference were clearly surprised at the scholarly interest being taken in Ford (one earnest young correspondent, representing a large eastern newspaper, asked me if I was writing about Ford only because all the better topics had been taken). The press spent most of their time talking with scholars and former members of the administration in an attempt to uncover tidbits of information on Ford's pardon of Richard Nixon and whether a deal had been made between the two men before Nixon's resignation from the presidency. Their accounts of the symposium, however, essentially ignored both the pardon and the rather substantive amount of scholarly material on Ford's domestic and foreign policies that had been presented. Rather, the vast majority of the stories written about the Hofstra conference proclaimed that the legacy of the Ford administration was, in the words of *Newsday*'s Arnold Abrams, that although there had been "no landmark legislation, no precedent-setting policy, no strong visual image frozen in national memory . . . Gerald R. Ford's administration will be given high marks by historians for restoring calm and maintaining political continuity in a country torn by turmoil."[1]

In the little scholarship that has been offered through the early 1990s on the presidency of Gerald R. Ford, the central theme usually has been this issue of healing. Ford's years in office are treated as a period that bound up the most festering wounds of Watergate and kept the Republic from impaling itself further on that butcher knife but that did little else—the classic caretaker view. Even after an international gathering such as the Hofstra conference, the vast majority of scholars treat Ford's tenure as that of a caretaker presidency. The assumption seems to be that healing the nation after the turmoil of Vietnam and Watergate was really an *easy* thing to do since we had a generally honest man in the White House; Ford's genuine honesty smoothed things over, and policy—an area in which Ford was never really *expected* to perform— need not be critically analyzed. To this point at least, Ford has simply not been subjected to the same rigorous analyses as either his predecessors or successors have been.

Thus it is safe to say that the tenure of Gerald R. Ford is one of the most misunderstood of any administration in American history. As is the case with the many presidencies that followed a period of strife in our history, the Ford administration clearly saw that it needed to offer the nation a "time to heal"—an opportunity to move the country away from the tumult caused by both Vietnam and Watergate and into a period of more stability. Given the transgressions of the past, the task of healing the nation would be monumental, and Ford never underestimated it. But never did the Ford administration see this role as its only one. The 865 days of the Ford presidency tell a story of an administration struggling to create itself, to escape the long shadow of the Nixon administration by offering its own agenda to the American people. The pardon, as we shall see, is the seminal event in the planning of both these objectives as Ford sought to evict the ghost of Nixon past from his White House and to begin anew, with a Ford administration.

In this book, then, I propose to analyze just how well Gerald R. Ford succeeded both in healing our nation and in establishing a Ford administration. For scholars of the presidency, such an approach would seem to suggest the obvious since, after all, I am proposing to study Ford's tenure in full, as any other American presidency might be. Yet as of 1994 there is no serious scholarly study of the Ford presidency. One wonders why, some twenty years after the fact, that this is the case—thoughtful analyses of the Carter and Reagan tenures, based on primary-source research, have been in print for several years, and there is certainly a surprising wealth of manuscript and primary-source material available on the Ford years, much of it at the Gerald R. Ford Presidential Library in Ann Arbor, Michigan. Perhaps there has been an assumption by scholars that it is enough with Ford merely to *like* him, to recognize, as did the pollsters at the end of his term, that he left office as one of our most personally popular presidents, and to give him credit for healing the land. Certainly the tone of much of the available Ford literature suggests this. Yet this assumption has done the Ford presidency and our history a grave disservice. The period from 1974 to 1976 deserves to be analyzed and understood fully by scholars; that task is only beginning.

There are many people to whom I am grateful. For financial support, I thank the Gerald R. Ford Foundation and Rockefeller University for their generous grants-in-aid. I am also grateful to the faculty and administration at Cazenovia College for their patience with me as I traveled, researched, and wrote. Particular thanks are due President Stephen M. Schneeweiss, Vice Presidents for Academic Affairs Carolyn B. Ware and Adelaide Van Titus, and Assistant Deans for Academic Affairs Frederic M. Williams and Margery Pinet.

Gerald R. Ford took the time out of his busy schedule to be interviewed. Within his administration, as well as from the circle of knowledgeable political players during the Ford presidency, the list of those who gave time to answer my questions is thankfully lengthy. I have cited their contributions in the notes to this book. I am also grateful to A. James Reichley for allowing me to quote from transcripts of his interviews with members of the Nixon and Ford administrations.

The Gerald R. Ford Library is the epitome of what a research archive should be. Not only is it automated (the Ford Library was the test site for a data-retrieval system called PRESNET, which allows archivists to search a manuscript down to the actual document level and to present researchers with a detailed report to aid their work), but it is incredibly user-friendly on the human level. The staff of Library Director Frank Mackaman is, for my money, the best in the business. I thank Supervisory Archivist David Horrocks and Geir Gunderson, Ken Hafeli, Dick Holzhausen, Karen Holzhausen, Bill McNitt, Nancy Mirshah, Jenny Sternaman, Helmi Raaska, and Leesa Tobin. It should also be noted that this book, thanks to the efforts of the staff at the Ford Library, is supported by a number of declassified documents, particularly in the area of foreign policy, that are appearing for the first time. I am also indebted to the staff of my home library at Cazenovia College. Library Director Stanley Kozaczka and Gina DeVesty, Martin Breen, Nan Bailey, and Jennifer Rice have been more than patient with the research requests of a full-time teacher. I also traveled to or otherwise consulted over fifty other archives that held material on the Ford presidency. A list of those people who helped me in that endeavor, particularly the research archivists who answered every question, no matter how trivial, would be too long to include here. Suffice it to say that without archivists, historians would be left only to surmise rather than to hypothesize.

The University Press of Kansas is a first-class house; working with them has been a pleasure. I would particularly like to thank Director Fred Woodward and Megan Schoeck, Susan Schott, and Claire Sutton.

Hearing a professor talk incessantly about his work is consistently pleasant only for the professor, and I am very grateful to my students for their patience with me. Several have written course papers over the years that have led me to rethink my conclusions on the Ford presidency; the work of Susan Basile and Rose Burdziakowski has been used here with much profit. One of these students has given more of her time and effort toward the completion of this book than I could possibly have hoped for. I am indebted to Elizabeth Harwick, who served as an outstanding research assistant, for her invaluable assistance throughout every phase of this project.

Over the course of the years during which this book was evolving, several portions of it have gone through a developmental stage elsewhere. Material in chapters 2, 4, and 11 dealing with the White House staff was originally presented to the Center for the Study of the Presidency's Leadership Conference in fall 1988. Material on the evolution of the Ford image was derived from an April 1989 address, "'A Nice Guy Who Worked at the Job': The Dilemma of the Ford Image," delivered to the Hofstra University Conference on the Ford Presidency. Finally, the material on Ford's Clemency Program found in chapter 9 was presented to an International Conference on the Vietnam War, held at Notre Dame University in November 1993. Professor Shirley Anne Warshaw of Gettysburg College read early drafts of the first chapters and offered many prescient suggestions. I am grateful to those panels and critics who read portions of this work in progress, but I am particularly indebted to Donald R. McCoy and Clifford S. Griffin of the University of Kansas and to Homer E. Socolofsky of Kansas State University—the general editors of the American Presidency Series. Their thorough and detailed assessment of the manuscript brought my effort into a much clearer focus.

Countless others have given me support both when I wanted it and when I needed it. A few of them are the people of Belleville, Michigan, Faith Dickinson, the Eisenberg family, Jesse Lott, Deborah Nygren, Margot Papworth, Herbert Parmet, Robert Shogan, Virginia Solomon, Donna Gates Thomas, Ronald Waite, the Webster family, and Dolores Weiss. It goes without saying, however, that the conclusions made in these pages bear my own imprimatur.

Ultimately, it is my family who makes my work as a teacher and as a writer possible by realizing its importance to me. It is to them that this book is—again—dedicated with love.

1

★ ★ ★ ★ ★

"THANK GOD, IT WORKED"

Leslie Lynch King was born in Omaha, Nebraska, on 14 July 1913. In 1914, his mother, Dorothy, left her husband (later the boy would remember that "I heard that he hit her frequently") and took her child to live in her parents' home in Grand Rapids, Michigan. Through her church, she met Gerald R. Ford, Sr., who owned and ran a paint and varnish company. They were married on 1 February 1916. Although he was never formally adopted by his stepfather, young Leslie took his name—Gerald R. Ford, Jr.[1]

During the Great Depression, Ford, Sr., showed perseverance and a desire to take care of his own. His company provided a necessity in the manufacturing of the city's primary product—furniture—but even so, Ford's company was no more immune from the financial calamity of the 1930s than any other small business. In order to keep his company alive, he took home only five dollars a week in salary, and he paid his workers the same amount. Although the bank foreclosed on his home and he and his family had to move to a more modest rental, he kept his business, and his income was steady. His financial situation was, as one Grand Rapids friend remembered, "better than most of us."[2]

As a result, Ford was able to keep his family relatively well insulated from the horrors of the depression. Throughout his youth, Jerry, or Junior, as his family and friends knew him, worked with his brothers in his father's business, gluing on labels and filing paint cans. He was a Boy Scout, attaining the rank of Eagle Scout. College was out of the question without outside help, but his high school awarded Ford a $100

1

per year athletic scholarship (equivalent to a year's tuition) to attend the University of Michigan. While studying liberal arts in Ann Arbor, Ford augmented this scholarship by working at a hospital and, every two or three months, by selling his blood.

It was football, however, not academics that consumed young Ford. While at South High in Grand Rapids, he was named All-City Center for three consecutive years and was chosen in his senior year for the All-State Team in 1931. At Michigan, Ford developed into one of the country's best centers. In the balloting for the 1935 Collegiate All-Star Game played against the Chicago Bears at Soldier Field, Ford was the number-four votegetter among fans around the nation (he played a few minutes toward the end; the Bears won, 5–0). Both the Detroit Lions and the Green Bay Packers of the National Football League offered Ford a contract (the football draft was not instituted until the following year). He assessed the situation as dispassionately and practically as he would any other decision of his career and decided that "pro football probably wouldn't lead me anywhere."[3]

Instead, in fall 1935 Ford accepted a position at Yale University. For three years he worked as an assistant line coach for the varsity team, head coach for the junior varsity team, and, despite never having boxed, as head coach of the boxing team—for a yearly salary of $2,400. He decided he would like to study law, and in 1938, he was allowed to register part-time for a few law courses on a trial basis. In 1939 he secured the school's permission to attend classes full-time, and he got his law degree in 1941, graduating in the top third of his class.

Ford returned to Grand Rapids after graduation and rekindled a friendship with a college fraternity brother, Philip Buchen. The son of a Sheboygan attorney, Buchen, who had been stricken with polio while a junior in high school, attended the University of Michigan for both his undergraduate and his law degrees, graduating Phi Beta Kappa and serving as editor of the Law Review. Ford and Buchen opened their own law firm in Grand Rapids, but thanks to Pearl Harbor, the firm existed for less than a year.

Ford enlisted in the navy in April 1942, and because he had a college degree, he was commissioned an ensign. Throughout 1942 he trained recruits in the V-5 flight school at the University of North Carolina, Chapel Hill. Not having a teacher's temperament, Ford requested active duty and was sent to Norfolk Naval Station for gunnery training and then assigned to the USS *Monterey*. On 18 December 1944, while on a mission in the South Pacific, a vicious typhoon caused the carrier to pitch wildly, and Ford was thrown from the flight deck onto the catwalk below; he narrowly missed being swept overboard. In December 1945 at age thirty-two, Ford was discharged as a lieutenant with ten battle stars on his theater ribbon.

Ford returned home to a political climate in Grand Rapids that was more favorable for challenging a sitting incumbent than it had been for many years. The congressman from Grand Rapids, Bartel Jonkman, was a four-term leading Republican member of the House Foreign Affairs Committee and an unreconstructed conservative who opposed aid to Europe. In 1948 Ford announced that he would challenge Jonkman in the Republican party primary. Despite Ford's vigorous campaign, Jonkman never took the challenge seriously. He returned home too late to campaign effectively, condescendingly refused to debate Ford, and angered Leonard Woodcock, the United Auto Workers' representative in western Michigan, with his cavalier attitude. As a result, both Grand Rapids newspapers not only supported Ford but predicted his victory.

For his part, Ford was not above capitalizing on his war record. His campaign headquarters was an old army quonset hut set up on a vacant lot in the downtown area. Ford was a tireless campaigner, once shocking a farmer when he offered to help him with the milking so that the candidate might make his pitch. In a major upset, Ford won the primary that September, outpolling Jonkman by 9,300 votes; his margin of victory in November was even wider. From that first victory, Congressman Ford would never poll less than 60 percent of the vote in any election in which he ran in Grand Rapids' Fifth Congressional District.[4]

On 9 September 1961 Ford was named the Congressman's Congressman by the American Political Science Association, undoubtedly one of his most cherished awards. This was the goal that he had set for himself from the first day of his entry into political life—to be the consummate national legislator. At first glance, Ford seemed the legislative technocrat, developing a knowledge of the intricacies of budgetary matters. He was appointed to serve on the Appropriations Committee, and he would eventually be put on the army panel of the Defense subcommittee as well as on the subcommittee to appropriate funds for the Central Intelligence Agency (CIA). Ford was no boring workaholic, however; he reveled in the clubby nature of Capitol Hill. He typified the legislator that *New York Times* reporter Hedrick Smith has described as "Old Breed"—the backslapping, innerroom-dealing pol whose strength lay not in a media-projected image but in an ability to play the insider's game.[5]

Ford's entry into this congressional club led to the forging of a relationship that would affect the rest of his political career. In 1947 fifteen junior Republicans had formed the Chowder and Marching Club, meeting each Wednesday to discuss upcoming legislation and to plan their tactics. Ford joined the group in 1949 and became acquainted with charter member Richard Nixon. Their relationship began in earnest toward the end of the Truman administration, when the two men worked together on a scandal surrounding the Federal Housing Authority. Ford was one of the first to support the idea of Nixon as Dwight Eisenhower's running mate in 1952, and despite that fall's crisis over the discovery of a secret fund set up by Nixon supporters, Ford joined Republican conservatives including Herbert Hoover, Karl Mundt, and Robert Taft in refusing to desert Nixon. Along with others he pressed Eisenhower to keep Nixon on the ticket in 1956. Returning the favor, Nixon floated Ford's name as a possible running mate in 1960. Although Ford was never Nixon's first choice, the attendant publicity thrust him into the national spotlight for the first time.[6]

The end of the Eisenhower presidency was the end of an era for the Republican party as well. The party's right wing, best represented throughout the 1940s and 1950s by Ohio senator Robert Taft, had consistently called for fiscal austerity, refused to sanction American intervention in world affairs, and preached vigilance against domestic communism. Despite the popular appeal of his views, however, the dour Taft had three times proven incapable of gaining his party's presidential nomination. Two party moderates—Thomas Dewey and Dwight Eisenhower—had carried the party's banner against the Democrats. The stunning margin of Eisenhower's electoral victories in 1952 and 1956, his immense personal popularity, and the ignominious collapse of the anticommunist crusade led by Wisconsin senator Joseph McCarthy had sent the Republican Right into hiding during the last years of the Eisenhower presidency. In 1960 they did not even bother challenging Richard Nixon—a converted Taftian conservative who had, as vice president, developed into an internationalist in world affairs—for the party's nomination. Nixon's loss to John F. Kennedy and the increase of Kennedy's popularity sent Republicans of all ideologies scurrying for a usable issue, however. No moderate could be found—New York governor Nelson Rockefeller showed no interest in a race against the popular president. Virtually by default, Arizona senator Barry Goldwater, heir to the Taftian conservatives, was soon being touted as the front-runner for the 1964 race against Kennedy. Yet in 1962 Goldwater's conservatism, a strident formula of anticommunism and ultrapatriotism, appealed to a much narrower segment of the party than had the conservatism of Robert Taft. It was soon clear that Goldwater could never defeat the popular Kennedy in 1964: stunning off-year gains for the Democrats in 1962, generally attributed to Kennedy's deft handling of the Cuban missile crisis that October, seemed to confirm this assessment. As a result, a large number of younger, more moderate Republicans—infinitely more interested in winning elections than in taking a philosophical stand—moved to recapture their party from its right wing.

In January 1963 a group the press dubbed the Young Turks engineered the victory of Ford, then forty-nine years old, over the sixty-nine-year-old chairman of the House Republican Conference (Caucus), Charles B. Hoeven of Iowa. The Turks included Michigan's Melvin Laird and Robert Griffin, New York's Charles Goodell, and Illinois' Donald Rumsfeld. The victory, stunning not only because of Ford's youth but because successful challenges to entrenched leadership were rare in the 1960s, made Ford the third-ranking Republican in the House.

Ford was no longer an anonymous midwestern congressman. Moreover, his status as one of the party's most upwardly mobile young leaders was only enhanced by the Republican party's massive electoral loss in 1964. In the months following the November 1963 assassination of Kennedy, Goldwater had worked tirelessly to broaden his base of support within the party, and his success, particularly with the party's younger members, was instrumental in his turning back a strong challenge from Rockefeller for the nomination. But although Goldwater had captured the prize that had so long eluded Taft, Republican conservatism was as yet unappealing to the mainstream American voter. Lyndon Johnson's landslide defeat of Goldwater and the accompanying Republican loss of thirty-eight seats in the House led to a renewed effort from a now larger group of Young Turks to rid themselves of the old Republican leadership in the House. Through their efforts (Ford contributed little, taking three separate vacations during the postelection period), Ford was elected minority leader in January 1965, ousting Indiana's Charles Halleck by a vote of 73 to 67.

Ford proved himself to be a vibrant, if somewhat predictable, leader of his party in the House. No iconoclast, he had been a safe choice to represent the House minority on the President's Commission to Investigate the Assassination of President Kennedy. Johnson did not appoint Ford to the Warren Commission because he was an administration favorite, however. Virulently opposed to almost every measure of Johnson's Great Society, Ford also argued against the administration's Vietnam policy on the grounds that the president was not fighting the war vigorously enough. Ford's attacks, often made in a nationally televised forum with Senate minority leader Everett Dirksen—dubbed the "Ev

5

and Jerry Show"—served largely to irritate the president. According to Ford, the shows prompted Johnson to lash out at him personally—thus Johnson's famous quip that Ford had played football once too often without a helmet. Brushing off the comment as pure politics, Ford professed to believe that such Johnsonisms were due to the president's "frustration."[7]

Aside from angering Johnson, Ford's attacks on the administration enhanced his growing reputation within his party. In 1968 Nixon was serious about adding Ford to the ticket and offered him the position at the Republican convention. By that point, however, Ford was eyeing the job of Speaker of the House; with just a shift of thirty-one seats, not impossible in the tumultuous political year of 1968, he would have the job. Thus Ford declined Nixon's offer.[8] The eventual choice of Maryland governor Spiro Agnew proved to be inspired. Agnew held the party's right wing in line, Nixon appealed to the moderates, and together they narrowly defeated Hubert Humphrey and George Wallace. Still, the closeness of the three-way race did not provide for a congressional majority for the Republicans, and Ford served the new president in the role of minority leader.

Nixon's White House staff thought little of the Republican leadership in Congress. White House Domestic Policy adviser John Ehrlichman noted in his memoirs that the first time he met Ford, "I was not impressed," observing that Ford "wasn't thrilled to be harnessed to the Nixon administration," and, echoing Johnson's slight, Ehrlichman judged that Ford "wasn't excessively bright."[9] Ford generally shared their disdain, writing that "the White House staff viewed Congress in much the same way that the chairman of the board of a large corporation regards his regional sales managers. We existed, they seemed to believe, only to follow their instructions."[10] Yet Ford was loyal to the Nixon administration to a virtual fault. He supported the president on 83 percent of House votes and was one of seventy congressmen who voted to sustain each of Nixon's vetoes during the politically difficult year of 1973.[11]

For his part, Nixon respected Ford's legislative talents and appreciated his loyalty. He was also quite willing to make use of that loyalty to carry out some of the more questionable goals of the administration. One such target was Supreme Court Justice William O. Douglas. Ford professed to be offended not so much by Douglas's liberal viewpoints as by his liberal lifestyle. Ford's midwestern values led him to find fault with Douglas's receiving payment for an article published in a magazine containing sexually explicit photographs and with the septuagenarian's fourth marriage to a twenty-three-year-old lawyer. When it was revealed in early 1969 that Douglas had been serving as paid president and director of a foundation that had links to Mafia chieftain Meyer Lansky, Ford quietly began an investigation into Douglas's past.[12]

Ford's activity on the issue played neatly into the hands of the Nixon administration, which was having problems of its own regarding the Court. On 18 August 1969 Nixon had nominated Clement F. Haynsworth to fill the vacancy created by the resignation of embattled justice Abe Fortas. Within three weeks, Haynsworth's confirmation chances hit a serious snag when it was revealed that he had held stock in a company that had had business dealings with a party to a 1965 suit before Haynsworth's Fourth Circuit Court. The charges were innocuous and had long since been resolved; however, they were used by Democrats, particularly Indiana's Birch Bayh, to attack the nomination and the administration.

Nixon moved to save the Haynsworth nomination by putting White House support behind Ford's investigation of Douglas. During a 9 October 1969 White House meeting, Nixon instructed Ehrlichman to "call Ford—talk now—impeach sitting Justice."[13] Robert Hartmann, then serving as Ford's chief assistant, later claimed, "I have no evidence that any direct contact [occurred] between Nixon and Ford on this matter."[14] Indeed, there is no solid evidence to support a claim that Ford was working under White House orders. Nevertheless, in early November Ford's previously quiet investigation found its way into the newspapers, the resulting publicity leading many in the press to conclude that Ford was holding Douglas hostage for Haynsworth. If either the administration or Ford had intended to use the threat of a Douglas impeachment to pressure Congress into confirming Haynsworth, it boomeranged; Haynsworth was defeated on November 21 by a 55 to 45 vote. Nixon nominated G. Harrold Carswell in January 1970, another southerner whose record on civil rights was even more flawed than that of Haynsworth. It was a poor choice, but Nixon could ill afford a second embarrassment. Many individuals close to both Nixon and Ford have privately speculated that Ford continued with his investigation of Douglas on orders from the White House, hoping to keep Congress' feet to the fire—however, once again there is no evidence to conclude this indisputably. Yet for whatever reason, be it his own puritanism or orders from the White House, Ford advised Hartmann to keep the investigation going over the winter months.[15] If the investigation was continued in order to put pressure on Carswell's foes, it again failed: Carswell's nomination was defeated on April 9.

Nixon was seething; demands for revenge were in the air. The White House may have approached another Republican congressman who had been calling for Douglas's head, Virginia's William Scott, to demand that Ford speed up his investigation of Douglas. Ford told Hartmann that Scott had indeed approached him and had given him an ultimatum: "If I wasn't willing to impeach Douglas, then next Tuesday, by God, they would do it in spite of me. And you know, they can." Rather than feeling gratified because his idea was coming to fruition, Ford was nervous about the prospect of a Douglas impeachment. He had hoped that his investigation would make Douglas resign, but he did not want an impeachment vote, a vote he believed would fail. Ford thought that this misfire would "widen the gulf between [GOP] conservatives, moderates, and liberals. . . . I had a duty to try to prevent that from happening."[16] Clearly such an outcome would do Ford's career little good.

Ford then took a step that can be seen only as damage control. In a speech on the floor of the Congress on 15 April 1970, Ford summarized the findings of his investigation and then called for a select panel to decide whether further steps toward impeachment were warranted. But events had moved beyond Ford, the Democrats having realized that they could severely embarrass the administration if a vote to impeach the justice failed. Accordingly, in the middle of Ford's speech, Democrat Andrew Jacobs of Indiana went to the hopper and dropped in a resolution to impeach Douglas. The administration lost absolutely no time in pulling out of the issue. According to speechwriter William Safire, Nixon had figured out "that he was better off outlasting Douglas, who was aging, than condoning an ouster effort."[17] On 16 April 1970, the day after Ford made his speech on the floor of Congress, Nixon was crystal clear as he ordered Ehrlichman and congressional liaison Bryce Harlow to "turn off Ford re Douglas."[18] The Douglas investigation slowly disappeared from the front pages, and Ford, whose investigation had been first appropriated and then abandoned by the Nixon administration, suffered an embarrassing defeat. Nevertheless, when the Watergate crisis hit, Ford would once again be called into service for the administration.

It was not the botched burglary at the Watergate Hotel that the Nixon administration tried for two desperate years to cover up. The break-in of 17 June 1972 was the final, almost comic act of an administration that had broken the public trust since its inception. With Nixon's full knowledge and cooperation, members of his administration or their paid underlings had bugged the phones of offending news reporters,

8

spied on the Black Panther and the antiwar movements, used their influence to overthrow a duly elected Marxist government in Chile, assembled a list of the administration's enemies, secretly bombed and invaded Cambodia, then a neutral nation, and had ransacked a psychiatrist's office in hopes of finding a tidbit of information that could be used against a former National Security Council member who had leaked a Defense Department report to the *New York Times*. Several of the burglars arrested at the Watergate had participated in one or more of these schemes; to a greater or lesser extent, each one was aware of the broad scope of the administration's abuses of power.

When Nixon learned of the burglary (there is no evidence that he had planned the stunt) and heard that it was money from his reelection campaign that had paid for it, he quickly realized the need to contain the public's knowledge of the crime to the break-in itself. If any of the several investigations of the burglary managed to ferret out the true extent of the burglars' relationship with the White House, the administration could crumble. His fears were well founded—it took the Federal Bureau of Investigation only three days to figure out that one of the burglars had been carrying large sums of money that had been laundered through a Mexican bank. On 23 June 1972 Nixon met with his chief of staff, H. R. "Bob" Haldeman, and ordered him to call the director of the Central Intelligence Agency, instructing him to squash the FBI's investigation. Nixon's actions were a clear obstruction of justice, and, as luck would have it, the conversation was taped. But that tape would not be made public for more than a year, and meanwhile there were other investigations for the White House to suppress.

In August 1972 Wright Patman of Texas, Democratic chairman of the House Banking and Currency Committee, assigned members of the committee's staff to investigate whether there had been banking violations as a result of the strange movement of campaign money through Mexico and into the bank account of a Watergate burglar. On August 30, Maurice Stans, Nixon's finance director, was interviewed by Patman's staff. The next day, Michigan Republican Garry Brown, a member of the Banking Committee, wrote a letter to Patman, claiming that even though Brown recognized that as chairman Patman had the authority to initiate such investigations, he was "shocked and dismayed" that such a probe had begun without informing the rest of the committee.[19] According to the reporter who discovered the actions of the Patman committee, Brown's letter "succeeded only in hardening Patman's resolve to pursue the investigation." Patman scheduled a hearing with Stans for September 14, but he still had no authority to subpoena Stans to appear. On September 11, Patman received a letter from Stans's attorney,

Kenneth Parkinson, declaring that Stans would not testify.[20] Without the subpoena power, Patman's investigation would die. On September 12, Patman circulated an eighty-page report to the thirty-seven members of his committee, arguing the need for public hearings and the subpoena power.

The rumbling of the Patman committee worried a White House that had already begun to cover up its Watergate-related tracks. Three days after Patman's report was circulated, Nixon held a strategy meeting with Haldeman and White House counsel John Dean, who would soon take complete control of the cover-up. Dean first surmised that fellow Texan and Nixon's secretary of the treasury John Connally might be able to dissuade Patman. Then Dean noted that "Jerry Ford is not really taking an active interest in this matter" and that Stans should get in touch with Ford to "try to brief him and explain to him the problems he's got." Nixon quickly agreed:

> Put it down. . . . Jerry should talk to [Republican William R.] Widnall [of New Jersey, who had been on the committee for some twenty years] and, uh, just brace him, tell him I thought it was [unintelligible] start behaving. . . . Jerry's really got to lead on this. . . . He's got to really lead . . . tell Ehrlichman to get [Garry] Brown in and Ford in, and then they can all work out something. But they ought to get off their asses and push it. No use to let Patman have a free ride here.[21]

The evidence strongly suggests that Ford quickly took the hint. Two weeks later, on 27 September 1972, Ford's office produced a draft of a letter to members of the committee, a call to "urge you to be present" at an October 3 meeting:

> Obviously, we desire to see those who have been involved in illegal activities brought to justice, but at the same time we must be careful not to impinge on the constitutional rights of those who have been indicted by reckless or irresponsible investigations motivated by political considerations. Because of the political overtones of this matter I think it would be imperative for all Republican members to be present at the committee meeting to assure that the investigative resolution is appropriately drawn.

In the upper corner of the letter was a query in Ford's handwriting: "OK—When do *they* want it sent out?"[22]

In his testimony before the House Judiciary Committee while undergoing the vice-presidential confirmation process, Ford defended his actions: "I was asked by several members on our side of the aisle on

that committee to call the committee together. That was and is a responsibility, as the Republican leader in the House, to get groups like that together when they have a problem. I did it. I presided . . . they thought
that Mr. Patman was going on a fishing expedition, and they had beliefs
they thought were sound, and, therefore, decided to vote to postpone
any action."[23] Ford's role at that meeting may well have gone further.
On October 3—the same day Ford attended the committee meeting—the
full House panel defeated the bid by Patman to get subpoena power,
thus squashing his attempt to hold hearings prior to the election. Patman immediately accused the White House of exerting undue pressure
on his committee members. Brown acknowledged in an interview with
the *Washington Post* that he had worked with both the Justice Department and with Ford to block the hearings. Brown denied a charge by
Patman that the White House had brought "all kinds of pressure" but
added, "I would have to presume that the White House wouldn't want
further attention paid to this. I'm not so stupid to have to be told."[24]

Concerning Ford's loyalty to Nixon there can be no question. Yet
loyalty to this president was, in many quarters, fast becoming the political kiss of death by summer 1973. Ford, however, had been able to lead
his president's party in Congress without making the host of enemies
that Nixon himself had made by then. This combination of loyalty and
likability thus led directly to Ford's next step on the ladder of political
success.

On 10 October 1973, pleading no contest to a charge of income tax
evasion, Vice President Spiro Agnew resigned. Nixon would now be the
first president to act under the Twenty-fifth Amendment, which allowed him to nominate a candidate to fill the vice-presidential vacancy
subject to the approval of both houses of Congress. Later that day,
Nixon asked Ford to coordinate recommendations from Republican
members of Congress, and told him that he wanted the recommendations by 6:00 P.M. the following day. After Ford left, Nixon spoke with
congressional liaison Bryce Harlow, presidential counselor Melvin
Laird, and Speaker of the House Carl Albert (D-Okla.); the three men
told the president that Gerald Ford was the only confirmable choice.
Later that evening, before Nixon had even seen the results of the congressional recommendations, he instructed Laird to call Ford to sound
him out about the nomination. Calling Ford at his home, Laird inquired
whether Ford would accept the vice-presidential nomination if asked.
Despite the protests of his wife, Betty, who said that she wanted him to

11

run for one more term in the House and then retire, Ford said that he would accept it.

The next day in the Oval Office, Nixon formally asked Ford if he wanted the job. Ford accepted and that evening, Nixon announced his choice to the nation. With his usual sense of melodrama, Nixon tried to keep his audience guessing; the first hint came when he said that his choice had twenty-five years of experience in the House. The guests in the East Room now knew that it would be Ford, despite Nixon's tweaking of the group not to be "premature, there's several here who have served twenty-five years in the House." When Nixon finally announced Ford's name, the guests cheered and whistled. Nixon turned to Ford and whispered, "They like you." Ford then briefly responded that he was "terribly humble" and added, "I hope I have some assets that might be helpful in working with Congress."[25]

It was, in fact, these assets that had won Ford the job. Nixon makes it clear that despite his respect for Ford, "John Connally had been my first choice" and that he instead chose Ford because "there was no question that he would be the easiest to get confirmed." This assessment was borne out not only by Nixon's own reading of the situation and the recommendations of Harlow, Laird, and Albert but also by the recommendations from Republican party leaders solicited by the White House. Of the approximately four hundred responses, Nixon remembered that "Rockefeller and [California governor Ronald] Reagan were in a virtual tie for first choice, Connally was third, Ford was fourth. Ford, however, was first choice among members of Congress, and they were the ones who would have to approve the man I nominated."[26]

Although respect for Ford ran deep on both sides of the aisle as well as in both houses of Congress, public and press suspicion of the presidency was at a fever pitch in October 1973. No one assumed that Ford's confirmation hearings would be a breeze. Ford remembered that "some 350 special agents from 33 of the Bureau's field offices had interviewed more than 1,000 witnesses and compiled 1,700 pages of reports."[27] Before the nomination could go to the floor of both houses of Congress, it had to clear the Senate Rules Committee and the House Judiciary Committee. The process would be painstaking; it was widely assumed, by Democrat and Republican alike, that in Ford, the Congress was confirming the next president.

In general, Ford said all the right things during his committee testimony. He argued that he saw himself as "a ready conciliator between the White House and Capitol Hill" and described himself as a "moderate on domestic affairs, conservative on fiscal affairs, but a very dyed-in-the-wool internationalist in foreign policy." He indicated a solid agreement with the policies of the Nixon administration, and he continued in his long-standing loyalty to Nixon when he made it clear that he thought Nixon was "completely innocent" of any wrongdoing in Watergate.[28] The votes to confirm Ford's nomination were overwhelmingly positive: the Senate Rules Committee supported him 9 to 0, and the House Judiciary Committee voted 24 to 8 nine days later. In the full House, the vote was 387 to 35; in the Senate, 92 to 3. All the nay votes were cast by Democrats.

Nixon wanted to have the swearing-in at the White House, lest he be booed when he walked down the center aisle of the House chamber with Ford. Ford requested the Capitol, however, and Nixon reluctantly agreed. In his 6 December 1973 speech to Congress and the nation after being sworn in, Ford introduced a theme that he would repeat during his presidential inauguration less than one year later: "In exactly eight weeks we have demonstrated to the world that our great Republic stands solid, stands strong upon the bedrock of the Constitution." He also tried to level any overinflated expectations of his performance when he quipped, "I am a Ford, not a Lincoln."[29]

During his eight months in office, more than five hundred groups in forty states heard the vice president speak. He also held over fifty press conferences and gave more than eighty interviews (no less an observer than Norman Mailer commented in the *Wall Street Journal*: "Someone ought to do Jerry Ford a favor and take his airplane away from him").[30] The White House assumed that Ford would use these opportunities just as he had done as minority leader, to strike back at Nixon's critics. During the first month of his tenure, Ford did fulfill that duty, using speeches that were largely written by Nixon's speechwriters. But on 15 January 1974 Ford delivered an address in Atlantic City in which he identified Nixon's antagonists as "a few extreme partisans," and he specifically named the AFL-CIO as an adversary. Response to the speech was overwhelmingly negative, particularly when the White House admitted having written it. So that he would not continue to be a "White House appendage," as he called it, Ford brought in his own speechwriters, Bob Orben and Milton Friedman, and made them responsible to Hartmann.[31]

The Atlantic City speech was a turning point for Ford; after that, he concentrated less on defending Nixon and more on attacking Nixon's staff. On 30 March 1974 Ford spoke to one thousand Republican party officials at the Hyatt Regency in Chicago, beginning with the somewhat startling question, "What lessons can the Republican party learn from

Watergate?" His answer: "The political lesson of Watergate is this. Never again must America allow an arrogant, elite guard of political adolescents like [the Committee to Reelect the President] to bypass the regular party system and dictate the terms of a national election." Ford told reporters later that he was "not blaming the president for CRP. . . . He picked people he thought would do a good job. Unfortunately, they made mistakes."[32]

Nixon's bunkered administration finally surrendered following the July 24 decision of the Supreme Court requiring that the president release the subpoenaed Watergate tapes to the Watergate Special Prosecutor and to those special congressional committees that had been formed to investigate the matter. Ever since the existence of the tapes had been made public almost exactly one year before, the fate of the administration had centered on the fight to control them. Most observers in Washington had long assumed that the administration had been stonewalling on the release of the tapes not entirely because of its famous demand for "executive privilege" but because the tapes included some bit of irrefutable evidence—the "smoking gun"—that would prove its guilt. They would now have their chance to prove their assumption as Nixon immediately announced that he would comply with the Court's decision. On July 27 the House Judiciary Committee turned out the first of what would be three articles of impeachment. Congress would surely vote to convict, and Nixon knew it. So did his vice president.

Ford spent the first days of August preparing for the inevitable. Though both he and his staff did their best not to seem to be forcing Nixon out prematurely, in retrospect Ford clearly was getting ready for Nixon's resignation. On August 1 and 2, Ford had several conversations with Nixon's chief of staff Alexander Haig. Their discussions centered on the available options that Nixon had, including the possibility of a Ford pardon. Within less than a month these conversations would return to haunt Ford (see chapter 3). On Friday, August 2, Ford met with the two leaders of the Senate, Democratic majority leader Mike Mansfield of Montana and Republican minority leader Hugh Scott of Pennsylvania, to discuss plans for the probable Senate trial of Nixon. It was agreed that Ford should not attend but should be waiting in the wings to take the oath of office when Nixon was convicted. Scott's eyes filled as he told Ford, "You're all we've got now, and I mean the country, not the party."[33] The next day, Ford, who had spent most of his vice-presidency acting as Nixon's surrogate campaigner for the upcoming congressional elections, kept to a scheduled campaign swing through Mississippi. He surprised many reporters when he repeated his contention that Nixon was not guilty of an impeachable offense (later, Ford would protest that "had I said otherwise at that moment, the whole house of cards might have collapsed").[34]

That following Monday, August 5, the White House announced that one of the released tapes contained the 23 June 1972 conversation between Nixon and Haldeman. The smoking gun conversation, in which Nixon ordered the CIA to block the FBI's investigation, was clearly evidence of an impeachable offense. Left with no other options, Ford now broke with the administration:

> I have come to the conclusion that the public interest is no longer served by repetition of my previously expressed belief that on the basis of all the evidence known to me and to the American people, the president is not guilty of an impeachable offense. . . . The business of government must go on, and the genuine needs of the people must be served. I believe I can make a better contribution to this end by not involving myself daily in the impeachment debate, in which I have no constitutional role.[35]

In his memoirs, Ford was more blunt: "No longer was there the slightest doubt in my mind as to the outcome of the struggle. Nixon was finished."[36]

The next day Ford attended what would be the final cabinet meeting of the Nixon administration. The meeting seemed almost surreal at first when Nixon announced that he wanted to talk about the "most important issue confronting the nation . . . inflation." After a few moments of rambling discourse, he shifted to the revelations of the tape of 23 June 1972, which he insisted showed only that he was concerned with national security. Ford then asked to speak. Clearly conscious of the historical gravity of the moment and also concerned that he not in any way have his words or ideas misrepresented or taken out of context, Ford spoke verbatim from typed notes:

> At the outset, I would like to make several points. First, everyone here please recognize the difficult position I am in; I am a party in interest. Second, no one regrets more than I do this whole tragic episode. I have deep personal sympathy for you, Mr. President, and your fine family. Third, I wish to emphasize that had I known and had it been disclosed to me what has been disclosed in reference to the Watergate affair in the last twenty-four hours, I would not have made a number of the statements that I have made, either as Minority Leader or as Vice President of the United States. Fourth, I do not expect to make any recommendation today to the president as to what he should do, and neither do I expect to make any such recommendation to any of the others at this meeting. Fifth, whether the full disclosures will

meet the constitutional definition of an impeachable offense is a matter that can only be finally resolved by the United States Senate in a
proceeding as provided for in the Constitution. Finally, let me assure
you that I expect to continue to support fully the administration's foreign policy and fight against inflation.[37]

According to Ford, Nixon sat back in his chair and said, "I think your
position is exactly correct."[38]

On August 8, after presenting the Congressional Medal of Honor to
the families of seven men who had died in Vietnam, Ford met with the
president at 11:00 A.M. Nixon told his vice president, "I have made the
decision to resign. It's in the best interest of the country." He paused
and then quietly said, "Jerry, I know you'll do a good job." Ford remembered that Nixon suggested that Kissinger was "absolutely indispensable," that Haig be kept as chief of staff, that Nelson Rockefeller be chosen as vice president, and that Ford avoid wage and price controls.[39]
Nixon later wrote that "Ford's eyes filled with tears—and mine did as
well—as we lingered for a moment at the door."[40] Ford returned to his
office in the Executive Office Building and immediately called Kissinger,
telling him, "Henry, I need you. The country needs you. I want you to
stay. I'll do everything I can to work with you." Kissinger responded,
"There will be no problem, sir. It is my job to get along with you and
not yours to get along with me."[41]

Ford then began to plan what would be the most extraordinary
presidential inauguration in American history. Although he wanted to
be sworn in a second time at the Capitol, there was no time to make
preparations; instead, the East Room of the White House was chosen.
Ford would have no one other than Chief Justice Warren Burger swear
him in; a government jet was sent to bring Burger home from a conference in the Netherlands. Ford quickly contacted *Detroit News* Washington correspondent Jerald terHorst, Buchen's recommendation for the office of press secretary; terHorst accepted. Congressmen were notified,
ambassadors were contacted, and Hartmann put the finishing touches
on Ford's inaugural address.

On the morning of August 9, Nixon said good-bye to his staff in an
emotional speech. Ford and his wife did not attend; rather, they waited
for Nixon's family one floor below in the Diplomatic Reception Room to
escort them to their helicopter. Ford remembered that Pat Nixon was
surprised that a red carpet had been rolled out to the helicopter and that
she remarked to Betty, "You'll see so many of these red carpets, you'll

get so you hate 'em."[42] Moments after the helicopter had whisked Nixon away, White House staffers, with eyes still damp from the drama of his farewell, filled the East Room. Burger walked in alone, wearing his full black judicial robe. When the Fords entered, they were met with a standing ovation. Smiling, Ford went to the podium and turned slightly to acknowledge the applause. As the oath was administered, Ford's voice never wavered, but the emotion of the moment soon caught up with the new president. Never a graceful speaker, Ford more than made up for his halting style with an abundance of sincerity in his delivery. He began by admitting that it would not be "an inaugural address, not a fireside chat, not a campaign speech, just a little straight talk among friends, and I intend it to be the first of many." Clearly cognizant of the already mounting criticism in the press that he was a mere congressional hack, not up to the job, Ford remarked that "if you have not chosen me by secret ballot, neither have I gained office by any secret promises." And then in words that for many would become both the symbol of the administration and the standard by which it would be judged, Ford attempted to wash Watergate out of the minds of the American people:

> I believe that truth is the glue that holds government together, not only our government but civilization itself. That bond, though strained, is unbroken at home and abroad. . . . In all my private and public acts as your president, I expect to follow my instincts of openness and candor with full confidence that honesty is always the best policy in the end. . . . My fellow Americans, our long national nightmare is over. Our constitution works. Our great republic is a government of laws and not of men. Here, the people rule.

As he closed, Ford came close to tears when he asked the country to pray for Richard Nixon and his family so that "our former president, who brought peace to millions, finds it for himself."

The room was thick with emotion—not once was Ford interrupted with applause. Yet his audience was moved as they had not been by a political speech in a long time. As the crowd filed out, many openly weeping before national television cameras, the military band played "God Bless America." When it was over, an obviously moved Warren Burger turned to Hugh Scott, grabbed the minority leader's hand, and said, "Hugh, it worked. Thank God, it worked."[43]

2
★ ★ ★ ★ ★

TRANSITION

Richard Nixon began his presidency hoping to heal America. He was convinced, as had been most conservatives, that the social introspection and the vocal protest of the 1960s had damaged America and that the time had come for tranquillity in the policy arena. On the night of his election, he told the nation that during the campaign he had been particularly touched by a sign held by an Ohio voter who wanted the new president to "bring us together." His first term was an attempt to initiate policies that would accomplish this goal. Specifically, he set out to undo those foreign policies that had led to the continuation of the Vietnam War and to the standoff in the cold war, and he intended to cut back government spending on domestic programs—particularly on an out-of-control welfare system—that had resulted in a rapidly rising rate of inflation and unemployment.

Nixon's policies did not heal the nation, however. Foreign policy was his passion and secrecy his major diplomatic tool. Yet his record in that area was mixed. Although his policy of deception and war on the periphery of Vietnam had indeed extricated the country from the conflict in Southeast Asia, it did not accomplish the goal that had been set since the nation had become involved in Vietnam in 1947; clearly, despite the 1973 peace treaty, the South Vietnamese government of Nguyen Van Thieu was still in danger of being overrun by North Vietnamese forces. Détente had been achieved by 1972, but this improvement in America's relationship with the Soviet Union and the People's Republic of China (PRC) was compromised in less than a year as the Soviet Union and the United States once again came to the brink of war over the actions of their allies—this time in the Middle East, an area the administration had virtually ignored. American support for the Israelis during the 1973 Yom Kippur War led to an instant retaliation: the Soviets threatened war, and the Arabs placed a boycott on oil imports to the United States that resulted in an immediate tripling of the price of American crude. Although the crisis was averted, by 1974 American-Soviet relations had chilled noticeably.

Nixon's domestic policies suffered both from neglect and from the methods of his foreign policy. His demand that he be able to conduct his foreign policy in secret angered a Congress that was already in open revolt against a perceived growing presidential power. This mood, coupled with Nixon's heavy-handed treatment of Capitol Hill in general, led to the defeat of much of his domestic legislation, particularly an innovative plan for welfare reform designed to require that welfare recipients get a job. Although the issue of black civil rights in the North was virtually ignored, Nixon attacked the brewing economic crisis by freezing wages and prices for the first time since World War II. Yet the measure was miscalculated and mishandled so that the administration completely lost control of the inflationary spiral. As Nixon left office, prices had risen 3.7 percent in July 1974 alone and showed no signs of stopping.

The nation that Ford inherited was saddled with more than the direct consequences of Nixon's policies. His desire to end the turmoil of the 1960s had led to a repression of dissent unparalleled in modern American history. Protest groups were spied upon, civil rights groups were infiltrated, and reporters were harassed—actions carried out in the name of national security and with the advice and consent of the Federal Bureau of Investigation and the Central Intelligence Agency. His was an administration conducted with a bunker mentality, and the "us versus them" mindset that Nixon had striven to eliminate from his relations with the Soviet Union and Communist China prevailed on the domestic front. As a result, the nation's wounds inflicted by the Nixon administration cut far deeper than mere failures of policy. As journalist Theodore White observed, Nixon's most heinous crime was a "breach of faith" with the American people.[1] The transgressions of his administration were so blatant—and ultimately so *provable*—unlike similar offenses committed by his predecessors—that the nation not only learned about their existence but also demanded that Nixon be held accountable for them. Americans certainly sighed with relief when Nixon resigned, but his resignation did not restore the nation's faith in their political institutions. A distrust that had begun under Johnson had crystallized under

Nixon—the overwhelming majority of Americans no longer believed the word of their president. Thus national self-doubt—not a new domestic and diplomatic steadiness—became Richard Nixon's most important legacy to his nation.

Little wonder, then, when *Time* magazine assessed the State of the Nation upon Nixon's resignation, it demanded a "time for healing." Like Nixon before him, Gerald Ford had promised that. But Vietnam and Watergate had left an indelible scar on American society. Its institutions had been altered, its economy compromised, and its citizenry made cynical about its destiny. Ford was expected not only to heal the damage done by Nixon's policies but also to heal the damage caused by Nixon's breach of faith. Yet, Ford's whiplashlike entry into the White House gave him virtually no time to reflect on the task at hand. Denied the luxury of being a president-elect and thus unable to plan for his own administration while his predecessor was still in office, Ford was forced to assemble an administration at the same time that the nation's wounds needed his immediate attention. This double demand made more difficult the two immediate tasks of his breathlessly short transition period—the construction of a Ford administration and the creation of an agenda for his presidency.

Ford's managerial style as a congressman had always been collegial: he preferred an open door to a memorandum, banter to a formal presentation. Despite Ford's many committee and leadership responsibilities, one trusted aide, Robert T. Hartmann, ran his office. When Ford became minority leader he brought the former Washington Bureau chief for the *Los Angeles Times* aboard as his legislative assistant. Hartmann's reputation as a hard drinker, his verbal tussles with his fellow staffers, and his late-night work habits were the stuff of Washington legend. Richard Reeves, one of Ford's most caustic critics throughout his presidency, was particularly harsh on Hartmann, noting that he served as the "dark side of sunny Jerry Ford. . . . [He is] nasty, vindictive and loud—and that was when he was sober."[2] The description was true enough, but he was also an outstanding speechwriter, a prodigious and usually successful manipulator of the Washington press corps, one of the shrewdest judges of the Washington scene, and unflinchingly loyal to Gerald Ford. Ford not only appreciated Hartmann but also, despite his personality glitches, found him indispensable.

Hartmann was superb in his role as Ford's congressional aide-de-camp; however, Ford was correct when he wrote that naming Hartmann chief of staff after assuming the vice-presidency was "a dreadful mis-

21

take."[3] His was not the personality suited for the confines of an executive office. Hartmann's sloppy hours, crocodilelike demeanor, and refusal to compromise made him an outstanding idea man but a rather poor administrator. The boss himself did little to help the situation. Hartmann noted in a 1985 interview that "members of Congress don't think in terms of organizational charts or structures. . . . The person who is drawn to a career as a legislator is usually not the type of person who rises to the top of a corporate or military structure. The essence of the legislator is compromise."[4] Ford himself did not have an executive mindset—that little bit of the corporate CEO that is so necessary to the smooth running of a large staff.

Because of the lack of managerial skills in both the vice president and his chief of staff, the vice-presidential staff quickly fell into disarray. Ford's press secretary Paul Miltich, a former schoolteacher and a reporter for the *Saginaw News* before coming to Washington for the Booth chain, proved incapable of keeping the Washington press corps from noticing the chaos. The *Wall Street Journal* was rather typical in its criticism: "[The] Ford staff is a lot like the boss . . . not especially noted for brilliance."[5] Ford, feeling a need to call in the cavalry, turned to his friend Philip Buchen to serve as his troubleshooter, as he would do many times during his administration.

Buchen had served as a perennial adviser to Ford throughout his congressional years, coming down from Grand Rapids whenever the need arose. At the time of Ford's vice-presidency, Buchen was serving as the chief counsel to the Domestic Council Committee on the Right to Privacy. Buchen observed that "every time I came down here . . . there weren't any staff meetings, people were just not knowing what to do, and never certain if the correspondence was getting answered promptly, and you know, it's a big thing. . . . And, of course, Ford was attracting a lot of attention. . . . It just seemed to be a terrible operation."[6]

Buchen suggested to Ford that his friend L. William Seidman be allowed to take a look at the situation, and Ford agreed. A graduate of Harvard and Dartmouth, the fifty-three-year-old Seidman had earned his wealth through his international accounting firm (one of his clients was billionaire J. Paul Getty). A polo player and yachtsman, Seidman was no stranger to politics, having worked for Citizens for Romney and having entertained the notion of running for Ford's vacated House seat.[7] Seidman put together a study that proposed to improve communications and efficiency on Ford's staff, a plan that took power away from Hartmann and spread it among several different staff managers. While serving as Lyndon Johnson's press secretary, Bill Moyers had dubbed such a system a "spokes to a wheel" approach in structuring an executive's staff.[8] Ford was the hub, and each staffer's influence and access to him was ideally equidistant from him.

Seidman's spokes concept suited Ford's managerial style quite well. Since each senior staff member had equal access to the vice president, the arrangement offered a certain amount of flexibility. There was only one problem with the system: if anyone in Ford's office did not accept an egalitarian distribution of power, the plan was doomed to failure. As Nixon and Ford chief of staff Alexander Haig would later observe, "Only a supreme optimist could have believed that such an arrangement would work out in a town in which ambition is mother's milk."[9] Hartmann simply refused to accept any lessening of the access that, only days before, had been complete and unfettered. Examples of Hartmann's running feud with Seidman are legion (after receiving from Seidman an agenda for a staff meeting that included a "speech session," Hartmann penned an angry reply: "If this meeting is to deal with speech content, I believe it should be under my auspices since this is one of my primary responsibilities. However, I question the need for group discussion in this area").[10] Hartmann grumbled to everyone—including the press—about Seidman's interference. Clearly, as events were pushing Ford's vice-presidency to a close, the spokes concept was failing; this staff would never be able to combine the speed, political sagacity, and rectitude necessary to prepare a transition plan for Ford's first days. But as that eventuality drew near, the need for such a plan became essential. Once again, Buchen stepped into the breach.

On 7 May 1974 Buchen had dinner at the Georgetown home of his friend Clay T. Whitehead, a Harvard Ph.D. who had worked at the Bureau of the Budget under Johnson, had worked on the 1968 transition, and had created the Office of Telecommunications Policy (OTP). As OTP director, Whitehead had an office directly across from Buchen's Privacy Council office, and the two men had become friends. Buchen asked Whitehead to help him form a group that would discuss possible options and make recommendations to Ford in the event that he acceded to the presidency; thus the first of three transition teams was born. Buchen had acted out of loyalty to Ford, a sincere belief that the vice-presidential staff could not undertake such a task, and confidence in the idea that since he was not then a formal member of Ford's staff, he would not get caught either by Ford or the press (Buchen believed that Ford would have "blown his top" if he had found out).[11] For his part, Whitehead remembered that "I really didn't want to do it. I felt it would be fundamentally wrong for the president to be hounded out of office."[12] He agreed, however, when Buchen told him that they would be working in secret.

Buchen and Whitehead recruited three young Republicans—Jonathan Moore, an aide to New York governor Nelson Rockefeller and to Attorney General Elliot Richardson; Brian Lamb, Whitehead's assistant at the OTP; and Larry Lynn, a former National Security Council (NSC) staffer—to join their efforts. They held their meetings in Whitehead's home—Whitehead's wife dubbed it the Ford Foundation. For about three months, they worked at a leisurely pace; there was a sense of history about their work but not of immediacy. Their deliberations were akin to an academic seminar on the presidency. Lamb remembers that "we would meet once a week . . . and just sit around and talk through what would be a president's—a new president's—main difficulty in the first . . . thirty days."[13]

The team's overriding concern team was the question of staff management. The personality conflicts on Ford's vice-presidential staff, high even by Washington standards, would be a problem if, as expected, Ford transferred the existing staff to the White House. And there were other problems, not the least of which was who would be in charge if Ford reorganized his staff. In the days following Watergate, the role of the president's senior staff had come under a microscope; many critics saw these people as evil gatekeepers who had insulated Nixon from the country, with Watergate resulting. Political sagacity dictated that Ford fire the Nixon people as quickly as possible and when he installed his own advisers that he steer clear of a Haldemanlike chief of staff. Yet Ford's transition period would be only a matter of hours; prudence dictated that someone be kept on to show him the ropes.

The formal result of the Buchen-Whitehead team's discussions was a sixteen-page working paper, "The First Week." Most interesting is the page entitled "Transition Organization." The team made suggestions for immediate first-day appointments to key positions expected to be left vacated ("People Needed"), including one suggestion for "Political Liaison"—then chairman of the Republican National Committee George Bush.[14] But the key recommendation regarded Chief of Staff Haig. As Lamb remembered, "We suggested [that] Haig go."[15] The team believed, quite simply, that given time the spokes-to-a-wheel approach to staffing would work—as long as Al Haig was not there to co-opt the process.

The August 5 release of the Nixon tapes with the smoking gun conversation changed everything. A Ford presidency was no longer a theoretical debate; it was an immediate reality that was only hours away. That evening, at Ford's house for dinner, Buchen told Ford about the transition team's plans. As Buchen remembered it, the general thrust of his message—and that of his team—was "you're not quite ready to go. . . . You better get some work done, even though I've done some work."[16] Sensing an immediate need for a more explicit transition plan, Ford was loath to leave such important work to a bunch of youthful strangers, no matter how dedicated they might be. He therefore directed Buchen to add to his team five men who had been close to Ford: William Whyte of U.S. Steel, Nixon congressional liaison Bryce Harlow, Secretary of the Interior Rogers C. B. Morton, Congressman John Byrnes, and Senator Bob Griffin. As he left, Buchen mumbled to his old friend, "It's happening."[17]

This group, nominally headed by Whyte, constituted a new, second transition team on which Buchen's team played the role of interested spectators. Whyte's goal was to use the ideas of the first transition team to prepare for Ford a succinct document—a road map for his first days in office. Yet as seasoned political observers and participants, the Whyte team was not about to endorse Buchen's staffing arrangement, which in effect left nobody in charge. At least at the outset, the Whyte team counseled Ford to keep Haig and to trust the continuity of the federal government rather than a spokes-to-a-wheel approach to management. On the morning of August 9, Ford met at his home with Buchen and Byrnes, who gave him a lengthy memorandum broken down into four parts: Transition Organization, the Business of Government, Old White House Staff, and Vice-Presidential Search Process. They recommended that although Ford should expect to receive resignations from the vast majority of the Nixon staff after a suitable grace period, Haig should be considered the "one exception. . . . Al has done yeoman service for his country. You should meet with him personally as soon as possible and prevail upon him to help you and your transition team, thus completing the holding-together he has done for so long. He will also be needed for liaison to Mr. Nixon and his family. However, he should not be expected, asked, or be given the option to become *your* Chief of Staff." Nevertheless, the Whyte team had assumed that eventually Haig would leave. They therefore proposed that although Ford should have no chief of staff—at least not in name—and that all senior staff members would have equal access to the new president, Ford would continue to need someone to oversee the staff. They offered several names for the eventual replacement of Haig; Ford placed a check next to the name of his friend from congressional days, former Young Turk Donald Rumsfeld.[18]

Ford needed little prodding to accept the recommendations of the Whyte team. On the subject of Haig, Ford recalls, "I knew we needed Haig, and I wanted him to stay as long as he possibly could."[19] He quickly gave Haig the responsibility, if not the actual title, of chief of staff. Buchen remembers that it was a simple, practical decision: "[Ford] didn't have anyone to take over the duties that Haig had, I mean the routine handling things, getting [paperwork] into his office, and all that."[20] Even Hartmann grudgingly agreed, telling future press secretary Ron Nessen that Haig had to stay because "he's the only one who knows how to fly the plane. We're not going to shoot him in the cockpit before we learn to fly the plane or design a new plane."[21] Ford's decision to retain Haig and his agreement that Rumsfeld would eventually succeed him clearly indicated that his White House staff would be spokes in name only; Ford had endorsed having a chief of staff. Acting on the Whyte team's recommendations, Ford asked both the cabinet and the key members of Nixon's senior staff to stay on for the foreseeable future. A third, more formal transition team headed by Rumsfeld generally agreed with the conclusions of the Whyte team.

Ford thus surrounded himself with one of the largest groups of senior aides of the postwar presidency. Each of Ford's senior advisers received appointments as presidential counselors with cabinet rank. Hartmann was given control of the White House Office of the Editorial Staff and later that year was also made the White House liaison with the Republican party. Buchen replaced J. Fred Buzhardt as White House counsel. Bill Seidman was made counselor for Economic Affairs, and former Virginia congressman John O. Marsh was named counselor for National Security and International Affairs. A conservative Democrat who quickly became an invaluable confidant for Ford, Marsh soon became Ford's congressional liaison. There were also four Nixon carryovers occupying "advocacy positions": Henry Kissinger as both secretary of state and presidential assistant for national security affairs (head of the NSC); Roy Ash as presidential assistant for management and budget and director of the Office of Management and Budget (OMB); Kenneth R. Cole as assistant for domestic affairs and executive director of the Domestic Council, and Al Haig.

Haig continued to run the Ford White House in the same brusquely efficient manner with which he had managed the declining months of the Nixon presidency. As it had evolved since 1932, the modern presidential staff had assumed an advisory as well as a managerial role. Yet Ford's staff was largely unable to help the president formulate a coherent policy direction for the administration primarily because, unlike its immediate predecessors, the Ford White House staff was loosely organized. Much of this was Ford's own fault. Jerry Jones, Ford's White House staff secretary, remembered that for all the attempts at reorganization,

> [Ford] didn't really want a structure that was a very aggressive, activist organization and took steps to ensure that it wasn't. Frankly, the

place, as a managed organization, did not work nearly as well as the Haldeman White House did. Ford rarely said "Hey, I want a program to do this," or "I want this to happen," or "I want that to happen." Things floated to him, he considered them, decided them, and they went back down. So the staff were the activists, in a sense, as opposed to Ford.[22]

Despite his desire to have a more businesslike and compatible staff, Ford refused to discipline his troops and hoped that he would be able to bring about a consensus after everyone had had his say. Ford never achieved that goal, however. He had to contend with a rollicking staff that had difficulty reaching agreement. One cabinet secretary later told Roger Porter, then executive secretary of the Economic Policy Board (EPB): "In some cases [Ford] almost asked for heartaches by encouraging debate among his top people to be sure what they were saying, rather than tip his hand and have them line up behind whatever decision it was that they thought he wanted. I have often said that I felt in the other administration [Nixon's] there were indications of where we were going and people lined up behind it. That was not as true in this administration."[23]

Equally important as the lack of strong organization was the fact that the spokes did not get along with each other. The biggest feud was between Hartmann and Haig, an enmity that Phil Buchen later labeled for an interviewer as "a natural."[24] As he had with Seidman, Hartmann begrudged Haig access to the president and believed that Haig had less than the president's best interest in mind. Although he recognized that Haig was temporarily necessary, Hartmann was particularly embittered by Ford's decision not to clean house immediately and fire all other Nixon appointees. Ford genuinely found it difficult to let go of the mass of Nixon people who occupied the Executive Office lest they be "tarred . . . with the Nixon brush. . . . So I made the decision to proceed gradually. Some of the people I didn't want on the White House staff had already left of their own accord. The others, I told Haig, would have to be gone by January 1."[25] Hartmann, however, blamed most of the failures of the Ford administration on these Nixon holdovers. In his memoirs, he dubbed them a Praetorian Guard who surrounded Ford and kept him from initiating his own presidency. To Hartmann, "there was never, for all thirty months he was President, a truly Ford Cabinet or Ford Staff. There was an incompatible, uncontrolled, contentious collection of Praetorians, many bitterly resentful of the few old Ford loyalists who hung on to the end. [They] stubbornly shielded Jerry Ford from his better self."[26]

Few participants in the Ford White House agree with Hartmann's assessment. Even Ford disagrees: "Bob is a brilliant, able, loyal, friend of mine. But he does have some fixations, and he has them against certain people. And I think his book brings it out. . . . He's totally loyal to me. And he . . . resented anybody that in any way whatsoever—indirectly or otherwise, he thought was undercutting what we were trying to do, I have a little broader perspective . . . and I respected his views, but I felt differently on some people."[27] It should be noted that not only did Hartmann indeed feud with most of the Nixon holdovers but that he also crossed swords with many of the original Ford staffers. Moreover, even had Ford desired to clean house, one wonders if he could have found any Republican replacements in 1974 who had not been Nixon people. Nevertheless, the issue is moot: Ford added the Nixon senior staff to his own, altercations followed, and disarray was the order of the day.

Many observers expected that the Ford administration would gain its stability and receive much of its policy advice from a strengthened cabinet. It was generally believed that Nixon's refusal to consult his cabinet along with the increase in the power of the White House staff had led directly to the abuses of power. Rumsfeld's transition team suggested greater access to the president for cabinet members with less White House involvement in the decisionmaking process.[28] There were hints during the honeymoon month that Ford intended to follow such a plan, and that message was constantly given out to the press by the White House. The idea of a strong cabinet was a large component of the honeymoon month as most of the country had come to view the Nixon White House as a fortress where access was forbidden and advice ignored. The press clearly wanted to believe that Ford was treating his cabinet better than Nixon had dealt with his. Dom Bonafede of the *National Journal* observed that Ford had "sought to restore some of the prestige" of the cabinet and quoted cabinet secretary James Connor that "it is a rule here that if a cabinet officer wants to see the president, he is entitled to see him."[29]

Yet one of the key developments of the modern presidency since 1932 was the subordination of cabinet government—the system by which policy is formed outside the White House in the departments and brought to the president for discussion and eventual action—to a system that allowed the White House staff to initiate the bulk of the administration's policy. The latter was certainly the case under Nixon. With the exception of Henry Kissinger (and even with him, more than Kissinger's hagiographers would have it), Nixon ignored his cabinet, preferring to use a rejuvenated National Security Council and a newly created Domestic Council to develop policy. Despite the press given to Ford's interaction with his cabinet, most insiders assumed that as the administration matured, the White House would continue to play the lead role in policymaking.[30]

The pattern that actually emerged in Ford's administration fell in between these extremes of policy development. Ford's style with his cabinet was neither as heavy-handed as Nixon's nor did it offer a collegial return to cabinet government. Unlike his predecessor, Ford did not ignore his cabinet. Attorney General Edward Levi played a major role in the development of the administration's civil rights policies; from the Treasury, William Simon provided an important conservative voice in matters dealing with the economy; Secretary of Defense James Schlesinger—despite Ford's dislike— was a key national security adviser; and even though by 1975 his influence was on the wane, Henry Kissinger, still holding the portfolios of secretary of state and assistant to the president for national security, continued to be the president's chief adviser on matters of foreign policy. Although Ford consulted his cabinet more often, he did not expect his department heads to initiate policy; nor did he turn to the White House agencies, the makers of policy under Nixon, to continue in that role. The Domestic Council was essentially ignored throughout the Ford presidency, and the influence of the National Security Council waned as détente was challenged by the Republican conservatives. Ford depended instead on his staff members and presidential counselors to present him with policy initiatives and options. Indeed, this close inner circle of White House advisers was infinitely more involved in the making of policy decisions than had been the members of the Nixon staff. Ford often consulted his staff in secrecy—a practice that angered his cabinet members no less than it had done in previous administrations—and in the wake of the national revulsion toward "all the president's men" of the Nixon years, the Ford team took great pains to present the administration as being open, one in which all forms of advice were both sought and heeded. In reality, however, even though Ford's relationship with his department heads was friendlier and more collegial than Nixon's had been, the White House staff continued to control policy.

Ford did have some innovations in mind, particularly in terms of the traditional role of the vice president. Yet the opening weeks of the administration were further complicated because for almost five months the administration was without a second-in-command.

Richard Nixon had paid Nelson Rockefeller his highest compliment when he quipped that "only three men in America understand the use of power. I do. John Connally does. And, I guess Nelson does."[31] The ultimate prize of the presidency had long eluded Rockefeller. He was hampered by his own strength of character, his outspoken bluntness, a controversial personal life and, ultimately, by his reputation as a freewheeling liberal in Republican clothing who had spent New York into a recession. To the end of his career, even though he was more personally conservative than many of his Republican peers (he would often joke that with his wealth, he had more to conserve than the next guy), Rockefeller was incapable of building a bridge to the conservative wing of the party necessary to win the nomination.

Despite his oft-quoted comment, "I never wanted to be the *vice* president of *anything*," the office was a job that Rockefeller had long coveted. In 1973 he had campaigned hard for the vice-presidential nod; that he did not get it centered less on his qualifications than it did on Nixon's judgment that he would not be easily confirmable. Rockefeller was bitter over being bypassed by Nixon, but he remained stoic, publicly supporting Ford. Not so Rockefeller's wife, Happy, who announced to Dan Rather of CBS News that her husband would never be tapped by Nixon because "weakness never turns to strength."[32]

When Ford began his search for a vice-presidential nominee, Rockefeller was once again on the short list. In a private White House poll of leading Republicans, George Bush received 255 votes and Rockefeller 181.[33] Bush was seriously considered, but *Newsweek* had released a story revealing that in 1970 the Nixon White House slush fund ("Operation Townhouse") had given Bush approximately $100,000 during his unsuccessful run for the Senate against Lloyd Bentsen.[34] Thus on August 17, Ford telephoned Rockefeller and offered him the vice-presidency; the next day, Rockefeller accepted. Rockefeller's acceptance of the second spot poses an interesting question. According to Rockefeller, he accepted because of the gravity of the "constitutional crisis."[35] But this explanation excludes Rockefeller's sizable political ambition. Rockefeller biographer Sam Roberts once told the story of a limousine ride he took with Rockefeller from the Capitol to the White House during which Roberts asked him if he still wanted to be president. The vice president replied with a smile, "Well, what do you think I'm doing here?"[36] Yet there was another, even more substantive reason. In a move that later was to haunt him, Ford promised Rockefeller that he would "head the Domestic Council and help put together my domestic legislative package."[37]

Rockefeller's nomination had sent the right wing of the Republican party, who remembered Rockefeller as Goldwater's nemesis in the bloody primary battles of 1964 and who saw him in 1974 simply as the spendthrift womanizer from New York, into fits. Nixon speechwriter Pat Buchanan, interviewed for a 1987 PBS special, "The Conservatives," observed that "there was no one who could rattle the cages of the Right" like Nelson

Rockefeller."[38] Rockefeller certainly agreed with that assessment; when George Will asked him in 1975 why so many conservative Republicans disliked him so much, Rockefeller smiled and replied, "It's sorta visceral."[39] The opposition from the Right was both vehement and vocal, one reason that Rockefeller's nomination took so long to get through the Congress.

The second reason, not surprisingly, was his wealth. On September 12, a preliminary figure of $33 million was released as the estimate of Rockefeller's personal net worth. One week later, the income from two trusts, real estate, and his art collection was disclosed, and the figure was upped to $182.5 million.[40] The final totals showed that Rockefeller had $64 million, almost half of which was his art collection; he was also the beneficiary of a lifetime trust fund set up by his father so that his total net worth was approximately $178 million.[41] Even Ford was stunned; one morning after reading his newspapers, he turned to White House photographer David Hume Kennerly and exclaimed, "Can you imagine, Dave. . . . Nelson *lost* $30 million in one year and it didn't make any difference."[42]

It did not take long for stories to appear dealing with Rockefeller's use of his wealth, including tales of gifts and loans to members of his staff and most notably to then-aide Henry Kissinger, amounting to approximately $2 million over the years. A delayed tax audit also disclosed that Rockefeller owed approximately $1 million in back taxes. Rockefeller explained that his financial largesse had not been "designed to corrupt . . . either the receiver or the giver."[43] As one observer wryly commented, "Countless politicians had been destroyed for being on the take—Nelson Rockefeller was in trouble for being on the give."[44] After promising to put his finances in a blind trust and to pay his taxes, Rockefeller was finally confirmed by both houses of Congress and on 19 December 1974 was sworn in as vice president.

The length of these hearings is significant. Between September 23 and December 5, Rockefeller testified on seventeen separate days, eight times before the Senate Rules Committee and nine before the House Judiciary Committee. Thus Ford spent the critical first four months of his presidency—months that spanned the pardon, the first steps on the economy, and, most important, the off-year congressional elections—without a vice president.

The transition from the Nixon to the Ford presidency was indeed rocky, yet few Americans were aware of any problems. For the first month both press and public fawned over the new president. Entertained by such scenes as a pajama-clad president on the front stoop of his Alexandria, Virginia, home retrieving the morning newspaper and waving to the press, America took no time at all in bestowing upon Ford the ultimate accolade from Middle America: he was christened a regular guy. In an article written immediately after he took office, *U.S. News and World Report* announced, "He's superbly average. . . . He's like Ike. He gives you an impression of solid dependability."[45] The *Washington Post*, fresh from seven years of Nixon bashing, breathed a sigh of relief when it noted that "Jerry Ford is the most normal, sane, down-to-earth individual to work in the Oval Office since Harry Truman left."[46] *Newsweek* concurred, with its observation that the new president was "nothing any different from your next-door neighbor."[47] America found itself having a warm relationship with its new First Family.

The Fords—often described by Betty as "one big scrappy family"—took over the White House with a freshness of youth the country had not experienced since the Kennedys. Susan, the youngest child at seventeen, was a student at a private girl's school in Bethesda until fall 1975 when she entered Washington's Mount Vernon College. Steven, the youngest boy at eighteen, was a high school student in Alexandria. Jack, twenty-one and a recent graduate of Washington State University, was called home to his father's inauguration from his summer job as a forest ranger. His older brother Mike was a student at Cornwall Theological Seminary in Essex, Massachusetts. Actions such as Susan's public refusal to stop wearing jeans around the White House and Jack's squiring of musician George Harrison to the White House made the children favorites of the press (Jack gave Harrison a WIN button; the former Beatle gave Ford a button with "OM" on it—the Sanskrit word for wholeness). Yet Susan later recalled with some regret that the White House was "a cross between a nunnery and a penitentiary."[48] Mike Ford, who had been married one month before Ford assumed the presidency, agreed—he even took a job under an assumed name to avoid the camera's glare.[49] The White House, on the other hand, often wished that Jack Ford was as eager as his siblings to remain anonymous. In May 1975 press secretary Ronald Nessen wrote Donald Rumsfeld that he had been called by a member of the Secret Service who was concerned about some of the interviews being given by Jack Ford, suggesting that he and his agents attended parties and smoked pot.[50] Such tidbits came as a surprise to an America used to having its teenage presidential scions hidden under a bushel basket, but the nation was not entirely disapproving of its new First Children. They were viewed as healthy, growing, American kids—a novelty in the White House.

Quite apart from her husband and children, Betty Ford would carve for herself an important niche in the history of American First Ladies. The former Elizabeth Bloomer was born in Chicago but grew up in Grand Rapids. Betty began to study dance at age eight, and by age seventeen she was choreographing her own routines. She studied dance at Vermont's Bennington College and then moved to New York City, where she became a member of the Martha Graham modern dance group and a fashion model. Returning to Grand Rapids, Betty met insurance salesman William C. Warren; they were married, but divorced after five years. She met Gerald Ford in fall 1947, while she was working as a fashion coordinator in a Grand Rapids department store. Ford proposed in February 1948, but they delayed their marriage until after he had won his congressional primary election.

Gerald Ford remembers that his values and goals and those of his wife "were almost identical and I felt good about that."[51] The American public, however, viewed their new First Lady as the polar opposite of her rather staid husband. Plainly put, she was fun. Fascinated by Citizen's Band (CB) radios, Mrs. Ford bought one and talked to the truckers driving through Washington; they christened her "First Mama." She appeared on the Mary Tyler Moore show, the first time that a member of the First Family had appeared on a network comedy. She reinstated dinner parties at the White House; the First Couple was invariably first on the dance floor and last to leave the party. She danced barefoot with a Chinese ballet company during her husband's state visit to Beijing and was photographed pushing a fully clothed president of the United States into a Camp David swimming pool.

The affection with which the nation viewed Mrs. Ford was put to the test when she became an outspoken advocate for women's issues such as the Equal Rights Amendment (ERA), then being considered in the state legislatures. Recent scholars have pointed to the moderateness of her support for the ERA, noting that she devoted only ten speeches—less than 10 percent of her total discourse—to the subject of women's rights.[52] Yet public candor on a political issue was a response that Americans had not yet learned to expect from a First Lady; Betty Ford broke new ground. The most famous instance of her frankness occurred on 10 August 1975 when she gave an interview on CBS's "60 Minutes." She told Morley Safer that she assumed that her children had experimented with marijuana, that she "wouldn't be a bit surprised" if her daughter Susan had had an affair, that *Roe v. Wade* was a "great, great decision," and that if she were young again, she would try pot.[53] There was a brief hue and cry from those Americans who believed that the president's wife should be neither seen nor heard. Ford mentioned to a Minneapolis audience that when he first heard the interview, "I thought I'd lost 10 million votes. . . . When I read it in the paper the next morning, I raised it to 20 million."[54] Mrs. Ford was unfazed, telling a reporter, "I don't like to dodge a question, and I guess I'm not astute enough to walk around it." In exasperation, Press Secretary Ronald Nessen told reporters on the record that the president "has long since ceased to be perturbed by his wife's remarks."[55] In the long run, the CBS interview did little to damage the respect that the country felt for its feisty First Lady.

It is quite possible that the nation, in a transitional period in its thinking regarding women's rights, accepted Mrs. Ford's candor because it had already been so impressed with her courage. In late September 1974 doctors found a nodule in her right breast and decided that surgery was necessary to determine whether it was malignant. During the September 28 operation traces of the cancer were found in two of the thirty lymph nodes, and she underwent a mastectomy. Following her recovery Mrs. Ford became an advocate for breast self-examination, which she believed had saved her life. In her many speeches on the subject, her calmness and good humor impressed the nation. For example, in New York in November 1975 she said, "It isn't vanity to worry about disfigurement. It is an honest concern. . . . When I asked myself whether I would rather lose a right arm or a breast, I decided I would rather have lost a breast."[56] The respect given Mrs. Ford for the dignity with which she faced her personal crises was solidified by her stoic behavior following two near-misses on her husband's life. With shades of Dallas in their minds, Americans watched news footage of Ford ducking from bullets fired by two separate San Francisco women in fall 1975. The nation was not only relieved that their president had been spared but also impressed by Mrs. Ford's manner when facing the press after the attacks. Comparisons were immediately made to Jacqueline Kennedy, but Betty Ford had placed the office of First Lady onto the pedestal first provided it by Eleanor Roosevelt.

The public could not get enough of their new First Family; it seemed as if ordinary people had taken over the presidency. In one sense, all the fawning over Ford is not surprising. New chief executives usually receive the benefit of the doubt during a honeymoon period, at least until they make their first controversial decision. Ford's inauguration was punctuated by the national sigh of relief that followed Nixon's exit; there is something to be said for the observation that in August 1974 anybody was an improvement over Nixon. Yet Ford's personality and image were immediately taken at face value by the press and public, and that warrants an explanation. One would expect that, given the imperious behavior of his immediate predecessors, the nation would be somewhat critical of Nixon's successor. The events of the 1960s would seem to have destroyed completely the public's faith in their president; certainly, polls show that press and public alike had stopped taking their president at face value by 1965. The simplest explanation seems to be that in summer 1974 no one wanted to believe that Ford was anything more or less than what he appeared to be. People wanted to believe that the Ford administration could heal America. Vietnam and Watergate had turned much of the country, particularly the press, into political cynics; Nixon's resignation gave Americans the opportunity to have faith in their government again.

Ford realized that he could lose this goodwill as quickly as he had gained it, however. The maintenance of the Ford image was left initially in the hands of Ford's first press secretary, Jerald R. terHorst. Like Ford, terHorst was born in Grand Rapids and was a graduate of the University of Michigan. He began his career as a reporter for the *Grand Rapids Press* in 1946, covered Ford's first race for Congress in 1948, and then became the Washington correspondent for the *Detroit News*. TerHorst had been with that paper for twenty-two years before Buchen recommended him to Ford, who chose him as his press secretary. TerHorst's comfortable, one-of-the-boys relationship with the White House press corps was largely responsible for the good press coverage that Ford received during his first month. Just before Ford's first press conference, terHorst suggested that the reporters' chairs be brought closer to the podium and that the blue curtain that had hung behind Nixon be discarded. Ford then stood on the other side of the East Room in front of the open doors that led to the grand entrance hall. The result was a more open atmosphere and a vastly improved working relationship between terHorst and the press. With remarkably few questions asked, both the press and the public grabbed the opportunity for a new normalcy in their lives and plainly relished the moment.[57]

That moment lasted for exactly one month. Americans wanted to believe that the Ford administration could indeed heal their nation. Yet before he could set about that task, Ford believed that he must first gain control of his administration. To do so, he decided to clear two pressing issues from his desk. By those acts—the issuing of two pardons, one to Richard Nixon and one to Vietnam-era draft evaders—Ford destroyed his honeymoon with the American people.

3
★★★★★

"FOR GOD'S SAKE, ENOUGH IS ENOUGH"

As the combat troops came home from Vietnam, they received a welcome that, for many, was as traumatizing as their combat experience itself. Their country was not as grateful for their service as much as it was relieved that the need for it had come to an end. Politicians all but ignored the Vietnam veterans; their plight was too graphic a reminder of the politicians' own policy blunders. It would take more than a decade for any organized show of appreciation to surface for the returned veterans, and even then they were welcomed from a distance, almost as if a hug or a handshake implied support of the war. Against this backdrop, the question of what to do about those people who had refused to serve was particularly volatile.

Comparatively, their numbers were small—1 percent of all draft age men failed to register, and 1 percent refused induction.[1] Yet unquestionably they had broken the law, and most people agreed that they would not be able to repatriate without making some sort of amends. Moreover, personal statements of protest had been made on different levels; subsequent governmental studies have identified four different categories of draft resisters. One group refused to report for the draft, heeding calls such as the Reverend William Sloane Coffin's to "resist illegitimate authority" and staying in the United States. These "resisters" burned their draft cards, wore black armbands, and joined in the antiwar protests. A second group also refused to serve and stayed in the country but did not join the antiwar resistance. Termed "deserters" by the press, they went underground for the duration of the war. A third group, barely noticed by the press, were those young men who had faced induction but could not face war. They were formally defined by the government as a "combat deserter" who had been "conspicuously absent without leave for more than twenty-nine days, or [who met] other specified criteria (e.g.: escapes from confinement, seeks political asylum in a foreign country, or has access to classified materials)." The fourth and most publicized group were termed "exiles" by the press. These young people, who preferred to refer to themselves as "political fugitives," avoided the draft by leaving the country, usually heading for Canada or Sweden.

Yet these distinctions generally went unrecognized in the immediate months following the January 1973 truce in Vietnam. Press and public alike lumped these groups together under the term "draft dodgers." And most Americans wanted the draft dodgers, like the veterans, to disappear from their consciousness, helping to end the Vietnam memory. For some people, that meant letting the "dodgers" stay where they were—"America, love it, or leave it!" For others, it meant finding the resisters, prosecuting them, and punishing them. For still others, it meant having the president issue a statement of amnesty and letting them all come home.

This latter solution would never come from Richard Nixon. In July 1972 Nixon received a research memo from speechwriter Ray Price on the issue of amnesty; Nixon's angry responses covered the margins of the memo. Regarding Price's contention that Abraham Lincoln had shown leniency during the Civil War, Nixon penned, "This is a very weak piece . . . amnesty for *rebels* is irrelevant to our situation. It was total and unconditional as a war measure. For *deserters* Lincoln required *either* a prison term or return to units for service—*Never* unconditional amnesty." Next to statistics showing that Harry Truman had established an Amnesty Board and had pardoned 1,523 persons who had evaded service during World War II, Nixon scrawled an angry "never."[2] During the 1972 campaign, Nixon had said many times, "Never, never will we grant amnesty . . . until this war is over, until we get the POW's back."[3] The public generally supported Nixon on this point; in June 1972 a Harris poll showed Americans to be against amnesty by a 3 to 2 margin.[4]

Congressman Ford joined Nixon—and most Republicans—in his opposition to amnesty. Two days before Christmas 1965, both Ford and his Michigan colleague Philip Hart registered a strong protest against a decision to cancel draft deferments for some students who had staged a sit-in at a local draft board. Ford's vice presidential papers offer many examples of his statements against amnesty, including his March 1974 response to a Boy Scout completing a merit badge: "I am opposed to amnesty for those who fled our country rather than obey its laws. . . . If they want to return to the United States now, I feel that they must also be willing to be tried in our courts."[5]

Despite entreaties from his three sons, who were vocally in favor of some sort of amnesty, Ford continued to be philosophically opposed to it; however, the political realities of August 1974 led him to soften his beliefs. Faced by a battery of questions from the press about the fate of Richard Nixon, several of Ford's key advisers, including Secretary of Defense James Schlesinger, argued that some sort of reentry plan for Vietnam-era protestors would cement Ford's image as a conciliator, giving him the opportunity to bring to an end one more part of the "long national nightmare" of the sixties. Most important, they argued that it was just the sort of dramatic jump start that the new administration needed, allowing Ford to draw a distinction between the Ford and the Nixon administrations that would be difficult to ignore.

Intrigued by this opportunity to clear a politically sensitive situation from his desk, Ford moved quickly. Even though a formal program had yet to be proposed, much less discussed, Ford indicated he would announce his intention to pursue a clemency plan during a speech on August 18 before the convention of Veterans of Foreign Wars (VFW). No doubt Ford saw himself as if he were Daniel walking into the lions' den; if he could win this audience, he would begin his administration with a major coup. But his staff was worried. In a 16 August memo to Haig, congressional liaison Bill Timmons warned that "it would not be surprising if this audience responded with boos."[6] To hold this possibility to a minimum, Ford kept his plan a secret, and the announcement was omitted from the text of his speech given to reporters who accompanied him to Chicago.

It was hard to tell who was the more stunned at the VFW convention—the delegates or the press. When Ford began to discuss the issue of clemency, the room became dead still:

> Some fifty thousand of our countrymen [have been charged with] offenses loosely described as desertion and draft dodging. All, in a sense, are casualties. . . . I want them to come home if they want to *work* their way back. . . . So I am throwing the weight of my presidency into the scales of justice on the side of leniency. I foresee their earned reentry—their *earned* reentry—into a new atmosphere of hope, hard work, and mutual trust. . . . As I reject amnesty, so I reject revenge.

Ford's instincts were right—there was no booing. In retrospect, that is not altogether surprising, and to better understand why, a bit of terminology is in order. Amnesty, which does *not* apply to the Ford program, comes from the Greek word meaning "forgotten." It refers to absolving a wrongdoer of his or her offense. Clemency refers to the "disposition to be merciful and to moderate the severity of the punishment due." In short, with amnesty, the punishment is terminated; with clemency, the punishment is made less severe. Ford never intended to forgive the sins of all the Vietnam-era draft evaders. His program would be designed to allow those who had deserted to the American underground and those who had exiled themselves to a foreign country to come home without being imprisoned or receiving a dishonorable discharge or both—the usual punishments for such offenses. *That* the VFW could accept. Yet it was far from the unconditional amnesty that many antiwar activists had hoped for; even before the details of Ford's program were announced, they dubbed it "shamnesty."[7] Their criticism became even more heated when Nixon received his own grant of presidential amnesty, and Ford was assailed with charges of political hypocrisy. Nevertheless, Ford never wavered from his intention to base his plan on an earned reentry program of clemency.

Announced in mid-September and dubbed the "Vietnam Era Reconciliation Program," the clemency plan was a bureaucratic nightmare. Anyone who had violated a draft-related law, civilian or military, was eligible for consideration. The first requirement was that to be considered for clemency, applicants had to turn themselves in—a condition that kept the number of applicants predictably low. Once applicants surrendered, they were required to take an oath of allegiance to the nation and to agree to a period of alternative service. If they did so, their cases were referred to one of three bodies, which deliberated if the applicants merited a punishment greater or less than the alternative service. The Department of Justice reviewed the cases of unconvicted civilian draft evaders and deserters; the Department of Defense reviewed the cases of the combat deserters who were still at large; and a newly created presidential commission, the Presidential Clemency Board (PCB), reviewed the cases of all convicted and punished draft evaders and combat deserters. These three bodies were to provide a recommendation to the president as to the applicant's form of restitution; the president would make the final decision.

The manner of dealing with an applicant's specific circumstances varied across the three agencies. Civilian resisters who applied to the Justice Department were allowed to remain free while their cases were reviewed: if the result was unfavorable, they were prosecuted; if favorable, any action toward their prosecution was simply stopped. The Defense Department was more stringent, incarcerating applicants on a military base while their cases were reviewed. Applicants were also given an immediate undesirable discharge upon surrendering. If their cases were reviewed unfavorably, that discharge could be "lowered" to a dishonorable discharge and court-martial proceedings begun. If their cases were reviewed favorably, applicants could apply for a clemency discharge—which did not confer veteran's benefits but left them with the same appeal rights that were available to them before—and prosecution was stopped.

Dealing as it did with both civilian and military offenders, the PCB had by far the largest possible clientele (98,700, as opposed to 4,522 civilian offenders for Justice and 10,115 combat deserters for Defense).[8] And since it was dealing with convicted offenders, it had the more delicate task of reversing or upholding a previously imposed punishment. In that regard, it sat as a quasi-appellate court and as such, the types of resolutions at its command were numerous. For successful civilian and military applicants, the PCB could recommend the granting of a full presidential pardon, the commutation of sentence, or both. For military personnel, it could recommend a clemency discharge or a Recommendation for Discharge Upgrade (although recommendation for an honorable discharge was not initially an option). For civilians, it could offer a Certificate of Executive Clemency (Civilian).

Ford named as PCB chairman his close congressional friend, the former Young Turk Charles Goodell. The appointment was particularly ironic as Goodell had been blacklisted by the Nixon White House for his opposition to administration initiatives in Vietnam and Cambodia. The original PCB consisted of nine members and fewer than one hundred staffers, but this was enough to deal with the number of men who initially applied to the board for consideration—eighteen. Veteran's Bureaus, generally opposed to the plan, participated under protest and were slow to help publicize it. Nevertheless, the records of the PCB show that those eighteen received a thorough hearing. On 25 November 1974 (too late, as several White House staffers noted, to use the results as ammunition in the fall congressional elections), Ford received the PCB's first recommendations. Of the eighteen applicants, twelve were recommended for alternative service ranging from three to twelve months; five received an unconditional pardon, and one received an unconditional commutation of sentence without a pardon.[9] Ford and Buchen were given the specifics on each case and agreed with the board's recommendations without exception. In a public ceremony on November 27 Ford signed the first Executive Warrants for Clemency.

The work of the PCB officially ended on 1 September 1975, with carry-over cases being transferred to the Department of Justice. Despite

41

its efforts to publicize the options that it could offer an offender, the PCB heard from only 19 percent of those eligible for clemency.[10] Nevertheless, the one-year record of the PCB was impressive. It disposed of cases from 13,589 convicted combat deserters and 1,879 convicted draft offenders (Defense would eventually process 5,555 cases, Justice, 706). It did not give carte blanche to its applicants, a fact that undoubtedly contributed to keeping the numbers of applicants down. In civilian cases 1,432 received an outright presidential pardon, 299 alternative service, and 26 no clemency. Of the military cases 4,620 received a pardon, 7,252 alternative service, and 885 no clemency. A well-run and dutiful commission, the PCB was true to Ford's promise of "earned reentry" for draft evaders. Yet in the early months of the administration, a bigger question hovered over Ford's political future: Would Richard Nixon be given the same opportunity?

The story of the pardon of Richard Nixon began before Nixon resigned. A series of key meetings in the first days of August 1974 clearly reveal that Al Haig's protest in the second volume of his memoirs—"where Nixon's pardon was concerned, I played no role at all"—is simply untrue.[11] On 1 August 1974 Nixon told Haig to "tell Ford to be ready. Tell him I want absolute secrecy. Tell him what's coming. Explain the reasoning. But don't tell him when."[12] Haig scheduled a meeting with the vice president for later that morning. Not wanting to leave Ford alone with Haig, Hartmann suggested that either he or Marsh sit in on the meeting; Ford agreed that Hartmann should be there. Haig was particularly upset that Hartmann came to the meeting ("I hardly knew him, but the little I knew I did not like"), yet he could hardly ask him to leave.[13]

The three men met for forty-five minutes in Ford's office on the second floor of the Executive Office Building. Haig announced "Things are deteriorating. . . . The whole ballgame might be over." He also said that he had been told that the tapes subpoenaed by the special prosecutor and Congress included one or more conversations that would directly link Nixon to the Watergate cover-up. Those conversations, according to the Supreme Court decision, now had to be turned over to District Court Judge John Sirica. Once that was done, it was only a matter of hours before the press and Congress had the evidence as well. Haig said that he had not seen the evidence himself, that neither he nor White House Counsel James St. Clair had ever suspected that there was any such smoking gun, that the tapes were being transcribed as they spoke and as soon as those transcriptions were available, Ford would have them.[14]

Before the end of the day, Haig requested a second meeting with Ford·—this time, without Hartmann. During this meeting, Haig revealed to Ford the gist of the smoking gun conversation of 23 June 1972. Ford was stunned by the content of the tape. Both men knew that Nixon would have to resign. Haig asked, "Are you ready, Mr. Vice-President, to assume the Presidency in a short period of time?" Ford replied, "If it happens, Al, I am prepared."[15]

Haig listed for Ford six options that he had offered Nixon after hearing the tape of June 23. The first five alternatives included riding out the impeachment process in the Congress, resigning, stepping aside temporarily and delaying a resignation until the impeachment process was further along, maneuvering for a censure vote in Congress, or pardoning himself and everyone involved in the abuses of power and then resigning. It is important that Ford's recollections of Haig's presentation of the sixth, and potentially the most troublesome, option be quoted directly:

> Finally, Haig said that according to some on Nixon's White House staff, Nixon could agree to leave in return for an agreement that the new president—Gerald Ford—would pardon him. Haig emphasized that they weren't *his* suggestions. . . . What he wanted to know was whether or not my overall assessment of the situation agreed with his. I had no doubts about his basic assumptions. . . . Pressure couldn't be applied [to Nixon to resign] directly. Haig agreed completely with that. Next he asked if I had any suggestions as to courses of action for the president. I didn't think it would be proper for me to make any recommendations at all, and I told him so. Because of his references to pardon authority, I did ask Haig about the extent of a President's pardon power. "It is my understanding from a White House lawyer," Haig replied, "that a president does have authority to grant a pardon even before criminal action has been taken against an individual." He didn't name the lawyer.[16]

Haig has recently written that this list of alternatives was prepared by J. Fred Buzhardt, then serving as Nixon's White House counsel; however, during their conversation Haig told Ford only that they had been prepared by a "White House lawyer." Haig continues to be adamant that Nixon did not play a part in the preparation of this list ("I did not presume to instruct him in these matters"). He argues that he never showed this "hypothetical" list to Nixon, and "as far as [I] am aware, he did not know it existed until it was published after he resigned." Haig admits that he hoped for a pardon, but "if Ford divined what was in my mind . . . it was not because I told him my thoughts."[17] Former White House Counsel Fred Buzhardt disagreed and told reporter Seymour Hersh in 1983, "I would assume that [Haig] would have discussed with President Nixon this matter before going to the vice president, because it was my observation that he just didn't make decisions on his own without taking them up with the president, at this time or any other time."[18] Regardless of who came up with the idea, a pardon for Richard Nixon was now unquestionably on the table. And rather than rejecting it out of hand, Ford ended the meeting by telling Haig that he would have to discuss the matter with his wife.

Ford then briefed Hartmann on the meeting. Angry with his boss, Hartmann maintained that Ford's refusal to reject the pardon issue immediately implied assent: "I think you should have taken Haig by the scruff of the neck and the seat of the pants and thrown him the hell out of your office."[19] (Ford casually dismissed Hartmann's response, noting, "That reaction was typical of Bob. . . . Bob was suspicious of everyone.")[20] Hartmann then told Ford that he should consult with presidential assistant Jack Marsh. Ford agreed, but by the end of the day he still had not had a chance to brief Marsh. After a dinner engagement, Ford went home and told his wife of the day's events; she counseled him to make no recommendations or promises to anybody. Immediately after this conversation, Ford recalls he received a phone call from Haig in which he told Haig that he could not get involved in the White House decisionmaking process; Haig said that he understood.[21]

Early the next morning Ford met with Marsh, who agreed with Hartmann that Ford's silence on the issue probably indicated to Haig that Ford had agreed to a deal. Marsh suggested that Ford ought to seek further advice; Ford said that he would call Bryce Harlow, who had served as congressional liaison for both presidents Eisenhower and Nixon and who was one of Washington's most respected politicians. Later that afternoon, Ford met with Harlow, Marsh, and Hartmann; Harlow agreed that Haig's floating of a pardon had been Nixon's way of finding out Ford's opinion on such an option. Ford then picked up the phone and called Haig; Harlow, Marsh, and Hartmann stayed in the room during the conversation. Ford left no room for doubt: "I want you to understand that I have no intention of recommending what the President should do about resigning or not resigning and that nothing we talked about yesterday afternoon should be given any consideration in whatever decision the president may make." Haig responded, "You're right."[22]

There are some individuals who still agree with the congressman who told reporter Clark Mollenhoff, "Jerry Ford will deal on anything, and don't forget it."[23] Nevertheless, the evidence, though contradictory in its minutiae, allows for only one conclusion: as Ford was later to testify before a House Committee investigating the pardon, "There was no deal, period."

The issue was far from over, however. Throughout the first days of the Ford administration, Nixon's legal fate hung over the administration like the sword of Damocles. It was a major focus of Ford's first cabinet meeting, and administration members were besieged with questions from the press on whether Nixon would be indicted by the Watergate special prosecutor and if so if he would ever stand trial. In the face of this continuous interrogation, Senate Minority Leader Hugh Scott snapped, "For God's sake, enough is enough. [Nixon's] been hung, and it doesn't seem to me that in addition he should be drawn and quartered." On "Meet the Press," vice-president designate Nelson Rockefeller voiced his agreement with Scott.[24] But more important, Ford was pressured from within his new administration. Virtually all the Nixon holdovers, either privately or in press backgrounders, argued for a pardon; Haig and Kissinger lobbied Ford consistently.

On August 28, matters came to a head. At the 8:00 A.M. senior staff meeting, former Nixon confidant Len Garment gave Buchen and Haig a memo in which he referred to Nixon's failing health—Nixon was being "hounded, perhaps literally, to death"—and asked Ford to consider a pardon.[25] When Haig took his copy of the memo, he told Garment not to worry—a pardon was certain.[26] But Haig was wrong. Buchen later remembered, "I took [the memo] to Ford . . . and I said, here's what Len Garment wants you to do, but I think it's premature to even consider it, don't you? . . . or something like that. And I gathered from his reactions that he agreed with me on that."[27] Within the hour, Haig called Garment back and said, "It's going to happen, but not today."[28]

It is clear that on the morning of August 28 Ford told both Buchen and Haig that he was not yet ready to pardon Nixon; however, his responses at that afternoon's press conference—his first as president—indicated he was changing his mind. The occasion turned into a question-and-answer session on the fate of Richard Nixon.[29] Ford started the conference with an attempt at humor (noting that both he and his wife had inadvertently scheduled their first press conferences for the same day, Ford quipped, "We worked this out between us in a calm and orderly way. She will postpone her press conference until next week, and until then, I will be making my own breakfast, my own lunch, and my own dinner"). But the press would not be deflected. The first question, from United Press International's Helen Thomas, drove to the heart of the matter: "Mr. President, aside from the special prosecutor's role, do you agree with the bar association that the law applies equally to all men, or do you agree with Governor Rockefeller that former President Nixon should have immunity from prosecution? And specifically, would you use your pardon authority, if necessary?" Looking a bit surprised, Ford replied that he "subscribed to [Rockefeller's] point of view" but that "until any legal process has been undertaken, I think it unwise and untimely for me to make any commitments." This satisfied no one in the room. Ford was asked if a pardon was "still an option that you will consider, depending on what the courts will do?" Ford replied that he was the "final authority" and that he was "not ruling it out. It is an option, and a proper option for any president." Yet it was the final exchange that upset Ford's advisers; the question came from Linda Wertheimer:

> Wertheimer: Mr. President, you have emphasized here your option of granting a pardon to the former president.
> Ford: I intend to.
> Wertheimer: You intend to have that option. If an indictment is brought, would you grant a pardon before any trial took place . . . ?
> Ford: I said at the outset that until the matter reaches me, I am not going to make any comment during the process of whatever charges are made.

The final sentence of this exchange was a line that Ford had rehearsed—that he could not make a commitment while the judicial process was running its course. Yet his "I intend to" was interpreted by many reporters as a guarantee of a pardon, as the headline in the next day's *New York Times* indicated: "Ford Says He Views Nixon as Punished Enough Now; Pardon Option Kept Open."

The press conference had left Ford stunned. He could see the immediate future only in terms of answering questions about the fate of Richard Nixon rather than as an opportunity to defend or to tout the accomplishments of his own administration. He recalled in his memoirs that the press conference "forced me to address the issue [of the pardon] squarely for the first time. I had to get the monkey off my back."[30] By the afternoon of August 28 Ford had made his decision.

He needed to build a consensus among his advisers, however. Several hours after the press conference, Ford met with Buchen. Professing

that "[I don't] know what I'll decide," Ford said he needed some information on the scope of his pardoning power. He also ordered Buchen to
meet with Watergate Special Prosecutor Leon Jaworski to learn what
criminal charges might be brought against Nixon and to get an estimate
on the length of a possible trial.

The next day, August 29, Ford met with Haig, Hartmann, Buchen,
Kissinger, and Marsh and informed his senior staff that he was considering pardoning Nixon in the immediate future. He then polled everyone in the room: Buchen and Kissinger were in favor of the decision;
Marsh and Hartmann had reservations about the timing of the decision.
Ford responded to Hartmann, "Damn it, I don't need the polls to tell
me whether I'm right or wrong."[31] After giving his staff twenty-four
hours to mull over his inclination, Ford clarified his intentions for Hartmann, Haig, Buchen, and Marsh. According to Hartmann, Ford "was
very much inclined to grant Nixon immunity from further prosecution
as soon as he was sure he had the legal authority to do so. . . . There
was a deafening silence." Haig asked to be excused—Ford refused to let
him go. Buchen then questioned the timing of the decision. Ford
snapped, "Will there *ever* be a right time?" Hartmann remembers the
reaction of the senior aides: "Outwardly, nobody was wildly enthusias-
tic, but neither did anyone violently object."[32] Ford had his consensus.

Time was now of the essence, and Buchen's research on the presidential pardoning power had to be completed quickly. Ford agreed to
bring in Benton Becker to aid Buchen in his investigation. A former trial
attorney for the Department of Justice's Criminal Division and a former
assistant U.S. attorney, Becker had done some previous investigative
work for Ford, most notably during the Douglas investigation and the
vice-presidential confirmation hearings. Becker spent most of that Labor
Day weekend poring over casebooks. His charge was to decide whether
a president could issue a pardon before a formal accusation was made
and whether a specific statutory crime had to be listed before the pardon was valid. Becker concluded that "neither issue was an impediment against a pardon." On Monday, September 2, Buchen and Becker
met with Ford to tell him of their findings, and Ford was satisfied that
he had the power to pardon Nixon before indictment, trial, or verdict.
But one major catch remained. The papers, files, and tapes of the Nixon
administration were not in San Clemente with the former president;
they had remained stored in the White House. Nixon demanded their
release, and the ensuing argument loomed between both the offering
and the acceptance of a pardon.

Before the presidency of Richard Nixon, there was no question as
to the ownership or the disposition of presidential papers—they were

the personal property of the president to do with as he pleased. Presidential papers had been sold at auction, donated to the Library of Congress or to a local historical society, or even destroyed, most often by a grieving spouse. In more current times, beginning with Franklin Roosevelt, they were donated to a presidential library, built by private funding and run by the National Archives, where researchers could consult the written records of the administration. The events that transpired during Richard Nixon's administration, however, would lead to changing the rules for the disposition of presidential papers and further complicate negotiations between Ford and Nixon over the pardon.

In 1973 Nixon had made the normal arrangements for the donation of his papers to the National Archives, outlining the procedure in a legal document that governed the disposition of his papers (his "deed of gift"). By 1974, however, his situation had drastically changed. Simply put, there was much in the White House Files that might be used as evidence in any number of upcoming trials—of White House staff members and if he was indicted of Nixon himself. Moreover, the Nixon material included the White House tapes, already under subpoena from several different courts and investigative bodies at the time of Nixon's resignation. Few people were surprised when, the day before his resignation, Nixon changed his original deed of gift so that he retained the sole right of access and photocopying of his papers until 1 January 1985.[33] As soon as Nixon returned to San Clemente on 9 August 1974 he called Haig and demanded that all his records, tapes, and papers be sent to him.

In the confusion of the transition to the Ford presidency, Marine Sgt. William Gulley, the administrator of the White House Military Affairs Office and also the person responsible for White House liaison with former presidents, had begun to send truckloads of Nixon's papers to a hangar at Andrews Air Force Base. The White House was also destroying documents—burning and using the chemical paper shredder—at a high rate of speed. The day after Ford's inauguration, on authority given him by Hartmann, Benton Becker went to the White House burn room and ordered the destruction stopped; he also ordered a truck that was being filled with presidential material to be unloaded immediately. Becker, remembering that Haig professed ignorance of the movement of the papers, was unfazed: "I had no illusions about Haig, and so I went outside and watched that son of a bitch unload." Yet this setback was temporary. Feeling loyalty to Nixon rather than to Ford, Gulley simply increased the pace of his shipments until an irate Becker marched him into Haig's office. Haig, claiming not to know about the transfer, ordered Gulley to unload the trucks and cease the shipment of materials.

By then, however, some 400,000 pounds of materials had already been shipped to San Clemente.[34]

Becker then inventoried the remaining tapes and papers. He found 900 reels of tapes stored on the ground floor of the Old Executive Office Building in a converted closet too small to have a room number. He also found that along with 2,800 boxes of material at a Federal Records Center in Maryland and 6,550 boxes awaiting shipment to the National Archives, there was a total of 7,678 boxes of material in the White House complex—46 million pieces of paper in storage.[35] If Ford could rid himself of this problem at the same time that he pardoned Nixon, so much the better.

On September 2, Ford told Buchen, "If you can get the papers and tapes question settled prior to the pardon, that's fine. . . . But I don't want to condition the pardon on his making an agreement on the papers and tapes, and I don't want you to insist on any particular terms."[36] The next day Buchen, Becker, and Jack Miller, who had been retained as Nixon's lawyer, began work on an agreement pertaining to the Nixon materials, and by the end of the day a two-key plan was agreed upon. Nixon's written materials would be shipped to an archives near San Clemente to await the creation of a Nixon Library. For three years, either Nixon or his agents would have sole access to the documents, but no originals could be removed. After this time, the papers were Nixon's to do with as he pleased, but everyone concerned assumed that he would then deed them to the National Archives. As for the tapes, Nixon and the government would each have a key and would each share ownership of the material. The tapes would be in the custody of the government for the first five years, and only Nixon or his designated agent could listen to them. After five years, the legal title to the tapes would belong to the government, but Nixon could order the government to destroy some or all of them. After ten years had passed or if Nixon had died, the original tapes would be immediately destroyed.[37]

Two days later, however, Ford undercut the entire process and threatened to set the negotiations back to square one. At 4:00 P.M. on September 5, during a meeting with Buchen, Haig, and Becker, Ford reversed himself and ordered Becker to extract a statement of contrition from Nixon (Haig warned, "You'll never get it").[38] Then Ford stunned his aides by rejecting the Becker-Miller agreement over the tapes; a clearly concerned Henry Kissinger had been lobbying the president. Becker remembers:

Near the end of the conversation, the President advised that the Bird [Kissinger] had expressed concern for himself and others with regard

49

to a public disclosure of all tapes. Although not personally incriminating, those tapes were potentially embarrassing to individuals remaining in Washington, after the Nixon resignation. The President instructed me that in my negotiations with President Nixon, at the very least, *prevent public disclosure of the tapes for 50 years*. That was counter to Buchen's and my negotiations with Miller to date and represented a major impediment, in my judgement, to a full resolution to the records and tapes problem.[39]

Acting on the intercession of a worried Kissinger, Ford had undercut the negotiations of his aides. When Becker flew with Miller to San Clemente later that evening to complete the negotiations, he was carrying a set of instructions from Ford that ran directly counter to the deal he had struck with Miller. It was no longer clear either to Becker or Miller whether Nixon would even *accept* a pardon under these new terms.

When Miller and Becker arrived in San Clemente that night, it was immediately evident that Nixon had gained advance knowledge of Ford's new instructions to Becker. Former press secretary Ron Ziegler came to the door with an abrupt greeting: "I can tell you right now that President Nixon will make *no* statement of admission or complicity in return for a pardon from Jerry Ford." Becker threatened to leave (he later called it the "biggest bluff of my life"). Miller calmed them down, and they began negotiations that very evening. Ziegler was surprised at the extent of the problem, and the first meeting ended with no resolution.[40]

Aware of the shifting position within Ford's Oval Office, Nixon upped the ante. Completely ignoring the deal worked out by Buchen, Becker, and Miller, Nixon refused to accept the two-key proposal and insisted on maintaining final approval for access even for the special prosecutor. Negotiations thus began for a new, third deed of gift. When the discussions were over, Becker had given Nixon everything he wanted. A new agreement on the papers was crafted: Nixon would give the material to the government but only as a trustee. If scholars wanted to use the materials, they would have to request them, and either Nixon or the government had the right to object. Then after five years Nixon could order the destruction of any paper or tape.[41]

Next came the sensitive task of crafting a public statement of acceptance that both Nixon and Ford would approve, and Nixon won a clear victory here as well. Ziegler drafted Nixon's statement; Becker worked out four more drafts before they felt the final one was the best they could do. There would be no statement of contrition for Watergate. Nevertheless, Becker recalled that when he called Washington and read the statement to Haig, he asked if Becker had put a gun to Nixon's head.[42]

Before leaving San Clemente, Becker met briefly with Nixon and thought that the former president resembled "a man whom I might more reasonably expect to meet at an octogenarian nursing home. He was old." After a short conversation, Nixon gave Becker a set of cuff links and tie bar with the presidential seal—the last from his personal jewelry box. Speaking later with Ford, Becker opined, "I really have serious questions in my mind whether that man is going to be alive at the time of the election." When Ford observed, "1976 is a long time away," Becker replied, "I don't mean 1976. I mean 1974."[43]

Even as Buchen and Becker were negotiating with Nixon, Buchen was doing some negotiating on his own—with Watergate Special Prosecutor Leon Jaworski. All the agreements would be for naught if Jaworski chose to see the legal process through. For his part, Jaworski had never been inclined to prosecute Nixon. Before the resignation, Jaworski had strenuously opposed indicting Nixon, arguing that damage could be done to the country by trying a sitting president. When Buchen had asked Jaworski for guidance about the areas in which Nixon might be open to future prosecution, Jaworski assigned the task to his assistant, Henry Ruth. On September 3, Jaworski received from Ruth a list of ten areas in which Nixon was vulnerable to an indictment, including tax deductions relating to the gift of prepresidential papers, the misuse of IRS information, and the misuse of the IRS through attempted initiation of audits of his political enemies. Ruth concluded, however, that "none of these matters at the moment rises to the level of our ability to prove even a probable criminal violation by Mr. Nixon."[44] On September 4, Jaworski met separately with Buchen and with Jack Miller. In his meeting with Buchen, Jaworski gave him Ruth's memorandum and a letter, researched by another member of his staff, estimating that it would take about nine months to prosecute Nixon.

Immediately after the pardon was announced, Jaworski told the press that he had given Buchen "no indication whether [he] intended to seek an indictment."[45] In his own press conference, Buchen claimed that Jaworski had not informed him whether or not an indictment was expected and that Jaworski had never been consulted about the pardon.[46] Both men were telling far less than the truth. Although there is no concrete evidence to prove that such a deal was struck, it is difficult not to agree with Richard Ben-Veniste, a member of Jaworski's team: "In retrospect, it seems unlikely that Ford would have gone ahead in negotiations with Nixon's counsel without some indication that . . . Jaworski would not stand firmly against a pardon."[47] In a 1988 interview, Buchen came tantalizingly close to a confirmation of this conclusion: "Well, I knew he wouldn't challenge it."[48]

Early in the morning of September 8, the White House began to call reporters, telling them on an off-the-record basis that the president was about to make a major announcement. After attending church, Ford was asked what he was going to be doing for the rest of the day, and he replied, "You will find out soon enough." His presidency was now one month old to the day.

At 11:00 A.M. Ford appeared on television, reading a statement to the nation that had been recorded for broadcast several hours earlier. Little emotion or passion showed in his voice. Ford noted that the anguish of the Nixon family was "an American tragedy in which we have all played a part. It could go on and on and on, or someone must write the end to it. I have concluded that only I can do that, and if I can, I must. . . . I deeply believe in equal justice for all Americans." He also mentioned that allegations "hang like a sword" over Nixon's head, "threatening his health." Ford then concluded, "I do believe that right makes might, and that if I am wrong, ten angels swearing I was right would make no difference." He then read the proclamation pardoning Nixon for all federal crimes he "committed or may have committed or taken part in" while in office and signed it.[49]

Immediately after the announcement, Buchen met the press: "President Ford has chosen to carry out a responsibility expressed in the Preamble to the Constitution of ensuring domestic tranquility." Buchen argued that there had been no personal contact between Nixon and Ford before the pardon was issued, and in answer to a direct question, he emphatically declared, "There were no secret agreements made."[50] Few in the room believed him.

4

★ ★ ★ ★ ★

"DOESN'T HE HAVE ANY
SENSE OF TIMING?"

With the stroke of his pen, Ford had destroyed his month-long honeymoon. No longer was he seen to be an average guy; he was suddenly treated as an average president. So christened, Ford immediately paid the price at the polls. His approval rating plummeted from 71 percent to 50 percent in less than a week. One man from Alabama was so incensed that he filed a civil suit against "Gerald R. Ford, alias Leslie King, Jr., a/k/a Former Congressman from Michigan, Private Citizen Prior to Being Appointed by Devious Means to the Office of the President of the United States," seeking to have the Twenty-fifth Amendment declared unconstitutional.[1]

Yet Ford paid a higher price for his decision than the cost in personal popularity indicated. His action had quite the opposite effect from that which Ford intended. Rather than ridding himself of the ghost of Nixon past, the pardon—negotiated in secret, crafted on advice from Ford's inner circle, and given on terms clearly in Nixon's favor—threatened to strangle any attempt to initiate a Ford presidency.

The so-called balance of powers in American government is not a static entity; throughout our history the balance of that power has shifted among the three branches of government. The effects of the New Deal and World War II stripped federal power from Congress and planted it squarely in the executive office. Yet after 1945 Congress grew restless over the increase in presidential power, particularly presidential appropriation of the constitutional duty of Congress to declare war. The Korean War began the debate; Vietnam brought it to the fore. The term "balance of powers" no longer seemed to apply; many observers viewed the presidency as a runaway office with virtually no controls placed on it—an institution that Arthur M. Schlesinger, Jr., had aptly labeled "imperial." It was an office that had sanctioned an unpopular war, spied upon and harassed those people who opposed that policy, and lied to the rest of the population about its actions. The 1971 publication of the "Pentagon Papers," which outlined a history of presidential deceit and misuse of power, confirmed for many individuals on Capitol Hill that the time had come to wrest power from the executive branch.

That movement was hastened by the disdain with which Nixon treated Congress throughout his administration—not as an adversary but as an enemy to be vanquished completely. Even before Watergate, Congress was taking the first steps toward a process that would become known as congressional oversight of the executive branch. The 1973 passage of the War Powers Act, severely curtailing the president's power to send military troops into battle without congressional authorization, was decried by Nixon as unconstitutional, yet he was powerless to prevent its passage. Moreover, the Budget and Impoundment Act of 1974 took the budgetary process out of the hands of the president by creating two budget committees on the Hill, a Congressional Budget Office (CBO), and restrictive timetables, and it terminated impoundment as a method of budgetary control, further limiting the president's powers. The investigation, impeachment, and resignation of Richard Nixon confirmed the assumption that an upheaval was occurring in America's balance of powers.

Nixon, then, bequeathed to Ford a new relationship between the executive and legislative branches of government, and Congress clearly had the upper hand. It was not simply because Ford, like Nixon, was working with a Congress that had had Democratic majorities since 1954. The new mood on Capitol Hill made any kind of a coalition virtually impossible even for such an experienced legislative hand as Gerald Ford. More so than at any time since 1945, American government was truly divided, and Americans in the mid-1970s were introduced to a new term to describe the relationship between their president and their congress—gridlock.

During the honeymoon month, the frigid relations between the White House and Congress, which had typified the Nixon administration, had indeed thawed. Ford worked the phones constantly, invited Democratic liberals to the White House whom Nixon had banned, and established a congressional hour, held every two to three weeks, which allowed members to bring in important constituents to meet the president. It seemed that this new style would bear immediate fruit. During the first week, Shirley Chisholm and Charles Rangel, both New York Democrats and prominent members of the Congressional Black Caucus, had sent Ford a telegram indicating their intention to ask the black community to give the new administration a chance. Ford immediately picked up the phone and called a stunned Rangel to thank him; the president then invited the caucus to the White House, a meeting that took place almost immediately.[2]

No serious observer expected an indefinite honeymoon between Ford and the Democratic Congress. Still, Capitol Hill's reaction to the announcement of the pardon was so stinging and so bipartisan that the White House was caught completely off guard. Congress stopped treating Ford as one of its own and struck out at the White House with particular venom. In the Senate the response to the decision was so vicious that when White House congressional liaison William Timmons sent Al Haig a cross section of senatorial statements on the pardon, the chief-of-staff jotted on the memo that the president should not be allowed to see them.[3] Tip O'Neill spoke for many on Capitol Hill: "Jesus, Jerry, don't you think it's kind of early?"[4] The upcoming congressional elections were also prominent in their minds. One example of the many messages given to White House congressional liaison Tom Korologos came from Sen. Marlow Cook of Kentucky: "My gawd, what are you going to do to me next? Here I've got Wendell Ford on the run in Kentucky and Jerry Ford has me on the run up in Washington. . . . Doesn't he have any sense of timing?"[5]

The congressional elections of fall 1974 confirmed that Ford would have little respite from his battles with Congress, at least for the rest of his first term. Ford had been campaigning for congressional candidates throughout his vice-presidency, but the Democrats were making every Republican candidate an accomplice in Watergate, and thanks to the pardon, labeling Ford as an accessory. Taking the lead in his first truly national campaign, Ford crisscrossed the country with indefatigable energy, traveling 16,685 miles and giving eighty-five speeches in twenty states. He seemed to believe that his vigor would buttress his sagging party and that if he, as president, claimed his party was not responsible for Watergate, then the electorate would be sophisticated enough to believe him. Yet as one observer noted:

> When Ford . . . raced across the country speaking for every Republican in sight (many begged him not to come), he had nothing to say. . . . It was a frustrating, Mickey Mouse system, and compound-

ing the frustrations of no input from Ford was the total lack of any-thing to say. . . . It's difficult to say with a straight face that the only way to prevent future Watergates is to send men to Washington who represent the party responsible for Watergate.[6]

In addition to Watergate, Ford was forced to defend his decision to deal with the worsening economy by raising taxes—a decision that certainly did not play well outside the Beltway. And the assumption made by the Ford team—that Rockefeller would be confirmed in time to be the White House surrogate campaigner—had turned out to be a false hope.

Even though only 38 percent of all eligible voters voted that fall, the lowest turnout in over thirty years, the results were a clear-cut disaster for the Republicans. The Democrats gained forty-three House seats and three seats in the Senate and won four more governorships. The Democrats thus had a majority of 23 in the Senate and 147 in the House. New York Democrat Bella Abzug was heard to mutter, "My God, the rein-forcements have arrived."[7]

The power that would be wielded by this new-look Congress had been manifested in the middle of the fall campaign and had struck out at Ford in an unprecedented manner. On September 16, congress-woman Bella Abzug, along with thirteen others, submitted a resolution to the House asking that the president give the House more information on the Nixon pardon. She was particularly interested in any details on when and if a pardon had been discussed with Nixon, Rockefeller, or both and in any material that had been given to the president to help him with his decision. The next day John Conyers (D-Mich.) submitted a second resolution, asking for "the full and complete information and facts upon which was based the decision to grant a pardon to Richard M. Nixon."[8] William L. Hungate (D-Mo.), chairman of the Judiciary Committee's Subcommittee on Criminal Justice, responded to Conyers's and Abzug's resolutions by writing Ford and asking him to answer five questions dealing with Abzug's resolution:

> Did you or your representatives have specific knowledge of any for-mal criminal charges pending against Richard M. Nixon prior to issu-ance of the pardon?
> Did Alexander M. Haig refer to or discuss a pardon for . . . Nixon or the representatives of Mr. Nixon at any time during the week of Au-gust 4, 1974, or at any subsequent time? If so, what promises were made or conditions set for a pardon?

When was a pardon for . . . Nixon referred to or discussed with . . . Nixon?

Who participated in these and subsequent discussions or negotiations with . . . Nixon?

Did you consult with Attorney General [William] Saxbe or Special Prosecutor Leon Jaworski before making the decision to pardon . . . Nixon?[9]

Rather than compound his political problems by ignoring Congress, Ford went against the advice of most of his senior staff, including Buchen, and decided to appear before the Hungate Committee.

On October 17, Gerald Ford became the first president to testify in person before a committee of Congress since Abraham Lincoln.[10] In his opening statement Ford explained the pardon by saying that its purpose was "to change our national focus" from the problems of a "fallen president" to other issues. He said that no conversations on the pardon had occurred until the 1 and 2 August meetings with Haig. In his final protestation he said, "In summary, Mr. Chairman, I assure you that there was never at any time any agreement whatsoever concerning a pardon for Mr. Nixon should he resign and I become President."

This claim, as we have seen, can be documented with a reasonable amount of accuracy. Yet much of Ford's testimony before the Hungate Committee was simply untrue. When he claimed that "at no time after I had been president . . . was the subject of a pardon raised by . . . Nixon . . . or people representing him," he had conveniently forgotten the negotiations between Becker, Buchen, and Miller. Ford also claimed that no one on his staff brought up the matter before the day preceding his first press conference—also clearly not true. Moreover, Ford said that "the pardon under consideration was not, so far as I was concerned, subject to negotiation" and that the disposition of the records of Nixon's administration was "not a condition"; yet Ford had insisted that both a statement of contrition and the fate of the tapes be conditions of negotiation when he had talked to Becker the night before the presidential aide flew to San Clemente.

But it was the issue of a deal that stuck in the mind of Democrat New York congresswoman Elizabeth Holtzman. Her voice shaking as she began her statement, she remarked that there were still "very dark suspicions" about a deal. As she went on, Ford sat frozen, licking his lips, until he could take no more. Red faced, he interrupted Holtzman to address the "question [of] whether or not there was a deal. . . . There was no deal, period, under no circumstances." The scene, in retrospect, was amazing. Congress had a president on the ropes, defending and explaining his most private decisionmaking. A new day had dawned, and Ford had to work in that new day—clearly, the locus of power in the federal government had shifted from the White House to Capitol Hill.

It was a spirited young group who came into Congress in January 1975. Democrat Timothy Wirth, then a freshman congressman from Colorado, remembered with some fondness that "it was a glory time. There was a tremendous sense of mutual mission."[11] These "Watergate babies," as the press dubbed them, wanted to be both seen and heard, and quickly. They forced a change in the House Democratic Caucus rules, requiring that committee chairmen would be elected by secret ballot at the beginning of each session. The freshmen asked the chairmen to address the new rule formally as they prepared to vote on each of their fates. When the majority of the chairs refused, the freshmen let it be known that they would not vote for any chairman who did not comply. Even after most of them finally appeared to address the rule, two chairs were ousted.

The caucus also changed those rules of the House that had limited the powers of the full membership of any committee so that the full membership of each committee would have the power to control its own budget, and most important, the power to determine the number of its own subcommittees. Thus was created a new congressional substructure. There were now 154 committees and subcommittees, and with this increase came a rise in the power of the professional congressional staff members who did most of the day-to-day work for each of these committees. Washington reporter Hedrick Smith coined the term "the Power Earthquake" to describe the new Congress created by the events of 1974–1975: "Congress finally revolted, and not just for the moment. . . . What emerged was a more fluid system of power, one which made the American political system harder to lead than just a couple of decades ago."[12]

The pardon also set off a firestorm of criticism in the conservative wing of Ford's own party. The Republican Right had been at odds with party moderates since 1964, when the Goldwater debacle had sent them into the wilderness, and Nixon's 1968 victory had offered no salve for their wounds. The pages of William F. Buckley's *National Review* and Irving Kristol's *Public Interest* raged against détente, welfare reform, and wage-and-price controls. The 1972 presidential primary challenge of conservative Ohio congressman Paul Ashbrook had been poorly planned and easily brushed aside by the Nixon juggernaut. But the Right continued to grumble against Nixon, and in Watergate they felt they had been vindicated. Most members of the right wing had hoped that John Connally, former Texas governor and Nixon's secretary of the treasury, would succeed Spiro Agnew. Ford, who had long been viewed by conservatives as little more than a moderate party hack, was immediately skewered as an inadequate replacement. Yet during the first month of his administration the Republican party was publicly united in its support of Ford, largely because of Barry Goldwater's strong public backing for the new president.

After the pardon and the fall electoral defeats, however, all bets were off. Ford had been politically wounded, and a newly emboldened right wing began to criticize the administration openly. The nomination of Nelson Rockefeller for the vice-presidency was being actively opposed by many conservatives, a move that contributed to the length of time it took to get his nomination through. The depth of the problem was indicated when the archconservative *Manchester Union-Leader*, one of the most influential newspapers in New Hampshire, where the first presidential primary in 1976 would be held, began to call the president "Jerry the Jerk."[13] But a more significant portent for the future was the seismic rumblings coming from California.

Ronald Reagan championed the conservatives in their resentment toward the moderate wing of the Republican party. An actor in B movies throughout the 1930s and 1940s, Reagan's screen career had faded after World War II. Friends found him a role as the host of *General Electric Theater*, and he went on the speaking circuit to publicize his new show. As Theodore White has noted, "They wanted him to talk of Hollywood; he talked of Hollywood but also told them that America was going to hell."[14] As Reagan perfected his speaking style, he also completed his conversion from liberal labor leader (he had served six years as the president of the Screen Actors Guild) to conservative celebrity. His speech in support of Goldwater in 1964 was considered by many observers the best speech made by any politician that year ("You and I are told increasingly that we have to choose between a left or right. There is only an up or down: up to man's age-old dream—the ultimate in individual freedom consistent with law and order—or down to the antheap of totalitarianism").[15] The speech catapulted Reagan into the California State House as governor in 1966 by the then unbelievable majority of 993,000 votes. The surprising viability of his 1968 campaign for president showed his national appeal, and his strong stand against the student protestors at the University of California at Berkeley endeared him to

59

many people in the middle class who, only a few years before, had thought him to be too far to the Right. His refusal to challenge Nixon in 1972 led no one to conclude that Reagan's desire for national office had been quenched.

After the pardon Reagan spent little time anguishing over whether he should challenge a sitting president for the nomination. By late 1974 Ford's policies had become regular targets for criticism in Reagan's weekly newspaper column. The antagonism was fueled by the fact that the two men genuinely disliked each other. Hartmann remembered that "Ford thought Reagan was a phony, and Reagan thought Ford was a lightweight, and neither one felt the other was fit to be President."[16] By the end of 1974 all the signs pointed to a Reagan candidacy in 1976. An intraparty bloodletting, the first since 1964, was looming, a potential contest that would have a profound effect on the development of the Ford administration's policies.

The most important result of the pardon, however, was the immediate change in the public's perception—the image—of Gerald Ford. Americans had perceived an average, honest man who wanted to heal the nation's wounds. This image was perpetuated by the national press and in equal parts by Ford's genuine inclination towards compassion and the efforts of press secretary Jerald terHorst. But Ford's decision to cut his own press secretary, and thus the press, out of the decisionmaking process surrounding the pardon signaled the abrupt end of the honeymoon month.

Even though the press viewed terHorst as a breath of fresh air, Ford himself did not feel as comfortable with his new press secretary. He did not tell terHorst about his decision to pardon Nixon until the night before the announcement during a staff meeting called specifically for that purpose.[17] Ford later wrote that terHorst was not told was because "I recognized that he would never knowingly tell a lie to a reporter . . . and public revelation of the truth—before the proper groundwork had been laid—could have been disastrous."[18]

Visibly shaken by the decision and by this demonstration of Ford's lack of faith in his ability to keep a secret, terHorst gave Ford his letter of resignation immediately prior to the pardon announcement. Ford dispatched presidential counselor Jack Marsh to try to dissuade terHorst, but to no avail. TerHorst delivered a second, handwritten letter to Ford immediately following the broadcast: "Regretfully, I find I must hold to my original resignation decision effective today despite Jack Marsh's intercession. I can see nothing in the next 24 hours that would change my mind. Louise [terHorst's wife], on my instructions, already has notified the children and our parents. God bless you, sir—again, I'm sorry it is necessary to for [sic] me to resign. I do not intend to release the text of my letter to you. Jerry tH."[19]

TerHorst's resignation was the first salvo fired in a war between the Ford White House and the press that would rage for the rest of his administration. Ford's image was the main casualty. Not surprisingly, many journalists stopped writing stories about English muffins and Ford as an average guy and began treating Ford as just another Nixon clone in the White House—deceitful, controlled by the leftover Nixonites, and in general no different from any of his immediate predecessors. The *New York Times* had not missed an opportunity to rush its approval of the new president in the first month: it had supported his accession to the presidency, his call for an inflation summit, his clemency program, his choice of Rockefeller—even his decision to stop having church services at the White House as had been the practice under Nixon. But the *Times'* anger over the pardon was unrestrained. The paper curtly criticized Ford's action as being "inappropriate" and in "contradiction to what a president's job consists of. That is to see that the laws were enforced and wrongdoers punished."[20] *Time* magazine, another supporter of the president in the honeymoon month, joined in, charging that by "taking such a sweeping action so soon, Ford damaged his efforts to restore confidence in the U.S. presidency and opened his own credibility gap."[21]

Much of this reaction was as inevitable as was the hostility between Ford and Congress. The presidency and the press have traditionally had competing agendas, and the relationship between the two institutions depends largely on the amount of respect that has been built up between the two. Like Congress, the press began with a genuine respect for Ford; like Congress, the press lost that respect as a result of the pardon. Yet many observers at the time believed that the press was overly harsh to Ford even after the sharpest criticism over the pardon had dulled, a response that can be explained by observing just how badly the press had been stung by Watergate. The White House reporters had completely missed the story of the depth of Nixon's abuses of power—Woodward and Bernstein were state and local reporters—and they lagged far behind in exposing the ensuing cover-up. As a result, despite their affection for Ford, the White House press corps was spoiling for a fight and felt, as did Congress, newly empowered by Nixon's resignation.

It did not take long for the press to concentrate on Ford's competence. References to Johnson's joke about Ford playing football once too often without a helmet began to pop up in print and on television and quickly led to the press's reporting of Ford's physical mishaps. When the president fell down an airplane ramp upon arriving for a summit meeting in Salzburg, Austria, one network news show played back the incident eleven times in one newscast—once in slow motion. Newspapers ran shots of Ford taking spills on the slopes at Vail during his Christmas 1974 vacation, and predictably, a plethora of jokes followed (one of the most popular was the observation that Rockefeller was just a banana peel away from the White House). These mishaps were parodied into the mythology of popular culture by comic Chevy Chase. In the first episode of NBC's experimental "Saturday Night Live," broadcast on 11 October 1975, Chase "reported" in his first "Weekend Update" that Ford's new campaign slogan was "If He's So Dumb, How Come He's President?" Chase followed this barb with a popular weekly impersonation of Ford, complete with jamming pencils into his hands and pratfalls, which helped cement the image of the president's incompetence in the public mind.[22]

No journalist did more to popularize the image of Ford as inept than did Richard Reeves; his piece for *New York* magazine in fall 1974 was seminal in that respect. Reeves followed Ford around throughout the last days of the congressional race and described him in "Jerry Ford and His Flying Circus: A Presidential Diary." The story was a day-by-day chronicle of Ford's speech errors and blunders, highlighted with commentary such as "it is not a question of saying the emperor has no clothes—there is a question of whether there is an emperor." As devastating as anything in the text, however, was the magazine's cover and the story's title page, both of which portrayed Ford as Bozo the Clown. Reeves concluded: "We have always cherished the promise that any one of us could be president. Any one of us now is."[23] This charge was prominent in Reeves's 1975 book, *A Ford, Not a Lincoln*, in which Reeves claimed that "it is fair to say that Ford is slow. He is also unimaginative and not very articulate."[24]

Few aspects about his presidency angered Ford as much as the beating that his public image took from the press. In his memoirs, he complained that "there was no doubt in my mind that I was the most athletic president to occupy the White House in years. 'I'm an activist,' I said. 'Activists are more prone to stumble than anyone else.'"[25] In a later book, Ford observed that Chase's antics "were sometimes hard for me and my family to take."[26] To a subsequent interviewer, Ford was even more critical as he remarked that while he was spending three or four hours skiing at Vail, "most of 'em [the press] would sit in the bar all day long, and when you would come in from three or four hours of skiing, they'd be sitting there or standing there trying to get a picture of you falling down."[27]

Yet Ford continued with the strategy that had been decided upon early in the administration—parry the barbs of the press with unexpected kindness and access. Ford held twenty-nine press conferences during his presidency, an average of 1.3 per month as opposed to Nixon's 0.5.[28] And he had a staggering two hundred, one-on-one interviews with reporters. Harry Reasoner of ABC News was invited to do an interview at Camp David (Nixon had kept the presidential retreat out of bounds to reporters), Jack Anderson was given a forty-minute interview, and in a move that the Nixon holdovers probably felt was the height of sacrilege, Ford approved a White House tour for Bob Woodward, Carl Bernstein, and their two researchers as they finished their work on *The Final Days* (however, Ford would not grant either reporter a personal interview for the book). Yet even such access—a marked change from the Nixon years—was not enough; Ford's relationship with the press continued to deteriorate. Furthermore, Ronald Nessen, terHorst's successor as press secretary, only made the situation worse.

A history major at American University, Ron Nessen started his career in 1956 as a reporter for United Press International. In 1962 he began a twelve-year tenure with NBC News, serving as a White House correspondent until 1965 and reporting from Vietnam from 1965 to 1966. In July 1966 he was wounded by a grenade fragment, suffered a collapsed lung, and was returned to the states for recovery. After a series of foreign assignments (including Mexico City) and a stint covering the 1968 campaign, Nessen was assigned to Washington, where he specialized in urban affairs stories. In 1973 he began to cover Vice President Spiro Agnew, and upon Agnew's resignation Nessen was assigned to the new vice president. When Ford was sworn in, Nessen returned for a one-month stint as NBC's White House correspondent and, on Hartmann's recommendation, was chosen to replace terHorst the following September.

The tone of the press office changed overnight. A workaholic with a famous temper, which more than once was displayed from the podium of the White House briefing room, Nessen was prickly, to say the least. Reporter James Naughton called him "a shield with a thin skin."[29] Tom Jarriel of ABC News was quoted as warning a Ford speechwriter, "That big mouth of [Nessen's] is going to get him into trouble some day."[30] The tone in the press room was soon as heated as it had been under Nixon; NBC White House correspondent Tom Brokaw characterized the situation as being akin to a "cock-fighting pit."[31] After several weeks of confrontations during the daily briefing, Nessen finally read an angry response to a stunned press room: "If these briefings are to continue, the atmosphere is going to have to change." He then accused the reporters of "blind, mindless, irrational suspicion and cynicism."[32] Nessen, however, did little to repair the situation. The next month, when accounting for his own negligence in informing the press that Ford had had a meeting with John Connally, Nessen charged that the "blind and irrational mistrust" and "cynical thinking habits" of the reporters were hurting the daily briefings.[33]

Nessen was also in regular trouble with key members of Ford's staff. Most members of the press, even those who disliked Nessen personally, admitted and reported that the flow of information to him obviously was often disrupted by either Rumsfeld or Kissinger or both.[34] Yet other Ford staffers fell by the wayside while Nessen survived. Despite his running war with the press, Nessen made himself invaluable to Ford as a personal confidant—a role that Ziegler had perfected under Nixon and that terHorst had had no interest in perpetuating. The situation, then, presented itself as a long-term problem: Nessen was staying, and Ford's relations with the press showed no signs of improving.

In retrospect, the chief culprit in the crisis caused by the decision to pardon Nixon was Ford himself. Although it was true that his senior aides were feuding among themselves, Ford had not sought their advice so much as he had informed them of his decision. He then complicated the matter by shrouding his decisionmaking process in secrecy, reminding the press of the Nixon years and increasing the bickering on the staff. Ford would never change his informal decisionmaking style, but even he recognized the need for improving his staff operations. After the pardon, the experiment with a multiple-advocacy system was dead.

Ford's first step toward bringing his staff into a more cohesive unit was to provide it with new leadership. The president had never considered keeping Haig on permanently as his chief of staff. Moreover, he had planned early on to nominate Haig for a position that would not require congressional confirmation—a fight that Haig, given his relationship with Nixon, probably would not have survived. At the end of September Haig was appointed Supreme Commander of the Atlantic Alliance at NATO, a position he assumed in December. On September 21 Ford asked Donald Rumsfeld to join the White House staff. The second transition team had listed Rumsfeld as one of it choices eventually to replace Haig, and Ford had quickly checked the name of his old congressional colleague as his preferred choice. Ford remembered that Rumsfeld initially did not want the job, however, arguing that he enjoyed his position as ambassador to NATO, and most important, maintaining that the spokes-to-a-wheel concept of organization "won't work."[35] Ford had long since concluded that Rumsfeld was right and offered him the opportunity to phase out the multiple-advocacy staff structure and to replace it with a system that would work. Rumsfeld agreed. Still wary of comparisons with a Haldemanlike chief-of-staff position, Ford announced nine days later that Rumsfeld had accepted the position of "staff coordinator."

Rumsfeld was a new type of political operative in the Ford White House. His experience working for Nixon (at the Office of Economic Opportunity, as a presidential counselor, and as director of the Cost of Living Council) had made him a charter member of Hartmann's Praetorian Guard. His ambition for higher office was taken for granted by most observers. Writer John Hersey summed up the prevailing view of "Rummy": "The eye [has] a glint that seems to say 'That big leather chair on the other side of [Ford's] desk looks comfortable. I wonder if it would fit me.' He is bright, jealous, crafty, and fiercely competitive."[36] Nevertheless, Rumsfeld brought with him political talents that Ford badly needed and, as Ford critic Richard Reeves astutely noted, talent that "Ford never wanted. Like John Kennedy or Richard Nixon, Rumsfeld could shed people without a tremor."[37] He could, and he did so quickly. Before 1 January 1975 Rumsfeld had cut the size of the staff from 540 to 480. A penchant for strict organizational discipline—a Haldeman trait—was the axiom in Rumsfeld's White House. In an interview published in *Princeton Alumni Weekly* in November 1975, Rumsfeld observed that "the problems of today don't fit [into] compartments. . . . It is therefore important that the White House serve the President by trying to bring the threads of a given problem toward him in a coherent way . . . that is digestible and workable, so he can make judgements in a timely fashion. [The president must serve as] the connection between those different spokes as they come in, because the decisions don't fit on any one spoke."[38]

Despite his being the agent of rather significant staff cuts, Rumsfeld was greeted by most of his new colleagues with a collective sigh of relief. They too had been worried about the inability of the staff to help Ford articulate his administration. Yet it was soon clear that the appointment of Rumsfeld had not solved the problems of the Ford staff; indeed it had created several new ones. Immediately noticeable was that Rumsfeld was unable to stop the feuding among staff members. Hartmann soon came to believe that in the reorganization, Rumsfeld had kept a disproportionate amount of power for his own office. Rumsfeld, for his part, had Hartmann moved from an office immediately adjacent to the president to a larger suite farther away. He also forced Hartmann to involve the entire speechwriting staff in the writing of any given speech and began to make serious editing changes in Hartmann's drafts.[39] Rumsfeld's appointment made Hartmann even more bitter, and Hartmann began to attack Rumsfeld in press backgrounders. Rumsfeld's somewhat imperious attitude irked other members of the staff also. Treasury Secretary Bill Simon complained to Ford personally that Rumsfeld had been undercutting him to the press. Henry Kissinger once remarked to Rumsfeld in a cabinet meeting, "Don, your wife was over measuring my office today" (Simon remembered that Rumsfeld "had not been amused by the remark").[40]

The major in-house battle, however, was Rumsfeld versus Rockefeller. There is no simpler way to put it—the vice president detested Rumsfeld. Rockefeller thought that in carrying out a job that traditionally had called for anonymity and subservience, Rumsfeld was transparently political. Rockefeller thus saw his problems with Rumsfeld as "not ideological but highly personal [because] it was hard to tell what Rumsfeld's ideology was; you couldn't read it on his sleeve."[41] For his part, Rumsfeld admitted that he was aware of Rockefeller's feelings and "felt badly that he felt that way. He said that he respected the way Rockefeller had pitched in and helped the President. He said that the hostility that had grown up between himself and Rockefeller need not have happened, he thought, but he wasn't sure how he could have avoided it."[42] The fight between Rockefeller and Rumsfeld spilled over into the policymaking area, however, and had a noticeable effect on domestic policy.

If Ford had waited for another month, had he explained his thought processes to the American people before he made his decision, had he consulted or at least informed Congress, had he not kept it a secret from the press, then the president might have spared himself the violent backlash from a decision made too soon. His staff might have had the opportunity to grow to maturity and offer Ford advice that would allow him to articulate his administration's vision for the future. Instead, after less than two months, Ford's administration showed all the signs of coming apart at the seams—a simmering interparty challenge, a bad press, a recalcitrant Congress, and a disorderly White House staff. As he faced critical policy decisions, observers wondered if the administration was up to the job.

5

★ ★ ★ ★ ★

STAGFLATION

Virtually uninterested in economics, Richard Nixon nevertheless had reacted to the inflation of the early 1970s in a novel fashion. Acting on the advice of his secretary of the treasury, John Connally, Nixon broke from the conservative laissez faire economics practiced by past Republican administrations, and on 15 August 1970 he froze wages, prices, and salaries for a period of ninety days. Renewing the freeze through April 1971 had helped little. Moreover, public pronouncements to the contrary, the Nixon administration did not cut spending to the extent needed to balance the budget. It took until 1974 to extricate the nation from Vietnam, which kept a continued drain on spending, and thus Nixon bequeathed to Ford an economy in which inflation had run amok.[1] The 1.3 percent rise in the Consumer Price Index (CPI) in August 1974 represented the largest monthly increase since August 1973 and the second largest monthly increase since the Korean War. By October it had risen another 0.9 percent. Wholesale prices were also rising. On the day Ford was inaugurated as president, it was announced that the Wholesale Price Index for the month of July had risen 3.7 percent, the second biggest monthly jump since 1946.[2]

A large factor in this spiraling rise in prices was the increase in the cost of oil. In the 1970s America was clearly in an energy-deficit situation. American demand for crude oil had sharply increased throughout the 1960s, but domestic sources were not close to meeting it. In 1974 the United States needed 17 million barrels of oil per day, a need growing at a rate of 4.5 percent a year. Yet roughly 35 percent of that need was being satisfied from abroad.[3] American dependence on foreign oil was brought into sharp focus when America was suddenly denied that oil. The Nixon administration's support of Israel during the 1973 Yom Kippur War led to the imposition of an embargo on oil exported to the United States, enforced by the member nations of the Organization of Petroleum Exporting Countries (OPEC). Even though the embargo had been repealed by the time Ford took office, severe damage to the American economy had already been done. The price of American oil had skyrocketed—indeed, about one-third of the rise in consumer prices that fed the inflation of the early 1970s could be attributed to world oil prices after the embargo.

If Ford had faced only rising prices in the economic sphere, his task would have been merely herculean. But conventional economic wisdom—which holds that in a period of rising prices there will be a corresponding period of low unemployment and relatively strong business—was wrong in the mid-1970s. In August 1974 the unemployment rate had reached 5.4 percent, a .01 percent rise from the previous month. Civilian employment declined by 125,000, and unemployment increased by 19,000. Business was also slowing. The Gross National Product (GNP) was dropping, the Dow Jones industrial average dropped ninety-nine points during August 1974, seasonally adjusted housing starts declined by 15 percent from July to August—the lowest since January 1970—and the U.S. trade deficit hit a record $1.1 billion in August.[4]

Even if he had been so inclined, Ford could not revert to laissez faire to curb the economic meltdown of the early 1970s. Given the situation, any of the standard methods of dealing with the problem were fraught with danger. If he chose to control inflation by raising taxes, severely cutting the budget, or both, he risked slowing down the already worsening business scene; if he cut taxes, a move that would spark slumping businesses, he risked feeding the fires of the inflationary cycle. Despite this seeming Catch-22 legacy he had inherited, Ford was well prepared for making economic decisions. Nixon had not disguised his boredom with the subject, but Ford, the former member of the House Appropriations Committee, enjoyed it. In fact, Ford understood the intricacies of economics and economic policy better than any president of the twentieth century. Yet the Democratic Congress had some ideas of its own, and they were drastically at odds with the conservative direction that Ford planned to take. The resulting confrontation provided a textbook example of political policymaking: the administration quickly learned that the economic policies they believed were best for the nation, the measures Congress would approve in that area, and the policies most efficacious in the political arena were irreconcilable.

Ford first moved to deal with the economic crisis by making a major change in the White House economic advisory system. The cabinet, the Domestic Council, and the Council of Economic Advisers (CEA) had failed either to foresee accurately or to deal effectively with the economic crisis. Another problem was that Ford had not yet developed a relationship with his inherited head of the CEA—indeed, Alan Greenspan had been in the job for less than a month. Greenspan had begun his career as a musician, studied at Juilliard, and toured for a year with a jazz band (playing the clarinet). After completing his studies at New York University, he started his own consulting firm. A longtime bachelor, softspoken and shy, Greenspan joined the CEA in July 1974. Nominated by Nixon to chair it, through the support of Chairman of the Federal Reserve Arthur Burns, Greenspan was confirmed by the Senate immediately before Nixon resigned. Ford decided to keep him on but knew so little about him that when he referred to Greenspan in his first press conference, Ford mispronounced his name.[5]

Concerned about a perceived vacuum in economic policymaking, William Seidman lobbied for a new White House agency that would take the reins in that area. Ford agreed, and on 30 September 1974 the president issued an Executive Order creating the Economic Policy Board. The new White House panel was to "provide advice to the president concerning all aspects of national and international economic policy . . . oversee the formulation, coordination, and implementation of all economic policy of the United States . . . [and] serve as the focal point for economic policy decision making."[6] Its membership included the secretaries of State; Interior; Agriculture; Commerce; Labor; Health, Education and Welfare (HEW); Housing and Urban Development (HUD); and Transportation as well as the director of the Office of Management and Budget, the chairman of the CEA, and the executive director of the Council on International Economic Policy.

Haig supported the creation of the EPB, but he also helped convince the president that although Seidman's new agency was necessary, someone still needed to "be in charge" of economic policy; in a September 15 memo Haig argued that Secretary of the Treasury William Simon should be that someone. A Wall Street banker, Simon had served as director of the municipal and government bond department of Salomon Brothers from 1964 to 1972. Nixon had brought him into the White House to help deal with the energy crisis and had promoted him to secretary of the treasury in April 1974. Ford had long been impressed with Simon's suave manner, and he fundamentally agreed with Simon's economic orthodoxy. Consequently, Simon was named the EPB's chair and Seidman its executive director.

Seidman is certainly correct in his observation that the EPB represented "the first time in the history of the modern American presidency that a cabinet level body had been engaged to run the economy."[7] Yet given Ford's proclivity for soliciting guidance from a rather closed inner circle of advisers, it bears noting that the EPB was a joint cabinet-staff body, run, in effect, by two chairs—one from the senior staff and one from the cabinet. It had also been formed because previous attempts by other advisory bodies to deal with the crisis of the economy had not worked. As such, it calls to mind the Executive Committee (Ex-Comm) under Kennedy—an ad hoc committee that cut across the departments and staff, formed to deal specifically with the Cuban Missile Crisis. The difference was that the EPB was a permanent body, now added to the NSC, the Domestic Council, and the OMB and soon to be joined by the Energy and Resources Council as one of the five formal White House bodies that existed to give the president policy advice.

Ford employed this same organizational strategy to deal with the worsening energy situation. Clearly Simon would continue to play a key role in this area, having been designated by Nixon as the administration's energy czar. Ford, however, came into immediate conflict with John Sawhill, his inherited head of the Federal Energy Administration (FEA). Even though the administration had promised that it would not be raising gasoline taxes in the near future, Sawhill publicly argued for an increase in the excise tax on gasoline of about twenty cents on the gallon, a stand which he refused to modify even on the direct request of the president. Ford fired Sawhill late in October and nominated Frank Zarb to head the FEA. A Former Wall Street executive, Zarb had served as Nixon's assistant secretary of labor from 1971 to 1972 and as the associate director of the OMB. Zarb joined Simon and Rogers Morton, then secretary of the interior and head of Ford's newly created Energy Resources Council, as a member of what one observer called Ford's "triumvirate" in dealing with energy matters.

As the administration charted its way through the economic landscape, it was clear that the Democratic Congress would not accept Ford's more conservative proposals. Simon, a truly doctrinaire conservative who most closely matched Ford in terms of economic philosophy, rarely counseled any form of compromise. Yet with a more finely tuned political antenna than Simon and with less need for economic orthodoxy, Greenspan and Zarb would counsel compromise, both with Congress and with the Republican Right. Ford's decision to side with these two advisers says much about the policy priorities of his administration and in many ways is the key to Ford's economic policy.

Ford's advisers began the administration in agreement that inflation was a greater threat to economic security than recession and that finding a way to lower prices would cure unemployment. They made their opinion clear to Ford during their first meeting on the day of his inauguration (Simon remembers asserting that "if we can't finally control inflation, we won't have an economy left to argue about"). Ford needed little convincing. On August 12, in his first address to Congress since his inauguration, Ford declared that inflation was "domestic enemy number one." There was also little debate in the early months of the administration over how to deal with the crisis. Once inflation had been identified as the enemy, Ford took the conservative approach of imposing austerity on the American people and on the government. One week after his speech to Congress, Ford leaked that he was thinking about raising taxes for the first time since 1968. He also let it be known that he would not use the revenue gained from those taxes to finance government projects to help unemployment. Later that week Ford told the congressional leadership that the objective of the administration was to cut the budget to under $300 billion, and he reminded them that it would "require some firm action."[8] He also asked Congress to impose a 5 percent ceiling on any increases in entitlement programs.

With congressional elections only weeks away, any candidate who supported either a tax hike or cuts in programs that benefited their constituencies stood to lose ground. Senate Minority Leader Hugh Scott spoke for many politicians when he quipped that "there [is] a reluctance to share the president's enthusiasm for sacrifice."[9] To try to mute the fallout that would certainly follow an announcement of any tax surcharge, Ford tried to position himself as seeking the widest range of advice on the issue. A White House "inflation summit" was held in early September, primarily because Ford had promised Congress that he would hold one. It offered little more than the usual positioning and platitudes (former Secretary of Labor George Shultz, who attended the conference as a private citizen, remarked that the whole range of economic forecasts discussed at the meeting could be covered by a hat).[10] Such presidential grandstanding was just that; Ford had made up his mind on the course that needed to be taken in economic policy, and in any case, he was out of time. The economic crisis had become acute, and the fallout from the pardon left him with a need to prove his strength on the policy front.

On 8 October 1974, in a speech before a joint session of Congress, Ford called for a temporary (one-year) 5 percent income tax surcharge on corporate and upper-level individual incomes and for cuts in federal spending that would shave $4.4 billion off Nixon's proposed budget, thus bringing federal spending below $300 billion. To take some of the sting out of the proposal and to lend a sort of New Deal spirit to his program, Ford announced that he had formed a national volunteer organization in which citizens could enlist by filling out a form in their daily newspaper. This organization would be committed to finding ways to keep prices down. The program, entitled "Whip Inflation Now," or WIN, actually began operations that night, evidenced by Ford's wearing a WIN button in his lapel as he spoke.

Clearly, Ford hoped to mix service with sacrifice and come out a winner before the congressional elections. It did not work, even though, for a moment at least, WIN was a popular diversion. Over the next nine days, 101,240 Americans mailed WIN enlistment papers to the White House, and the number of requests for WIN buttons was staggering.[11] But WIN was little more than a propaganda stunt, offering merely an opportunity for people to wear a button and show their concern. Indeed the program was derided in the press as an inadequate response. Ford blamed the press, which he later noted "gets bloodthirsty and they have to chew on something and . . . I happen to think the WIN program did some good. Despite what the press said."[12] Despite the president's defense of it, WIN simply offered nothing of substance to deal with the problem at hand.

Infinitely more important was the vehement congressional attack on Ford's proposed tax hike. The Watergate babies immediately scorched the Ford plan as being too little, too late, and too uncaring to boot. Republican congressional candidates who dared to defend the president's proposal were made into lackeys of the party of taxes and Watergate, and it played a large part in the defeats incurred by the GOP at the polls that fall. Reeling from the shock of the congressional election, the White House recognized that the economy would continue to be an issue in the 1976 presidential campaign. Among Ford's economic advisers, only Seidman seemed to see the need for readdressing the issue, calling for Ford to develop a "contingency plan" to meet the crisis. Nevertheless, Ford continued to side with Simon and Greenspan, who argued that inflation was still the number-one enemy and that Ford should stick behind his announced tax hike.

In retrospect, it is perplexing that Simon and Greenspan continued to argue, in the face of seemingly overwhelming evidence, that the country was not in a recession. The explanation given by EPB staff member Roger Porter—that "at a time when double-digit inflation persisted with no slackening in sight and the unemployment rate was less than 6 percent, the state of the economy seemed to justify the analysis" of Greenspan and Simon—is unconvincing.[13] Throughout that fall, it was apparent that a recession had hit the country. In August the unemployment rate was 5.4 percent; by November it hit 6.5 percent.[14] Ford's own team also privately accepted as a given that the rate of unemployment would continue to increase. On October 16, the EPB Executive Committee was informed by its staff members that unemployment would soon rise from 5.8 to 7 percent.[15] As a result of rising unemployment, the overall state of the economy continued to tumble. By the end of October the index of leading indicators reported the largest decline in any single month in twenty-three years. Clearly, the country was spiraling into a rare situation known as stagflation—slow economic growth and rising prices—and Ford's economic team had yet to accept that fact.

It was political reality that kept Ford from publicly admitting the obvious. In the midst of a brutal congressional campaign, Ford could ill afford to admit that he had been wrong in creating a plan that centered on inflation at the expense of unemployment. For example, during an October 9 press conference, an unpersuasive Ford argued, "I do not think the United States is in a recession." Yet Ford had suffered at the polls because he was seen as doing too little to help. Acting once again upon the advice of Seidman, Ford decided to search for another path.

As a first step, Ford publicly acknowledged what had long been evident. On November 11, in his daily press briefing, Nessen admitted that the most recent data supported the assessment that the economy was in a recession. The next day Nessen announced that Ford was "not wedded to the 5 percent surtax. He is wedded to a surtax or some other method of raising money for his program." In an interview later that week, Ford said that he would agree to a "modification or change" in his surtax proposal, "as long as they [Congress] don't abandon . . . the revenue."[16] In a December 11 speech to the American Business Council, Ford finally declared, "We are in a recession. Production is declining, and unemployment, unfortunately, is rising. We are also faced with continued high rates of inflation greater than can be tolerated over an extended period of time." Ford promised no quick fixes but announced that he "intend[ed] to keep my experts working over the holidays . . . to augment and update the economic package that I will place before the Congress within the next two months."

That new plan was far from the modification that he had earlier suggested. He had long since decided, with the unanimous support of his advisers, not to accelerate the level of federal spending as a way to jump start the economy. Yet despite the continued advice of both Simon and Greenspan not to forsake the fight against inflation, Ford had decided to abandon the conservative orthodoxy of his October 8 tax hike—a proposal that had cost him dearly both at the polls and in the press—and to embrace the more salable notion of a tax cut. Over the holidays, both at Ford's Winter White House in Vail, Colorado, and in Washington, the debate over the efficacy of a temporary tax cut raged. Those who were against the cut, including Simon, argued that it would drastically increase the already growing budget deficit. Those on the EPB who supported such a cut, including Zarb, Seidman, and now Greenspan, argued that it would not add to the deficit because the stimulation would provide revenue from the income generated. After an agreement to modify the tax cut to include a cap of one thousand dollars per person, Ford's mind was made up.

During this same time span, Ford decided to wed his new economic plan to his strategy for dealing with the rising price of oil. In summer 1971, controls had been placed on the price of crude oil, refined heating oil, and gasoline as a part of Nixon's wage-and-price-control plan. At the time that the controls were placed, however, the price on gasoline was high (because of summer travel), and the price on heating oil was low. Thus since 1971 the oil industry had found it more profitable to refine gasoline instead of heating oil. Winter shortages had appeared, but the controls—an integral part of Nixon's thinking about the economy—stayed.

Both Ford and his advisers had long advocated the decontrol of domestic oil as a measure to help alleviate the energy crisis. The idea appealed to Ford on two levels. First, as an economic conservative, Ford supported the across-the-board deregulation of business as a matter of principle. Second, decontrolling oil was seen to be a moderate, workable response to the energy crisis as opposed to other solutions—such as gasoline rationing—that were being discussed. If Nixon's controls were lifted, the price of both heating oil and gasoline could be expected to rise. Ford did not move on the issue before the congressional elections were over; however, after the election he started thinking about the energy crisis in the long term. Once the market readjusted and domestic oil was being purchased by American refiners at a rate that exceeded foreign oil, gasoline prices would drop and inflation would be affected positively. Concerned about the short-run political costs of his program, Ford also proposed that the oil producers, already seen by the public as profligates who were economically benefiting from the crisis, pay higher taxes on their profits.

On the evening of January 13, the night before he was scheduled to make his State of the Union address, Ford delivered a talk billed as a "fireside chat" from the White House Library. No chances were taken with this critical speech: special logs were brought in—made of compressed sawdust so that they would not crackle—and, much to Hartmann's anger, his original speech was redone by both Rumsfeld and Nessen.[17] The first sentence was designed to set the proper tone of crisis management: "Without wasting words, I want to talk to you tonight about putting our domestic house in order." Ford's new plan was an eclectic mix of ideas. He proposed a one-time $16 billion tax cut for businesses and individuals, a cut that could mean rebates of up to one thousand dollars to individuals on their 1974 tax payments. On the energy front, Ford proposed a three dollar per barrel rise in levies on imported crude oil—the first dollar to go into effect on February 1 and then one dollar per month until April—the lifting of controls on domestic oil prices, and a windfall profits tax on the oil producers.

Conservatives, led by Simon from within the administration and Reagan from without, contended that Ford had abandoned conservative orthodoxy and the tax surcharge before it had been given a chance to bring inflation under control. Certainly the argument had merit. In accepting a tax cut, Ford had strayed from conservative economics and embraced the more politically pragmatic strategy of Seidman—to battle recession rather than inflation. The right wing also criticized the windfall profits tax as being a penalty placed by government on the successful and were quick to point out that Ford's plan would mean a jump in the price of heating oil and gasoline.

Yet it was the perceived lack of direction on the economy from the administration that did the most damage as the press pounced on Ford's "flip-flop." James Reston's comments in the *New York Times* are indicative: "President Ford has not turned the economy around with his new energy and economic proposals, but at least he has turned himself around. He was on a collision course with the new Democratic Congress, but they are now proceeding on parallel tracks in the same direction."[18] The criticism was valid; Ford's move was a reversal. He had abandoned a plan calling for a 5 percent surtax and had adopted a plan calling for a 12 percent tax rebate.

The Democratic leadership in Congress had been caught off guard by Ford's proposal, a measure they had been advocating for several

years. Yet they quickly took the line that although they had long supported a cut in taxes, Ford's cut was not enough. Al Ullman (D-Oreg.),
chairman of the Ways and Means Committee, introduced an alternative
plan in late January that made Ford's proposal look pale by comparison—a sharp increase in government spending for domestic programs
and a permanent tax-cut plan of $19.4 billion, deficit financed and
sharply favoring the lower-income classes.[19] Late in March Congress approved a tax cut of $22.8 billion—larger than either Ford's January re-
quest or Ullman's proposal.

Ford was livid. In a meeting with the GOP leadership, Ford fumed
about the effects that Ullman's tax bill would have on the economy:

> What was intended as a responsible tax cut is now something differ-
> ent. Up around [a] $100 b[illion] deficit. A tax cut is the best way to
> stimulate the economy. . . . But when you couple $22.8 [billion] tax
> cut and astronomical spending, I don't know if I can, in good con-
> science, sign it. . . . If we could recommit, then I'd promise not to call
> back to session, and let Congress reconsider later in a calmer atmo-
> sphere.[20]

The political dilemma was clear. If Ford vetoed the congressional tax
cut, all arguments about gratuitous government spending to the contrary, it would be easy for the Democrats to position him as a hypo-
crite—willing to support only his *own* tax cut. Thus Burns, Greenspan,
and director of OMB James Lynn urged Ford to sign the bill. They argued that a veto carried two risks: Ford could lose his credibility and
Congress could pass an even bigger tax cut just before the election. Simon, however, urged Ford to veto the bill, because of the size of the tax
cut and because failure to do so would give further ammunition to the
Republican Right. Although he agreed philosophically with Simon,
Ford concurred with his other economic advisers that it would be political suicide to veto a tax cut. Therefore he signed the tax-cut bill into law
on March 29 but with what he called a "condition. . . . I will resist every
attempt by the Congress to add another dollar to the deficit. I will make
no exceptions."

Given Ford's relationship with Congress, this was an empty threat.
The Democrats were clearly approaching the economic crisis from the
polar opposite of Ford's point of view—despite the growing deficit, they
believed that the recession should be brought under control by spending more money on programs that would create more jobs. Thus began
a flood of Democratic spending proposals. Ford complained to the GOP
leadership: "When you add up all the spending proposals, it's unbeliev-

able. We will swallow something on the tax side, but fight against increases on the spending side."[21] Yet because of the new budget rules under the 1974 act that greatly constricted presidential action and because of the Democratic plurality he faced, Ford's only weapon for dealing with the situation was the veto. Acting on Greenspan's advice, the president began to use his veto power in a systematic fashion to deal with the considerable number of spending measures passed by the Democratic Congress.[22] The result was mixed. Ford vetoed a total of sixty-six bills over two-and-a-half years; he was overridden twelve times. Ford's veto was sustained mainly on spending bills, including Democratic plans for higher farm-price supports, large housing subsidies, and more public-service jobs.[23]

Congressional Democrats attacked Ford's energy proposal using a strategy that had been perfected under Nixon—claiming that Ford had exceeded his constitutional power by promising to impose a tariff on oil imports without first seeking congressional approval for the measure. On 19 January 1975 Democratic senators Henry "Scoop" Jackson of Washington and Edward Kennedy of Massachusetts announced that they would introduce a joint resolution to block the tariff, "at least temporarily."[24] Their measure called for a ninety-day freeze on Ford's power to impose a tariff on oil imports. Despite the fact that the first one-dollar-a-barrel increase went into effect on February 1, Congress passed the Jackson-Kennedy bill.

Simon counseled Ford to hold his ground, demand both a tariff and decontrol, and be true to his philosophy of deregulation of business. Zarb, however, was worried that the situation was so volatile that Ford would be unwise to proceed with either decontrol or the tariff right away. As Zarb later remembered:

> We had a handshake with Speaker Carl Albert and with Mike Mansfield on . . . control. While four of us were in the Oval Office, the President reached an agreement. [The] President wanted twelve month deregulation, and we would have accepted eighteen months. They wanted forty-eight months and, as I recall, we finally settled on thirty months. . . . And we shook hands, and within a couple of weeks they both came back to the President and said they couldn't deliver the package.[25]

Fearing that a presidential veto on the issue would be overridden, Zarb counseled Ford to wait.

Again, Ford agreed with Simon that immediate decontrol was best for the nation's long-term economic health. But Zarb's argument—that only a phased-in policy of decontrol would be passed by the Congress—

77

carried the day. Ford vetoed the Kennedy-Jackson bill on March 4, but he included in his veto message a promise to delay imposing the second and third tariff increases for sixty days, and he would indefinitely postpone his plans to decontrol domestic oil. On April 30, Ford directed the FEA to take steps to decontrol oil over a twenty-five-month period and announced postponement of the second dollar on the import fee for about another month.[26] It was not enough for Ullman, who, on May 12, sent to the floor a bill that called for the reimposition of quotas, a gas tax increase of up to twenty-three cents a gallon by 1979, and a tax on 1978 model cars with low fuel efficiency—the gas guzzlers' tax.

The Democratic Congress, responding more quickly than the administration had expected, had painted Ford into a corner. He had been forced to accept a tax measure that was anathema to his conservative beliefs. At the same time, he faced a congressional energy plan that would not allow him to decontrol the price of oil immediately and that would end up raising gasoline taxes. Both measures threatened to alienate the Right even further. Yet as the presidential election grew closer, Ford needed to be able to claim victory on the economy. He decided to deal with the Congress on energy but confront them over taxes. In both cases, he came up short.

By the end of summer 1975 the Democrats were doing everything possible to drown their own energy bill, having suddenly noticed that it was as weighted down with tax increases as was Ford's. When it passed the full House on June 19, it was immediately stripped of both the tax increase and the gas-guzzler tax. No Senate Democrat wanted to touch the emaciated bill, and it died in committee. The administration quickly seized the opportunity to gain passage for its oil-decontrol package. In a July 8 meeting with Zarb, Ford agreed to increase the period of phased-in decontrol from twenty-five to thirty months, with all controls on old oil expiring on 31 January 1977.[27] Ford sent the package to the Hill on July 16.

On the day the plan was presented to Congress, Ford asked Zarb for his assessment of its chances; he replied that the bill was "headed for confrontation."[28] That turned out to be an understatement. Still smarting from the retreat on the energy package and keeping an eye on the upcoming election season, Congress refused to accept the administration's compromise. On July 22, the House rejected Ford's phased decontrol plan, 262 to 167. Three days later, Ford submitted a second decontrol plan, increasing the length of time budgeted to phase out controls to thirty-nine months; it took the House only a week to reject this plan as well. The House then passed a simple six-month extension of controls. Ford vetoed this measure and instead accepted a forty-five-day extension of controls.

Repeated defeats on the energy issue had become a political liability for the administration. Many of Ford's staffers counseled him to accept a Democratic energy bill and thus to put the issue behind him before the presidential election. Early in November Congress passed an Omnibus Energy bill, a measure that would roll back domestic oil prices to $7.66 per barrel but that would give the president the authority to gradually decontrol over a forty-month period. The debate over the bill in the White House was furious. Zarb counseled that political realities dictated that Ford sign the bill. During a November 13 staff meeting on energy, Zarb observed that it was the "best bill we're going to get out of the Congress before the election. Max [Friedersdorf] and I agree—[we] couldn't sustain [a] veto."[29] Simon, who had been defeated at every turn on energy and economic policy, demanded that Ford veto the bill, but Zarb's reasoning once again carried the day. Ford signed the bill on December 27 for "a number of reasons," according to Zarb. "First he believed he'd be overridden. . . . [Also] he concluded that he could live with this bill because it allowed him the authority in his initial period of the next four years to dismantle the whole structure."[30] Ford later remembered that Simon agreed to "support it 100 percent"; Simon did so publicly, albeit grudgingly. He would later write in his memoirs, "that a Republican President should have signed it [is] tragic."[31]

While trying to win an acceptable energy package through negotiations, Ford decided to throw Congress on the defensive over taxes. On 6 October 1975 Ford addressed the nation on television:

> Much of our inflation should bear a label, "Made in Washington, D.C." . . . Tonight, I propose permanent tax reductions totalling $28 billion—the biggest single tax cut in our history. . . . We must recognize that cutting taxes is only half the answer. . . . I propose that we halt this alarming growth by holding spending in the coming year to $395 billion. That means a cut of $28 billion below what we will spend if we just stand still and let the train run over us.

This combination of tax cuts and budget cuts—Ford's third try at stopping stagflation—was rather unique. It also astonished his more conservative advisers. White House speechwriter Jack Casserly wrote in his diary that Ford's announcement "stunned . . . Simon and . . . Burns," as it "far exceeded any of their suggestions."[32] Ford was also not spared the obvious irony of his situation from the floor of Congress.

On the same day that his plan was introduced, Tip O'Neill told the House, "I am glad that this time the President agrees with Congress on the need for a tax cut. Just a year ago at this time, when we were headed deep into recession, President Ford was calling for a tax increase."[33]

There were two differences, however, between this plan and the first two. First, this tax cut was both enormous and permanent. Second, the election season was now upon Ford, and this would be his last chance both to improve the economy and to score a major political victory just before the election. In an October 7 meeting with the Republican Congressional leadership, Ford pleaded, "I need help. It's the only basic solution. It is politically a good position. It is substantive and right. I will fight down the line. This is a reduction only in growth and it's time to take action."[34] In a December 10 Republican strategy session on the plan, New York congressman Barber Conable advised Ford not to "apologize for your strategy. We must have the confrontation now. . . . Shoot Santa Claus now, and not in May closer to the election." Ford replied, "In 1947 Truman vetoed a tax reduction bill that was overridden and he won in 1948. In 1954 Congress passed the biggest tax reduction and the GOP got beat. This is not a bad approach: a tax cut and spending ceiling all in the same sentence."[35]

The following week, Congress gave the president but half a loaf. It approved his $28 billion tax cut but without the proposed spending cuts. On December 17, Ford vetoed the tax cut's extension and on the same day insisted that it be linked to spending cuts. Faced with an economic crisis that promised only to get worse, even the Democratic Congress could not override the veto and was finally forced to agree to language that pledged cuts in fiscal year 1977. The next week Congress passed the Revenue Adjustment Act of 1975 calling for a $9 billion tax cut as opposed to Ford's $28 billion. But as Ford rationalized, "The important thing was that the lawmakers had committed themselves to trim spending simultaneously with any further extensions of the tax cut measure after next June 30." Simon counseled against signing it, arguing that the bill did not go far enough. But Ford's more moderate advisers counseled that this was the best bill he could hope to get from Congress this close to an election. Ford signed the bill.[36]

The long run would show that the tax cut bill of 1975 and the Omnibus Energy bill of 1975 would help to bring the economy out of the recession. The CPI had dropped from its 11 percent high in 1974 to 9.1 percent in 1975, and it continued its fall until it hit 5.8 percent by late

1976. Also, 4 million more people had jobs in early 1976 than during the low point of the 1975 recession.[37] Nevertheless, neither bill was Gerald Ford's. He had been forced to accept Congress' offer in both cases, hamstrung by the knowledge that one more overridden veto would confirm in the public mind the image of an administration with no direction. This view is not entirely fair—on the economy, Ford initially had a direction—he simply abandoned it out of political necessity. In so doing, however, Ford had opened himself to charges of flip-flopping on the issues and had exposed himself to attacks from the Republican right wing. His social policies presented him with the same dilemma and met much the same fate.

6

★ ★ ★ ★ ★

"BRUSH FIRES"

In one of the most innovative moves of the transition period, Ford had promised his vice-president designate that he would be, in effect, the administration's domestic policy czar. Nelson Rockefeller recalled in a 1977 interview that Ford had told him, "I want you on the domestic, and Henry on the foreign, and we can move things."[1] Thus, although Kenneth Cole was retained as the Domestic Council's executive director, Ford named Rockefeller vice chairman of the council, with immediate responsibility for overseeing the day-to-day work of its staff. This appointment represented a major delegation of power to Rockefeller. Therefore, when he proposed that he also assume the duties of the executive director, replacing Cole, Rumsfeld was resistant. Hearing of his opposition, Rockefeller charged into Rumsfeld's office and demanded that, as vice president, his plan be accepted. Rumsfeld's response was cool: "That's not the way we do things around here."[2] Taken aback, Rockefeller modified his proposal, suggesting instead that Cole be replaced by two men; one would be an assistant to the president for Domestic Affairs and the other would serve as his deputy—both would be picked by Rockefeller. This time, however, both Rumsfeld and Buchen opposed the vice president.

Rockefeller was indignant over interference in what he viewed as a promise from Ford to oversee domestic policy. The matter was taken to the president, and on the surface at least, it seemed that Ford had sided with Rockefeller. James Cannon, a Rockefeller intimate, was named executive director of the Council and was also appointed to the White

House staff, serving as an assistant to the president for Domestic Affairs; a second Rockefeller lieutenant, Richard Dunham, was made deputy director. But Ford gave a second deputy's spot to James Cavanaugh, who had joined Nixon's Domestic Council in 1971 as a health policy specialist and was widely viewed as a Rumsfeld ally.

Cannon now found himself is a miserable position. He had two deputies instead of one, each man allied to the two competing arms of power within the administration. More important, tying Cannon to the president's staff stretched his own loyalty. He worked for Rockefeller on the Domestic Council, but he was also a member of Ford's inner circle. As a result, the lines of responsibility and communication were muddied. Cannon, not a hands-on administrator, also had difficulty asserting his authority.

Ultimately, however, the executive director's problems did not really matter. According to Cannon,

> Rockefeller . . . aimed to make the Domestic Council the equivalent in domestic affairs of the National Security Council. This was really impossible, because what President Ford wanted the Domestic Council to do was essentially to deal with putting out brush fires, to move paper back and forth between the departments and the White House. Rockefeller, on the other hand, was uninterested in this kind of work. He was more interested in the long-range implications of domestic policy.[3]

Ford's promise of a free hand for Rockefeller in the realm of domestic policy had been an empty one. Many observers believe that Ford never intended for either Rockefeller or the Domestic Council to be the organ of domestic policy development. As Dick Cheney bluntly put it: "Ford gave [Rockefeller] a mandate to come up with new starts but, on the other hand, there weren't going to be any new starts."[4] Rockefeller admitted that the Domestic Council under Ford developed into an agency to put out brush fires, and he knew precisely whom to blame: "That obviously was Rumsfeld's concept of what the staff of the Domestic Council should be used for. . . . Rumsfeld did not openly or officially take this position, but it was clear that was the way he wanted the Domestic Council to operate."[5]

The Domestic Council, then, was a minor player in the Ford administration. For example, Cannon was not even consulted when Ford made his October 1975 decision to propose a permanent tax cut—a charge that Cannon pointedly made in an angry memo to Rumsfeld.[6] In terms of policy development, Rockefeller was ignored for the rest of the administration as a domestic adviser. He was not replaced, and for all

intents and purposes, no one was in charge of Ford's domestic and social policies. In his economic policy, Ford had begun with a conservative
agenda only to have it sacrificed to political expediency; yet he never offered any coherent social agenda, and the possibilities for a conservative
social agenda simply never happened. Ford's desire to reform the system of federal regulation of business was essentially abandoned when
his efforts met unexpected opposition from businesses, which balked at
administration interference in business in any way. Education policy
had no real administration advocate, and an administration bill that
would have cut monies to federal programs such as the Right to Read
Program and Native American education was stopped by Congress. On
24 June 1975 Ford vetoed the Emergency Housing Act of 1975, arguing
financial exigency. Yet after compromises in conference committees,
Ford grudgingly signed a bill that was remarkably like the original bill
he had vetoed. Environmental policy received short shrift, and with the
exception of Betty Ford's high-profile support for the Equal Rights
Amendment, women's rights organizations did not have a true advocate
in the administration.[7]

For the most part, Ford's domestic policy was less an articulated
agenda and more an exercise in crisis management—dealing with brush
fires in areas such as civil rights, urban issues, and labor problems. Depending on the situation, Ford turned to a staff member or a cabinet
member to deal with the flare-ups. Depending upon the person responsible for the situation, the outcome was different each time.

Until the late 1960s, the legacy of *Brown v. Board of Education* (1954)
had been an uneven one. The case was clearly the legal spark that
started the fires of the civil rights movement blazing, but the Court had
refused to announce a definite timeline for the completion of school desegregation. Instead, in *Brown*'s reargument, the Court called only for
school systems to desegregate with "all deliberate speed." For the presidents who followed *Brown*'s order, including Nixon, having no timeline
for desegregation suited them. In 1969, however, the Burger Court demanded immediate desegregation. In *Alexander v. Holmes County*, the
Court ruled that "the obligation of every school district is to terminate
dual school systems at once and to operate now and hereafter only uni-
tary schools" and that separate but equal schools were "no longer con-
stitutionally permissible."

Forced to deal with a situation he would have preferred to ignore,
Nixon made a public distinction between the South, which had laws
hampering the pace of desegregation (de jure segregation), and other

areas of the country in which segregation was a social rather than a legal fact (de facto segregation). Nixon made it clear that as president, he had the power to attack de jure, but not de facto segregation. His moderate approach was accepted with more tolerance by southern leaders than the more strident tactics of Kennedy and Johnson had been. Thus by the end of Nixon's tenure, the percentage of African-American children attending segregated schools had shrunk from 68 percent to 8 percent.[8]

The problem of segregated schools in the North was virtually ignored by Nixon, however. Despite the Court's 1971 order in *Swann v. Charlotte-Mecklenburg County School District*, which ruled that busing to achieve racial integration was legal, and its commitment to extending integration in the North, as voiced in *Keyes v. Denver School District* (1973), Nixon dragged his feet. Northern school districts were faced with a dilemma of major proportions—if they obeyed the law and ordered a school to desegregate, they could expect little help from Nixon's Justice Department. At the time of Nixon's resignation, the situation was made to order for an inner-city explosion of sizable proportions. That convulsion awaited Ford in Boston.

Boston journalist Alan Lupo has observed: "The real story of Boston is the story of two cities. It's a story of the traditional, alleged liberal, abolitionist Boston, the progressive Boston. . . . But the other Boston is a very hidebound, distrustful, turf-conscious, class-conscious, parochial city, full of people who did not make much progress over the years. I'm talking about white folks."[9] Public schools in Boston had clearly remained both separate and unequal. In 1965 one in four of Boston's students were black and yet only one in two hundred teachers were black and there were no black principals. A group of parents, led by Ruth Boston of the Boston Branch of the National Association for the Advancement of Colored People (NAACP), initiated a heated exchange with the Boston School Committee over educational disparity in that city as well as over the books and supplies that their children were forced to use (in one popular textbook, a teacher found the song "Ten Little Niggers Sitting on a Fence" being used to teach arithmetic). Nevertheless, the popular chair of the School Committee, Louise Day Hicks, declared that the texts were adequate for classroom use and refused to speak to the blacks if the word "segregated" was used to describe Boston schools. In response, many black parents organized their own alternative schools, but they were too expensive to keep operational.

The battle then shifted to the public schools. In early 1972, under NAACP guidance, black parents filed a class action suit in federal district court that demanded the right for their children to attend suitable public high schools. Chiefly this move would directly affect the two most racially charged neighborhoods in the city, predominantly black Roxbury and Irish-American South Boston, separated by less than a mile. Everyone knew that if the NAACP won their suit, black students would have to be bused from Roxbury to the mostly white South High; it was just as obvious that that decision would lead to violence.

In June 1974, U.S. District Court judge Arthur Garrity, Jr., found the city of Boston guilty of unconstitutional segregation of the city's schools and ordered the immediate development of a busing plan. The School Committee refused to comply. Ignoring the committee, Garrity worked out a plan with the State Department of Education, which called for integrating only those schools that were near each other, thus requiring a minimal amount of busing. This solution, however, led to the coupling of communities such as Roxbury and South Boston. The polarization was quick and brutal. Antibusing groups such as Restore our Alienated Rights (ROAR) and probusing groups such as those centered in a Roxbury community center known as the Black Pentagon were formed. Massachusetts senator Edward Kennedy, a Democrat whose children attended private schools, also positioned himself as a proponent of busing. An attempt by ROAR to secure federal legislation to reverse Garrity's order led to a march on the Federal Building three days before school was slated to open. Kennedy made an appearance, but the crowd quickly turned on him and chased him inside, pounding on the barricaded glass doors until they shattered.

On opening day, September 12, Roxbury was quiet. Black parents met the few white students who arrived and accompanied them to their new classrooms. But at South Boston High, most white students were kept from the classrooms while their parents took to the streets around the school. Incoming black students were assailed with jeers and flying missiles; the ensuing riot injured nine children and damaged eighteen buses. Thus began the organized white boycott of the city schools, patterned, ironically, after the black boycotts of the segregated schools in the South in the 1960s. Throughout the year, black students were met by white adults holding bananas, calling the children apes, and chanting obscenities. Fights were common, and metal detectors were installed in the doorways of most schools. It was only weeks before the violence spread to Roxbury, sparked by the October 7 beating of a Haitian man who had been pulled from his car by a South Boston mob.

It has been argued that Ford's stand against busing was another calculated political decision. After all, there were no liberal votes to be had for the Republican party on the issue, and a probusing stand would endear him only to liberals. This being said, Ford's stand on the issue of busing was nothing if not consistent. Ford often remarked about how well served he was by going to a neighborhood school in Grand Rapids. As a congressman, though he voted for the Civil Rights Act of 1964, he also spoke out against busing that same year in a speech to the Republican National Convention.[10] During his vice-presidential confirmation hearings, Ford testified that he opposed forced busing of school children to attain racial balance but favored "compensatory education" for the disadvantaged.[11] During his first press conference as president, he noted that he "respectfully disagreed" with Garrity's order, a stand that he would take several times later in the conflict.

According to White House Counsel Philip Buchen, "The guiding principle that [Ford] finally adopted with regard to busing was that it should in all cases be limited to correcting the effects of intentional segregation. If segregation result[ed] from other causes, he did not think that busing should be applied as a remedy. This would be a form of overreaction."[12] Ford, then, followed the same line of argument as had his predecessor, arguing that he could respond to de jure segregation but not to de facto. Yet by fall 1974 the situation in Boston had gone too far to be solved by such legal hairsplitting, and Ford's reaction to the situation satisfied no one. The question remained, however, whether or not the Justice Department would intervene and initiate proceedings legally binding the Boston schoolboard to obey Judge Garrity's order.

When Ford looked at the Department of Justice he had inherited from Nixon, he found a department that had been ravaged, more so than any other in government, by Watergate. It was from his position as attorney general that John Mitchell had either planned or overseen some of the more blatant abuses of power of the Nixon administration. Mitchell's immediate successor, Richard Kleindienst, was also an accessory in Watergate-related abuses, and neither Elliot Richardson nor William Saxbe, both chosen by Nixon for their confirmability, had succeeded in restoring either the luster or the morale at Justice. Ford could only have been pleased when Saxbe became the first member of his inherited cabinet to resign in August 1974 to accept the appointment as U.S. Ambassador to India.

The January 1975 appointment of Edward Levi, then serving as president of the University of Chicago, as Ford's attorney general was Rumsfeld's idea. Levi had been a staff member of the House Judiciary Committee and between 1940 and 1945 had served as a special assistant to the attorney general. Levi made it clear to Ford early in the nominating process that he would not take the job unless Justice was made apo-

litical.[13] It would seem that he held true to his position during the busing crisis. He remembered that Ford had told him "The decision is all
yours," and that he made his decision without any interference from
the president. Levi decided that Boston was on its own; the federal government would not intervene. Levi also maintained that he had not considered political factors when he waited several months before issuing
his order on the busing situation. Arguing that "the department did not
have a copy of the record in the case," he had therefore decided not to
act in haste.[14] Ford agreed with Levi and defended his attorney general
in cabinet meetings in which other advisers, most notably secretary of
transportation William Coleman, the only black member of the cabinet
and a former civil rights advocate before the federal bench, argued that
Ford had to intervene. In fact Ford was ready to intercede if violence
broke out. He had ordered the Department of Defense to put fifteen
hundred troops of the Eighty-second Airborne on an increased state of
readiness, which would allow them to be in Boston in nine hours.[15]

On 11 December 1974 the violence hit. A fight at South Boston
High led to the non-fatal stabbing of Michael Faith, a white student. A
mob of angry white parents surrounded the school, refusing to let the
black students leave and threatening to storm the building. Louise
Hicks appeared and announced, "I want you to allow the black students to go back to Roxbury." Now at a fever pitch, the mob ignored the
entreaties of their nominal leader and began to smash police cars. The
students were saved only by the quick thinking of rescue volunteers,
who sent school buses to the front door; when the buses were stormed,
they whisked the students out the back.[16]

Democratic congressman Charles Rangel of New York, a leading
member of the Black Caucus, wrote Ford immediately following the incident, charging, "It is a disgrace to our nation that the tragedy of Boston continues without firm action on the part of the President of the
United States." Rangel called for Ford to send in the National Guard.[17]
Swayed by the argument that the violence had been less than expected
and was now contained, Ford refused. Nevertheless, it was Judge Garrity who eventually won the day. On 27 December 1974 Garrity held
three members of the Boston School Committee in contempt for refusing to comply with his desegregation order. Late in January the Boston
School Committee submitted a desegregation plan to Garrity. The next
fall an expanded busing program began in Boston, with no real violence. Many white parents continued to keep their children out of
South High, but the number attending was still three times as many as
had attended the previous year.

Despite the advent of busing in Boston, Ford refused to capitulate.

He ordered Levi to "look for an appropriate case in which to present arguments to the Supreme Court respecting the type and scope of the equitable remedies being applied by the lower courts which remedies included mandatory busing along with other forms of relief."[18] Justice's choice of cases left something to be desired. In June 1976 the Court ruled in *Spangler v. Pasadena City Board of Education* that a school board need not review an acceptable desegregation program annually. Three days earlier, in *Runyon v. McCary*, the Court ruled that racially segregated private schools denying black admittance are unconstitutional. These cases were significant setbacks to the Ford/Levi strategy of waiting the issue out; as the administration came to a close, the Justice Department was still looking for a case that would test whether federal judges were ordering too much busing.

The Boston busing crisis showed that Ford remained philosophically consistent; despite pressure from moderates and liberals within his own party, he refused to intervene in a matter he felt to be under the purview of the local authority. This was not so with the New York City fiscal crisis. Although Ford originally dealt with the unfortunate results of the city's mismanagement by publicly refusing to intervene, his position shifted quite dramatically as the presidential election year approached.

In the mayoralty campaign of 1965, candidate William F. Buckley charged that "New York City is in dire financial condition as a result of mismanagement, extravagance, and political cowardice. . . . [It] must learn to live within its income, before it goes bankrupt."[19] New York's income, however, had shrunk to the point at which it could not come close to handling the demands of a population that by 1975 was the size of Sweden's with a budget as big as India's. Since 1965 expenditures had increased by an average of 12 percent a year, while revenues had increased by less than 5 percent. The federal government already contributed $3.5 billion per year—or 25 percent of the city's budget—to help fund its social programs. By 1973 the city had to keep afloat $3 billion in accumulated budget deficits as well as provide for a reliable cash flow for income. Between 1965 and 1975 seven major studies came to the same conclusion: the rate of the city's expenditures was growing at a much faster pace than its revenue base. To make matters worse, the number of private-sector jobs had decreased 11 percent between 1969 and 1975.[20]

In November 1973 Abe Beame, a two-term city controller, campaigned as a fiscal wizard and was elected mayor. But even Beame's talents could not stave off inevitable disaster. Early in 1974 the city began to sell notes and bonds to pay the pensions and salaries of city employees, which enabled it to tread water until the end of the year when its borrowing increased dramatically. On 2 December 1974, $600 million in new notes were offered for sale at a record 9.48 percent rate of interest. On December 18, the city announced that it planned to coax the city's pension-fund trustees to use part of that $600 million to buy $250 million in city obligations.

Upset that the city had to sell its notes at the highest interest rates in the country, Mayor Beame contacted treasury secretary William Simon. Beame requested that the Treasury buy the notes; Simon refused. The city thus did not have the revenue to secure a February 1975 $260 million note sale, and both Bankers Trust and Chase Manhattan refused to underwrite a loan. Beame's immediate problem: where to find $1 billion to meet payrolls in mid-May and to pay on existing municipal debts before the end of the fiscal year on 30 June. In April and May 1975 the New York State Assembly advanced the city a total of $800 million, but it was nowhere near enough.

Accompanied by New York's Democratic governor Hugh Carey, on 6 May 1975 Beame met with Simon and other senior administration officials; they were looking for federal legislation that would provide New York City with the necessary $1 billion. Simon, Burns, and Greenspan simply did not believe that New York City would cease to exist if it had to default. Two days later, with the knowledge and consent of the president, Simon turned the request down.[21] Carey and Beame demanded to meet with the president.

Ford met with the two New York leaders at the White House on May 13. The president spoke first: "As an old Appropriations Committee member, I am sympathetic to the people. I think I have an understanding of the problems." Carey responded, "as though we are heading for a cliff." Then the governor requested a $1 billion, ninety-day loan for the city, which would enable it to adopt a balanced budget for the 1976 fiscal year. Beame chimed in: "I think I've gone as far as I can. Otherwise it will disintegrate in social services. I know what's going to happen to me, but I don't give a damn!" Then he murmured that no one came to the United States to visit Detroit or Columbus, Ohio. Rockefeller, also at the meeting, chastised him: "Don't get carried away, Abe." A flustered Beame finally cut to the point: "All we're asking, we don't want any more . . . is an expression of support for action, even congressional action." Ford recommended raising the subway fare and charging tuition at community colleges. Beame was furious at the suggestion, calling the free tuition at the City College of New York a "one hundred twenty-eight-year tradition . . . I wouldn't be here today if it weren't for free tuition." Ford concluded the meeting by saying that he could not make a commitment from the "general terms" of their argument and that the "first requisite before I can make a commitment is to see it in black and white." He offered no decision on the spot, but the tenor of Ford's mindset was clear from his final comment: "I want to help you. But officials in New York City have to face hard decisions."[22] It took Ford only a matter of days to refuse Carey and Beame's request. On September 2, Carey met again with Ford, now advocating the same idea that Rockefeller had suggested two months earlier—federal guarantees for the municipal bonds. Ford again refused.

All avenues for the city's financial relief were now closed in the Ford White House; the state of New York was thus forced to intervene. In June 1975 the state assembly created the Municipal Assistance Corporation (Big MAC), a temporary borrowing agency for the city that began to restructure New York's debt by turning over its short-term debt into long-term MAC bonds, but it offered city leaders little solace. Sales of these famous New York City bonds were slow as the investing public showed that it had little faith in the power of MAC to back itself up; by August only $2 billion worth had been sold. On September 9, Carey signed the New York State Financial Emergency Act for the City of New York. The bill provided for an intricate package, including a new MAC bond issue, amounting to $2.3 billion, which would be used to meet New York's most urgent financial needs. It also created the Emergency Financial Control Board, which gave much of the control of the city's financial fate to the state. The bonds were still unattractive to private investors, however, and the state had now exhausted its borrowing power.[23]

Ford refused to budge, but Rockefeller was undergoing a change of heart. During Ford's first meeting with Beame and Carey, Rockefeller had intimated to the president that "the state of New York has the capacity to do exactly what the governor is asking you to do."[24] With his expert's command of the New York state fiscal situation, Rockefeller believed this to be true; nor was he inclined quickly to pull either Beame or Carey—two Democrats Rockefeller had publicly quarreled with and privately insulted—out of their political quicksand. Yet as the crisis dragged on, Rockefeller began to drift away from the administration's position. Some observers attribute this change to a desire to help the city that he loved; others note that it was a reaction to his loss of influence regarding domestic policy and his anger that this particular policy was being set by others in the administration rather than by the former governor of New York. Rockefeller himself later pointed to his belief that

Ford's strong stand on New York was being manipulated by the vice president's enemies in the White House, most notably Simon and Rumsfeld, "to knock me off, my political base off."[25]

Whatever the reason, Rockefeller's advocacy for some sort of federal assistance for New York represented a startling break with the administration. On June 3, he proposed to Ford the creation of a Federal Guarantee Program to assist the city; Ford immediately squashed the idea. On September 4, Rockefeller proposed a joint Domestic Council-OMB task force to review the situation; Ford also refused. Disgusted and essentially defeated on the issue, Rockefeller told a Rochester, New York, audience on September 5 that the impending default would have "very serious implications" for both state and nation.[26] During a September 17 cabinet meeting, Rockefeller argued that "the political impact is far more serious than anyone thinks." He suggested a "quiet task force" and further stated that if the city "got their house in order" then Congress should give the president authority to act so that he could assist in transferring approximately one-third of their floating debt to long-term debt by advancing medicaid payments.[27] Despite both his position and his passion, Rockefeller was ignored by Ford and his advisers; the frustrated vice president then went public. In a Columbus Day speech in Manhattan—which, according to speechwriter Jack Casserly, was given "without consultation or clearance of any kind from the President"—Rockefeller demanded congressional action to bail out New York.[28]

Rockefeller's speech set off further rumbles within the White House about the vice president's loyalties, but, as expected, no initiatives were taken to solicit congressional action. On October 24, Ford held a meeting on the New York crisis in the Cabinet Room. Nessen, Rumsfeld, and Greenspan were present; Rockefeller was not. Ford opened the meeting with the multimillion-dollar question: "Before we decide what to support after default, does anyone think we should support any legislation to prevent default?" There was silence in the room, unbroken until Rumsfeld responded: "Not just 'no' but 'Hell, no.'" Greenspan lamely suggested that a bankruptcy plan would have an unwritten provision for the federal government to buy indebtedness certificates from the court; Ford retorted: "We'll pretend that you didn't even say that."[29] New York would be left to fend for itself; the city would have to be told. Ford addressed the National Press Club on 29 October 1975 and declared that he would "veto any bill which had as its central purpose a Federal bailout of New York City in order to prevent a default." The headline of the next day's *New York Daily News* overstated the actual case but accurately summed up most New Yorkers' views of the situation: "Ford to City—Drop Dead."

To the surprise of virtually everyone in the White House, Rockefeller continued his public opposition to Ford's decision. That weekend on ABC's "Issues and Answers," Rockefeller was asked several times if he agreed with the president's actions. Each time he answered carefully: "I share his concern that the federal government cannot bail out cities." But later in the show, in an unguarded moment, he said that he strongly felt that if New York City went down, the results would be "chaotic."[30] On November 4, in a meeting of the GOP leadership, Rockefeller again defended New York City, saying that "chaos" will erupt if the state did not receive help. Ford reacted harshly to his advice: "I'm not going to change my position. I will not be locked in a corner."[31]

The ground was being laid for yet another Ford change of mind, however. By late November the state of New York had begun to shape a $4 billion plan that would provide for the long-term solution of the crisis by promising that the city's budget would be balanced no later than July of the following year. The plan included new taxes of $200 million, changes in certain pension-fund provisions that would free the city of $85 million in contribution obligations, additional layoffs of city personnel, partial wage and price freezes, and an increase in the transit fare from thirty-five cents to fifty cents.[32] Rockefeller told the *Washington Post* on November 11 that he hoped that Ford would reconsider his decision "if the city balances its budget and takes other measures to restore fiscal integrity."[33]

In a move that can be viewed only as a stunning, complete reversal of policy, one that rivaled the tax-hike/tax-cut flip-flop earlier that year, Ford did reconsider. The *New York Times* reported on November 17 that Ford was "leaning toward a program of short-term federal assistance to New York City that would include $2.5 billion in loan guarantees for a three-year period."[34] On Thanksgiving eve Ford announced that he would ask Congress for the authority to "provide a temporary line of credit to the State of New York to enable it to supply seasonal financing of essential services for the people of New York City" in an amount not to exceed $2.3 billion through 30 June 1978. Two days later during a senior staff meeting, Ford expressed amazement at a *Washington Post* article claiming that the plan was not really the answer to the city's problem—ignoring the fact that Ford had been presenting that same argument until forty-eight hours earlier. Ford put the best face on his reversal: "I hope they understand this is it. Come hell or high water, this is it."[35] The bill, the New York Seasonal Financing Act of 1975, was rammed through Congress in only five days. The media certainly did not ignore Ford's latest reversal. The *Washington Post* reported that New

York "looked the nation in the eye and promised, cross-its-heart-and-hope-to-die, that it will be good from now on."[36]

Why did Ford change his mind? Ford claims that after seeing that the state had taken some of the initiative itself, he decided to back a bill that would help it. He would later recount with some glee that the federal government had actually made money on the interest paid them from the loans to New York.[37] Though this may be true, it does not resolve the somewhat illogical political point of view manifested by the reversal. Ford's harsh stand on aid had won him favor with conservatives, and he had cemented his desire to appease that group early in November by requesting that Rockefeller remove himself from the fall ticket. Thus there was no longer any need to pacify Rockefeller, though one could conclude that Ford, seeing that the state had begun to help itself, chose to give Rockefeller a bone without costing the federal government much money. Since the administration had completely ignored Rockefeller throughout the crisis, however, such an explanation lacks credulity.

Ford may have used the moment to placate another politician whose influence was valued infinitely more in fall 1975 than was Rockefeller's. New York senator James Buckley, a fiscal conservative but a political gadfly of sorts, had been marked by Ford's political team as a swing vote, both in the upcoming New York primary and at the Republican National Convention. If Buckley, who had been elected as the conservative party's candidate, could be kept in the Ford camp, it would shake Reagan's claim as the heir to the conservative cause. Therefore Buckley's opinion was actively sought on the New York City crisis. In a 23 October 1975 meeting with Ford's congressional liaison team, Buckley suggested that the president "minimize his rhetoric relative to New York City and talk more about the need to assist the millions of innocent citizens in the city who are the real victims of years of mismanagement and corrupt political leadership." He then hinted that, "given certain considerations," he could support Ford in a New York primary.[38] This development may well have been the reason for Ford's flip-flop. Once the state had taken primary responsibility for the bailout, Ford took the opportunity to act on Buckley's suggestion for remarkably little cost. Once again, Ford had exercised political policymaking. As had been the case with the economic and energy policies, the demands of presidential politics had dictated policy in the New York fiscal crisis. It would be so with the issue of common situs as well.

In February 1975 Ford appointed Harvard economics professor John Dunlop to replace Peter Brennan, his inherited secretary of labor. Dunlop had been brought into government by George Shultz, one of

Dunlop's former students. *Time* was straightforward about him: "He's abrasive as hell."[39] Yet despite his caustic temperament (he was nicknamed Tiger), Dunlop had earned the respect of many people while he was on the Wage and Price Board.

The central labor crisis of the Ford administration had also plagued his five immediate predecessors—the issue of common situs picketing, the practice of picketing an entire construction site even though a union might have a dispute with only one contractor on that location. In 1951, in *Denver Building Trades* v. *U.S.*, the Supreme Court declared that common situs constituted an "illegal secondary boycott" and was thus unconstitutional. Each subsequent administration had tried to amend the Court's decision through legislation. Both Truman and Eisenhower supported some sort of situs legislation, but it never made it through Congress. In 1959 then senator John Kennedy introduced situs picketing legislation only to have it squelched by then majority leader Lyndon Johnson (who, probably not coincidentally, had the nation's largest construction firm located in his congressional district). As president, however, Johnson recommended a situs picketing bill; again, it was not acted upon by the House.

On 10 April 1975 Congressman Frank Thompson (D-N.J.) introduced a new common situs picketing bill calling for the amendment of the Taft-Hartley Act to allow for situs picketing and restricting the application of the secondary-boycott prohibition of the law to the construction industry. Thompson's bill would allow a single union to close down every employer involved in a construction project; in other words, the bill authorized a form of secondary boycott in the construction industry. Wildcat strikes still would be illegal—local unions could not strike unless they received permission from the national union, and a labor-management panel would be set up to preside over the collective bargaining process.

It was in Ford's best interest to keep labor happy during the tough economic times, and the issue allowed him to show decisiveness in a troublesome area of domestic policy. Ford remembers that Dunlop came to him and said that he could draft an alternative bill that would satisfy both labor and management. The president had replied: "If you can do that, it'll clear a problem off the agenda that's been there for years. Furthermore, I'll support the bill openly."[40] In testimony before the House on June 5, Dunlop proposed a compromise in which common situs picketing would be allowed, but labor would have to provide management with ten days' advance notice before picketing would commence and the picketing would run for no more than thirty days. These amendments were eventually adopted into the administration bill that went before Congress.[41]

Soon after the bill's September 5 introduction into the House, it hit a logjam. The board of the Associated General Contractors of America, which had originally endorsed the legislation, reversed its position and now mounted a huge lobbying campaign against the bill. Their efforts resulted in a spate of criticism against the measure. The *Miami Herald* called it an "unfair labor practice"; the *Wall Street Journal* warned that "politicians should be advised that the only way to deal with common situs is to spray it, swat it, [and] stamp on it."[42] Jim Cannon wrote in a memo that two governors and at least thirty-five congressmen and senators were calling for a veto, "many indicating you will lose their support if you do not veto."[43] Dick Cheney remembered that the White House received more mail on common situs than they had on the pardon; in fact, the common situs issue generated more mail than any other single issue during the entire administration.[44] On October 1, the day that the bill was reported out to the Senate floor, congressional leaders bluntly warned Ford that if he did not veto the legislation, he would be damaged politically and that Reagan would not hesitate to use it as an issue.[45] Ford was faced with the political necessity of having to veto a measure that his own secretary of labor had written and introduced, ostensibly with the president's support.

Ford vetoed the common situs bill on 2 January 1976. In his veto announcement, he admitted that "during the course of the legislative debate, I did give private assurances to Secretary Dunlop and to others that I would support the legislation if the conditions specified were met." Although Ford admitted that "virtually all of these conditions have been met," he nevertheless was "reluctantly" vetoing the bill because of the "vigorous controversy surrounding the measure, and the possibility that this bill could lead to greater, not lesser, conflict in the construction industry." This response was disingenuous on Ford's part: common situs was a casualty of politics; it was sacrificed in order to stave off the challenge from the Right.

The decision, however, cost Ford his secretary of labor. Dunlop remembered meeting with Ford just before he announced that he would veto the measure:

> He spent ten minutes telling me what a fine bill it was and I did what he wanted him to do, and then he spent fifty minutes going through state by state the caucuses and primary situations, and what the problems were. Then he told me clear turkey, "I don't have anything

against the bill, I think it's a good bill, you did what I told you to do. But if I sign the bill I won't get nominated."[46]

Incensed, Dunlop resigned on January 14, saying that "since the veto an atmosphere and a set of attitudes have developed, and are likely to persist, that seems to me to preclude constructive and cooperative policies and administration" in labor-management relations.[47] Once again, Ford's policy had been held hostage to politics.

One area in which Ford scrupulously avoided any overt political posturing was in the judiciary, in his sole appointment to the Supreme Court. On 1 December 1974, while on vacation in Nassau, Associate Justice William O. Douglas suffered a stroke that paralyzed his left arm and leg. Ford, who had spent a considerable amount of time as minority leader trying to end Douglas's career on the bench, nonetheless sent an air force jet to bring Douglas and his wife home (when he found out about it, Douglas remarked to his wife, "My God, you know they'll drop us in Havana"). Douglas was admitted to Washington's Walter Reed Hospital and did not leave until March 24; however, he was in and out of the hospital for the majority of the remainder of the 1974 term. The caseload was backing up, and Douglas showed no intention of resigning, despite Chief Justice Warren Burger's urging him to do so. At the start of the new term in October 1975, Douglas returned to the Court, but his condition had severely worsened; he slept through the majority of oral arguments and had to have opinions read to him aloud. Finally, on October 28, doctors told him that his condition would never improve—he would be paralyzed and in almost constant pain for the rest of his life. On 12 November 1975 Douglas announced his retirement from the Supreme Court. He could not bring himself to deliver the letter to Ford, so he asked his wife to deliver it to the Department of Justice.[48]

Ford was under pressure from the Democratic Congress to replace Douglas with another liberal; he was under an equal amount of pressure from the Republican Right to name a conservative, thus continuing the swing to the Right begun with Nixon's four appointments. Ford resisted the urge to appease either group and essentially left the decision up to his attorney general. Levi submitted a short list of possible nominees to Ford, who annotated it and ranked the contenders.[49] The main competitors were Solicitor General Robert Bork, Judge Arlin Adams, and Judge John Paul Stevens. Bork, who was championed by conservatives of the Reagan Right and those individuals within the administration who saw an opportunity to appease that wing of the party, was eventually excluded because of his close ties to the Nixon administration. Adams, of the Third Circuit Court of Appeals in Philadelphia, was also considered a conservative but without Bork's associations. He was reputed to be somewhat flashy and overly self-confident, however. Levi pushed for Stevens, a moderate jurist who had taught at the University of Chicago during Levi's tenure as president. Introspective and modest, Stevens was born and raised in Chicago. In 1941 he graduated Phi Beta Kappa from the University of Chicago and enlisted in the navy, earning a Bronze Star. Stevens graduated first in his class at Northwestern Law School in 1947 and had clerked on the Supreme Court for Justice Wiley Rutledge during the 1947 term. In his private practice in Chicago, Stevens specialized in antitrust and commercial law and taught part time at both Chicago and Northwestern. Moreover, as two reporters have noted, Stevens's "anonymity would ensure a quick confirmation."[50] Ford met both Adams and Stevens at a White House reception and instantly liked his fellow midwesterner. On November 28, Ford called Stevens at his Chicago law office to offer him the nomination; Stevens instantly accepted. Later that afternoon, Ford announced his choice.

Both Illinois senators, Republican Charles Percy and Democrat Adlai Stevenson III, eagerly supported the nomination. The only objection came from several women's groups, who protested that several of Stevens's opinions were sexist. The judge responded: "I think women should have exactly the same rights as men and equal economic opportunity, but I don't think they should win every case they file." On December 17, Stevens was confirmed by the full Senate, 98 to 0, and was sworn in two days later.

7

★★★★★

"A ROGUE ELEPHANT"

By the end of 1974 it was clear that Congress, not the Ford administration, controlled the nation's agenda. Congress was also threatening
to further its challenge to the president's powers that had begun during
Vietnam and had continued with Watergate and that still bedeviled
Ford. We have already seen two examples of Congress as the beneficiary
of this Power Earthquake—Ford's command performance before the
Hungate Committee, and Senators Jackson and Kennedy's attempt to
nullify Ford's oil tariff. The most important example, however, deserves
extended treatment as more than any other event it led to the creation of
a formal system of congressional oversight regarding the actions of the
executive office—the 1975 investigation of the Central Intelligence
Agency.

In November 1944 New York attorney William J. Donovan was
asked by Pres. Franklin Roosevelt to suggest a plan that would lead to
the coordination of the government's intelligence-gathering efforts.
Donovan proposed replacement of the Office of Strategic Services
(OSS), then an arm of the Joint Chiefs of Staff (JCS) and responsible for
the collection of wartime intelligence, with an intelligence operation under the direct control of the president. This new agency, in the words of
the proposal, would have authority to direct "subversive operations
abroad," but it would have "no police or law enforcement function, either at home, or abroad."[1] The CIA, created by Congress under the Na-

tional Security Act of 1947, had included in its charter this limitation on its domestic authority. Cloaked in secrecy, the CIA became a favorite target of critics, both conservative and liberals alike, who agreed with the *Chicago Tribune* that the agency had the possibility of becoming an American "gestapo."[2] The only protection the agency had was its secrecy, however. Throughout the first years of its existence, it was answerable only to the two Armed Services Committees of Congress, both of which treated intelligence matters with a great amount of deference and secrecy themselves. For all intents and purposes, the president and his director of Central Intelligence (DCI) were able to work together in developing an intelligence program insulated from the glare of the media and the scrutiny of Congress.

That situation, like so many others, changed with Watergate. Because of the participation of former agency employees in the break-in at the Democratic National Committee headquarters, rumors of CIA involvement in the burglary circulated from the outset. In the course of the investigation into the break-in, it was learned that the White House Plumbers had used CIA equipment and disguises in their earlier botched burglary into the office of the psychiatrist of Daniel Ellsberg, who had leaked the "Pentagon Papers" to the press. These revelations gave the public its first sense that perhaps the CIA had violated its original charter and had participated in domestic intelligence gathering operations of questionable legality.

As a result of these revelations, Nixon was forced to remove Richard Helms, appointed DCI by Lyndon Johnson; Nixon replaced Helms with James R. Schlesinger, whose background for the position was sound. The author of *The Political Economy of National Security*, he had been a professor of economics at the University of Virginia, director of Strategic Studies at the Rand Corporation with a concentration on strategic and nuclear problems, acting director of the Bureau of the Budget, and chairman of the U.S. Atomic Energy Agency. He was the first DCI not to have served in either the OSS or the CIA, which sent the message that the White House believed the CIA needed to be overseen by someone other than an agency insider. Scholarly and austere, Schlesinger first learned of the Watergate-related revelations when the presiding judge at the Ellsberg trial released the information on 27 April 1973. Schlesinger was caught off guard and was furious that his deputy director of operations, William Colby, could have missed such relevant information during his collection of material on Watergate during the preceding summer. He told Colby that he would "tear the place apart and fire everyone if necessary," but he had to find out if any other such secrets were waiting to explode in the newspapers.[3] On 9 May 1973, two days before Nixon announced that Schlesinger would be named as his Secretary of Defense, the DCI ordered a study of all clandestine domestic activities by the agency that had operated outside the scope of the law. The project was then bequeathed to Colby, named as Schlesinger's successor.

An OSS veteran who had parachuted behind enemy lines in World War II, Colby had spent his entire career with the agency in clandestine services. From this vantage point, he had developed into a severe, uncompromising cold warrior and was a true believer in America's cause in Vietnam. Colby ran the CIA's pacification program—Operation PHOENIX—in Vietnam, a plan which, according to Colby's later testimony, killed some 21,000 people. It was an unquestioning loyalty to country that led to the brutal effectiveness of PHOENIX. This same loyalty to the agency led Colby to undertake his purge of the CIA's darker elements in 1975, a purge that made Colby persona non grata with many of his colleagues in the intelligence world as well as with his new colleagues in the Ford White House.

The project that Colby inherited from Schlesinger was called the Skeletons within the agency; when news of the study broke a year later, the press dubbed the project the Family Jewels. David Belin, soon to become executive director of the Rockefeller Commission, accurately described the report as "page after page of confession."[4] At 693 pages, the report covered every possible transgression by the agency, ranging from affidavits regarding stolen typewriters by agency secretaries to disclosures concerning more significant projects. Among the latter, the study included details of the surveillance of columnist Jack Anderson, the breaking and entering of Washington offices, and the wiretapping of the telephones of two newsmen. Also revealed was information on a mail-opening program (Project POINTER), the monitoring of dissident groups in the D.C. area to protect CIA installations, personnel, and information (Project MERRIMAC), and the placement of individuals into dissident groups to establish credentials for operations abroad (Project LODESTAR).

Although such revelations clearly showed that the CIA had violated its charter, two portions of the report were particularly disturbing. The first was documented evidence that the CIA had planned, though had not successfully carried out, assassination plots against President Rafael Trujillo of the Dominican Republic, Patrice Lumumba of the Congo, and Fidel Castro of Cuba. These hits were planned through a subcommittee called the "Special Group" during both the Eisenhower and Kennedy administrations. The report also showed that Kennedy had hired organized crime bosses John Roselli and Sam Giancana to arrange Castro's execution and that Judith Campbell Exner, lover of both Kennedy and Giancana, was used as the go-between for the operation. The second revelation regarded material documenting the progress of a program code-named Operation CHAOS. Started in 1967 by Johnson to trace links between the student antiwar movement and international radicalism, the program had developed into a domestic spying operation. Even though DCI Richard Helms had instructed in 1972 that CHAOS be redirected toward its original charge of an investigation of international terrorism and even though the program had been terminated in March 1974, the information would not play well during Watergate.[5]

Colby decided that he should share the content of the report with the chairs of the congressional Armed Services Committees. Accordingly, he briefed Stuart Symington (D-Mo.) of the Senate and Lucien Nedzi (D-Mich.) of the House on a confidential basis. According to Colby, Symington accepted the briefing, along with Colby's assurance that such excesses would never happen again. Nedzi, however, argued for the immediate public release of the report, but Colby talked him out of it. Until the story broke in the press, the contents of the CIA study were known only to these three men.[6]

It can be argued that in the midst of Watergate, it made little sense to continue to keep outdated secrets; certainly it seemed that way to Schlesinger and Colby. Moreover, secrecy was rapidly becoming impossible. In June 1974 the *New York Times* reported the existence of the Family Jewels; in September it was revealed in the press that the CIA had participated in covert actions in Chile from 1970 to 1973; at the end of the year a *New York Times* reporter had published many of the details of CHAOS. Yet apparently, the findings in the study bothered Colby from a moral standpoint. Many observers agreed with Henry Kissinger's assessment: "Colby has a human need to confess."[7] Regardless of his motive, Colby's decision to talk voluntarily to the committee chairs, even behind closed doors, caused a major rift at the agency among those who believed that secrets were meant to be kept, no matter what the cost. It is important that "no one thought to brief the president," as Colby noted in a 1989 interview.[8] The revelations of Seymour Hersh would make such a briefing an immediate necessity.

On 22 December 1974 an article by Hersh appeared on the front page of the *New York Times*, charging that "the Central Intelligence Agency, directly violating its charter, conducted a massive, illegal domestic intelligence operation during the Nixon Administration against the antiwar movement and other dissident groups in the United States, according to well-placed government sources." The spirit of Hersh's article was essentially correct—certainly CHAOS had evolved into such an operation. Yet Hersh greatly exaggerated its size. Also, despite citing one of his sources (inside the paper, on page 26) who stated that "anything that we did was in the context of foreign counterintelligence and it was focused at foreign intelligence and foreign intelligence problems," Hersh gave the distinct impression that CHAOS (not directly named in the story) was a domestic operation from the start—an error of fact.

A rage of criticism appeared in the press, and an editorial in the *New York Times* caught the prevalent mood: "This illegal surveillance operation and the failure to institute legal proceedings until after its public disclosure suggest an intolerable breakdown of institutional checks and balances."[9] Already bruised by the press's reaction to the pardon only three months earlier, the administration attempted to coordinate its response. In a memo to Rumsfeld, Kissinger cautioned, "We are concerned that we not act in such a way as to give credence to the allegations that a major problem actually exists and that the Ford administration is confronted with a scandal of major proportions." He then directed that rather than making a statement, the White House "take Q and A's in a normal press conference procedure."[10]

Colby was furious at the tone of the story and with Hersh, with whom he had spoken regarding the article. Even more furious was Ford, who was spending his Christmas vacation at Vail. Having no prior knowledge of the CIA study, Ford was caught completely off guard by Hersh's story. He moved quickly to rectify that situation, ordering Colby on December 23 to produce a written report explaining the story.[11] The next day Colby responded to the president in a six-page letter: "While the CIA has made certain errors, it is not accurate to characterize it as having engaged in 'massive domestic intelligence activity.'" He listed several areas where, as he put it, "there were individual cases in which actions were taken which overstepped proper bounds." Colby divulged that during the course of Operation CHAOS, "files were developed on American citizens. The total index of these Americans amounts to 9,944 counterintelligence files." Colby informed Ford that many of the programs that Hersh cited were not a part of CHAOS (although Colby did not deny that these programs had been in existence) and that Ford was not to worry: "As I stated to you on the phone, Mr. President, you have my assurance that the Agency is not conducting activities comparable to those alleged in the *New York Times* article."[12] Colby accompanied his letter with an unexpurgated copy of the report and with a sanitized version of it prepared for press release. He then waited in Washington for a summons to Vail; it never came.

It is possible that after the Hersh story Ford saw an opportunity to reform the intelligence community. Yet it is highly unlikely that Ford would have availed himself of this opportunity had it not been for the tempest that Hersh's story was causing. Ford thus had to involve the executive branch in investigating the CIA, if for no other reason than to beat Congress to the punch. With the 1976 election in mind, the president could not afford to bring up the rear on this issue.

Reluctantly but quickly, Ford issued an Executive Order on 4 January 1975 creating the President's Commission on CIA Activities within the United States. As described in its final report, the charge to this blue-ribbon panel was to "ascertain and evaluate any facts relating to activities within the U.S. by the CIA which give rise to questions of compliance with the provisions of [the statutes establishing the CIA in 1947] . . . to determine whether existing safeguards are adequate . . . [and to] make recommendations."[13] Naming a presidential commission in order to avert a congressional inquiry of the CIA was nothing new (in 1967 a proposed investigation into the CIA's relationship with education and labor organizations was preempted by Johnson's appointment of a commission chaired by Undersecretary of State Nicholas De B. Katzenbach).[14] Ford's choice to chair the panel caused quite a stir, however.

Nelson Rockefeller certainly knew how the CIA worked. As special assistant to Pres. Dwight Eisenhower on cold war strategies, he had served on a watchdog commission that oversaw the CIA's clandestine activities. In the Nixon administration he had served on the President's Foreign Intelligence Advisory Board (PFIAB), a position that also afforded him regular access to briefings on covert activities. Ford noted in his memoirs that it was precisely because of such experience that he chose Rockefeller.[15] Yet because of this background many critics questioned the vice president's appointment to head the inquiry, quickly dubbed the "Rockefeller Commission" by the press, noting that he had been so close to the intelligence process that he would not run an unbiased investigation. At this point, Rockefeller was embroiled in problems of his own; his influence was being questioned, his control over the Domestic Council had been limited, and his spot on the 1976 ticket was in jeopardy. Many vice-presidential staffers thought that Ford deliberately gave Rockefeller a high-profile assignment that would do little except weaken him in an attempt to get him to resign; as one observer put it, "It was a no-win issue and Rockefeller took the bait."[16]

For those people who hoped for a thorough probe of the CIA, the Rockefeller Commission was a disappointment. The membership was distinguished enough, but it was clearly constructed with the 1976 election in mind, notably with the inclusion of Lane Kirkland, secretary-treasurer of the AFL-CIO, and of Ronald Reagan. David Belin, who had served with Ford on the Warren Commission and was now named executive director of the Rockefeller Commission, lost several early battles with Rockefeller—the meetings were kept closed, and no court reporter could take notes when witnesses testified.[17] Perhaps most disturbing is the evidence suggesting that the commission ignored evidence that it did not want to hear. For example, Colby has written that during his testimony, Rockefeller took him aside and expressed his concern that the director was telling too many secrets: "Bill, do you really have to present all this material to us? We realize that there are secrets that you fellows need to keep and so nobody here is going to take it amiss if you feel that there are some questions you can't answer quite as fully as you seem to feel you have to."[18]

The Rockefeller Commission was at its most cautious in dealing with the disclosure of the assassination plots. To protect the commission, Ford took the risky step of leaking information to the press himself during an extraordinary luncheon held at the White House on 16 January 1975. The president's guests were seven *New York Times* reporters, including managing editor Abe Rosenthal, Max Frankel, and Tom Wicker. Ford defended the commission's caution during its investigation, noting that there were incidents on the CIA's record that would "blacken the name of every American president back to Harry Truman" and that must be kept from the American people. Wicker remembered later that Ford specifically used the word "assassinations." Though the rumors were nothing new, the fact that Ford had brought the subject up with representatives of the *New York Times* was little less than astounding. Wicker remembers struggling at that point to remember just how much of the conversation had been off the record and came away with the conclusion that "maybe he *wanted* us to print what he was saying about the CIA."

After the lunch only Rosenthal believed that the story should be used. Editor-in-Chief Clifton Daniel called press secretary Ron Nessen, who, professing shock, said that of course the meeting had been off the record. This settled the matter for Daniels, and the *Times* did not use the story. On March 1, however, Daniel Schorr of CBS broadcast that Ford had warned "associates" that the CIA investigation might disclose assassination plots, and on May 4, Schorr wrote in a *New York Times* op-ed piece that Ford had first mentioned the issue at a luncheon conversation with *Times* reporters.[19] With the story out in the open, Ford told Belin that he and the commission could investigate the assassination plots.[20]

Belin's investigation eventually corroborated the tie between organized crime and the plots to kill Castro and uncovered evidence that linked Robert McNamara, Robert Kennedy, and Lyman Lemnitzer—one of Kennedy's Joint Chiefs of Staff and himself a member of the Rockefeller Commission—to the plot.[21] The commission also reexamined the available facts surrounding the assassination of John F. Kennedy and the CIA's role in it.

The report of the Rockefeller Commission, submitted to Ford on June 6 and made public on June 10, dissatisfied everyone but the White House. Generally, the report was favorable to the agency, and proclaimed that the "detailed analysis of the facts has convinced the commission that the great majority of the CIA's domestic activities comply with its statutory authority." One entire chapter spelled out in detail the evidence suggesting that the Soviets had the capability to violate the privacy of U.S. citizens, and the report made it clear that "a vital part of any intelligence service is an effective counterintelligence program, directed toward protecting our own intelligence system." Yet the commission did admit that "the CIA has engaged in some activities that should be criticized and not permitted to happen again. . . . Some of these activities were initiated or ordered by presidents." CHAOS was defined in detail as were the mail openings, some of the illegal wiretaps, and the help that the CIA had given to Nixon's Plumbers. The commission also exonerated the CIA from any participation in the Kennedy assassination or in the planning and cover-up of the Watergate break-in. The report concluded that the National Security Act of 1947 be amended to "make explicit that the CIA's activities must be related to *foreign* intelligence" and that the president "should, by Executive Order prohibit the CIA from the collection of information about the domestic activities of U.S. citizens." Yet it was the material omitted from the Rockefeller Commission's report—a full disclosure of its findings on the assassination plots—that cast a shadow on the commission's credibility. In its report the commission claimed that although it did investigate the allegations and that "the president concurred in this approach . . . time did not permit a full investigation before this report was due."[22]

This claim was little more than a committee cover-up, and the press did not buy it. On June 15, about a week after the report was made public, Rockefeller appeared on NBC's "Meet the Press." Unusually quiet and serious, he was grilled about the commission's choice not to pursue the assassination plots. Rockefeller's protestations were far from convincing. At the beginning of the program, he claimed that the committee was not supposed to investigate the domestic aspects of covert operations (forgetting, for the moment, its lengthy report on Watergate,

Ellsberg, and the Kennedy assassination) and that "we were not able to get information that would justify conclusions or recommendations." Yet later in the interview Rockefeller admitted that some of the American leaders who had been involved in assassination plots had themselves been assassinated. In a particularly dramatic moment, Clifton Daniel of the *New York Times* asked Rockefeller if he would be willing to name those leaders. Visibly shaken by this question, Rockefeller again cited a lack of "conclusive information . . . but the President of the United States and the Attorney General of the United States were both tragically assassinated in this country." The reference to the Kennedys brought a noticeably long silence from the program's panelists. When George Will finally asked the inevitable follow-up question—What kind of "involvement" might either Kennedy have had in planning the assassinations of foreign leaders—Rockefeller resumed his defense of "inconclusive evidence" and noted, as had the commission's report, that the committee had chosen not to follow up on the assassination allegations and that Ford had "concurred."[23] The inference, however, was clear—the Rockefeller Commission had uncovered evidence of the assassination plots under Kennedy, and Ford would not allow it to be published. According to David Belin, who had argued in favor of releasing the material, Ford was influenced by Henry Kissinger, who felt that it would be "inappropriate for a presidentially appointed commission" to release the information.[24]

The Senate followed quickly on the heels of Ford's creation of the Rockefeller Commission, voting to create the Select Committee to Study Governmental Operations with Respect to Intelligence Activities. The committee was supposed to be headed by Philip Hart (D-Mich.), but for several reasons the chair went instead to Frank Church (D-Idaho), a legislator with decidedly presidential ambitions. Not all observers agreed with the need for a congressional investigation that would cover ostensibly the same territory as that trod by the Rockefeller Commission. Church justified the probe in an interesting correspondence with entertainer Bing Crosby, who had written Church and asked, "What useful purpose is served by all these investigations and disclosures? . . . Believe me, 90 percent of the American public doesn't care to know." Church responded to Crosby at some length:

> I and the other members of the Committee believe in the right of the public to know what the instrumentalities of their Government have done. Our democracy depends upon a well-informed electorate. . . .

> We on the Committee have considered and rejected the contention that the facts disclosed in the investigation should be kept secret because they are embarrassing to the United States. Despite the temporary injury to our national reputation, the Committee believes that foreign peoples will, upon sober reflection, respect the United States more for keeping faith with its democratic ideal than they will condemn us for the misconduct revealed. . . . A body with a cancerous growth is made healthier by its removal; so too, will the elimination of the misguided practices of our intelligence agencies make them healthier and stronger.[25]

Despite the committee's lofty goals, Ford had always been concerned that Congress would turn its investigation into a political witch-hunt. Indeed, the Church committee confirmed Ford's fears. Unquestionably, the committee was used by its chairman to advance his presidential aspirations. It engaged in theatrics that won headlines but did little to advance a serious investigation. Many of these performances were engineered by committee staffer F. A. O. "Fritz" Schwartz, who, according to a White House staffer close to the process, was "there to advance the career of Frank Church."[26] It was Schwartz, for example, who planned the appearance of a previously secret CIA electric dart gun in the committee's chambers (when Church found out about the weapon's existence, he exclaimed to Schwartz, "I want that gun there!").[27] The next day's *Washington Post* had a front-page picture of committee member John Tower (R-Tex.) playfully shooting at Church.

There was immediate conflict between the Church committee and the White House, most of it centering on the committee's demands for executive office documents. The question of executive privilege had helped bring down the Nixon White House when Nixon had refused all requests to listen to the tapes or to view classified documents. Ford could ill afford to make the same mistake, but he was clearly of the same mind as Nixon had been regarding the release to Congress of White House documents—he simply would not do it. In his dealings with a related House investigation, Ford had been successful; his quiet denial of key documents sent an already disheveled panel into a tailspin from which it never recovered. Church, however, was more persistent—and more public—with his demands. On 12 March 1975 Church requested access to a lengthy list of documents: the Colby report, all Executive Orders and other White House directives pertaining to covert activities, and more.[28]

The White House sought to give the appearance of cooperation without actually providing the committee with any substantive documentation. Buchen and several lawyers from the Office of Counsel to the President were initially put in charge of the process. On April 2, Buchen informed Ford that they had reviewed the material requested by Church and that they were recommending that a "significant number" of those documents be turned over to the committee as early as April 8.[29] Yet the release of even a small number of documents was unacceptable to Ford. To regain some control over the situation, Ford placed Jack Marsh, his presidential counselor for National Security and International Affairs, in charge, making him chairman of the Intelligence Coordinating Group (ICG). Quite simply, Marsh's task was to give Church as little as possible without causing a stir. The ICG was more successful at this than Buchen's staff had been; during the second meeting of the Church committee, held on April 23, Phil Hart observed that the White House had "given us two go-to-hells. What is our response going to be?"[30]

Information that Church did not get from the White House, he got from Colby, at least in part. The DCI cooperated with the Church committee in a fashion that angered the White House beyond repair. Colby met for the first time with the committee in a May 15 executive session, giving them an overview of the agency's covert activities. Colby returned to the committee on May 21 to discuss specifically the assassination plots. With the material already obtained from the Rockefeller Commission, the small amount of new material that had been obtained from the White House, and Colby's testimony, the Church committee pieced together a relatively full picture of the assassination plots. Surprisingly, Ford apparently had given little thought to the idea that Church might want to publish the material. During the course of an October 13 meeting with his intelligence advisers, Ford fumed, "I turned over [assassination] materials [to the Church committee] with the proviso they are responsible to handle [them] responsibly. . . . I never assumed Congress could publish assassination materials. [There has been] no negotiated agreement on this." Ford asserted "I always felt assassinations materials [to be] in [a] different category. Committee to handle as we did—non publication."[31] Ford's point of view was not opposed from within his inner circle. On October 31, he wrote to Church asking him not to publish the report on the assassinations, which he felt would do "grievous damage to our country. It would likely be exploited by foreign nations and groups hostile to the United States in a manner designed to do maximum damage to the reputation and the foreign policy of the United States."[32]

His request was denied. On 20 November 1975 the full Senate met in secret session, only the twelfth since World War II, to discuss whether to release the Church committee's interim report, "Alleged As-

111

sassination Plots Involving Foreign Leaders." The debate was furious, but the Senate refused to take action on the proposal; Church, however, simply released it without a Senate vote. As one committee staffer remembered, "The minute the secret session ended at one o'clock, the committee staff had been instructed to give out copies to anyone with press credentials. It was a masterful tactic on Church's part, though one that failed to endear him to many of his colleagues."[33] The report included most of the information that had been suppressed by the Rockefeller Commission. It would not be the last time that Church would release assassinations-related material. Indeed, many critics have argued that it was the way the committee published its information—not all at once but in pieces throughout their investigations so as to maximize the political effect throughout the 1976 primary season—that mattered more than the information itself, which was reported in the *New York Times* a day before the Rockefeller Commission released its report. In December 1975 the Church committee finally published a full report of its findings. The six-volume report offered 183 recommendations for improving intelligence. A key suggestion called for Congress to step in and take control of an agency that Church termed "a rogue elephant." According to the report, "Congressional oversight is necessary to assure that in the future our intelligence community functions effectively, within the framework of the Constitution."[34]

No single event in the Ford administration delivered an impact greater than the CIA investigations did. At the most basic level, Colby's cooperation with Hersh and the Church committee cost him his job. He was replaced in November 1975 by George Bush, then ambassador to the People's Republic of China. A more long-lasting result was the establishment of a formal congressional oversight for intelligence affairs, as the Church committee had recommended. The CIA would now come under the scrutiny of six (later eight) separate oversight committees, including a permanent Select Committee on Intelligence in both houses. The establishment of these congressional committees was to become one of the most important developments in American politics of the 1970s. The impact of this congressional oversight was first tested under Ford when Congress clashed with the administration over the handling of CIA intervention in Angola.

Mozambique and Angola, both rich in petroleum and minerals and strategically close to the sensitive areas of southern Africa, had been colonies of Portugal for almost five hundred years. Hoping to foster American investment in the region, the Nixon administration supported Portugal's president, Marcello Caetano, in his vision of a continuing Portuguese empire. Nixon's policy paid off during the Yom Kippur War, when Portugal was the only NATO ally that allowed American planes bound for Israel to refuel on its territory. Portugal's dreams were better suited to the nineteenth century than to the mid-twentieth, however. The struggle for independence within Portugal's colonies was a major reason for the fall of the Caetano government on 25 April 1974. Most of the coup leaders had served in Africa, and they demanded a government that would end the costly colonial conflicts. On 7 September 1974, Portugal, now headed by coup leader Gen. Antonio de Spinola, agreed to free Mozambique by 25 June 1975.

The situation in Angola was infinitely more complicated than that in Mozambique. Following Spinola's coup, there was little question that Portugal would eventually withdraw from Angola. But three nationalist groups whose membership was based largely on tribal loyalties had long been vying for control of post-Portugal Angola. To complicate matters even further, each of the proindependence groups had allied themselves with one of the major world superpowers. The Soviet Union, Cuba, and Mozambique had supported the Popular Front for the Liberation of Angola (MPLA) since the 1960s. China and Zaire supported the National Front for the Liberation of Angola (FNLA). Hedging its bets, the United States had kept the leader of the FNLA, Holden Roberto, on retainer as an intelligence source, but had also bankrolled the third group, Jonas Savimbi's National Union for the Total Independence of Angola (UNITA). Any hope of Portugal to grant an orderly independence in Angola depended on a truce among the three warring factions, but their superpower support made such a truce highly unlikely.

In January 1975 Portugal announced that it would allow Angola to become independent that November. Until that time a tripartite transitional government, made up of the three proindependence groups, would rule Angola until elections could be held on November 11. But because of the dynamic of world-power politics, this coalition, the Alvor Accord, was doomed from the start. The United States was the first to violate the agreement. Days after the Alvor Accord was established, the 40 Committee—the interdepartmental group that until the reforms of 1976 coordinated covert activity—authorized the payment of $300,000 in covert aid to Roberto's FNLA. This aid was kept secret from both the American people and the Congress; when it was discovered, Kissinger protested that it was for political purposes only. Such an explanation was disingenuous in the extreme. Only days after receiving the money, Roberto used it to launch a full attack on the MPLA. By March his forces had been reinforced by regular army forces from neighboring Zaire, and

113

Angola was engulfed in a full-scale civil war. The MPLA, headed by Agostino Neto, asked for and received both supplies from the Soviets and troops from the Cubans. The quick application of Soviet monies and Cuban troops saved the MPLA from certain annihilation at the hands of the FNLA. By July the MPLA had pushed back Roberto's forces on almost all fronts, and by mid-August, the FNLA was in full retreat.

African affairs had never been a high priority either to Nixon or, until this point, to Ford. One White House analyst, writing in April 1975, complained when asked to review a draft of the President's State of the World address: "I recognize that the President should not be required to mention every part of the world every time he addresses foreign policy matters, but since the record on Africa is so bleak, I believe this speech would be an appropriate occasion to break the trend. . . . We should recognize that our relations with Africa are not all that good."[35] Angola had increased the stakes, however. The Angolan Civil War had appeared on the American agenda only weeks after the fall of Saigon. Both Kissinger and Ford wanted to use the Angolan arena to show the world—and the U.S. Congress—that the Ford administration was still in command of its foreign policy. Even though the Church committee was in full swing, Kissinger recommended using the American intelligence community, without Congressional consultation, to force the Communists out of Angola.

On July 14, the 40 Committee directed the CIA to propose an appropriate covert response to the situation in Angola within forty-eight hours. Three days later DCI Colby presented his plan, code-named Operation FEATURE, to the president. Ford immediately approved a budget for FEATURE of $14 million and three weeks later, on August 20, authorized an additional $10.7 million in expenditures.[36] Coordinating its efforts with the South Africans, who were supporting both UNITA and the FNLA, the CIA advertised for mercenaries in *Soldier of Fortune* magazine. By fall the CIA had begun to reinforce the ranks of the FNLA. But the American aid did little good. In October South African troops crossed the border and began their own drive toward Luanda (an intervention that sources later told one writer had been begun on the basis of an "understanding" with the United States).[37] By November the FNLA and South African forces were in heated fighting against Cuban regulars; on November 11, the MPLA marched into the capital city of Luanda and proclaimed the country to be independent. That same month, a frustrated Ford approved an additional $7 million for FEATURE.[38]

Despite the high priority now given the Angolan situation by the

administration, Operation FEATURE fell victim to the new mood of congressional oversight. Indeed, Congress used the Angolan affair to reas-
sert its influence over foreign policy. Following up on a September 25
New York Times report of U.S. collusion with the South Africans in Angola, Sen. Dick Clark (D-Iowa) went to Africa and returned convinced
that the story was true. His outspoken criticism of the policy led the
press to pick up on the story, and in testimony before the full Senate
Foreign Relations Committee, Colby and Assistant Secretary of State Joseph Sisco admitted the involvement. The November 2 firing of Colby
did little to placate Clark. In December 1975 Clark and California's John
Tunney sponsored an amendment to the Defense Appropriations bill
for fiscal 1976, which called for the termination of the Angola operation.
It passed the Senate by a vote of 54 to 22 and passed the House the following month. Assured by his staff that a veto would be overridden,
Ford signed the bill into law on 9 February 1976—the first time that a
covert action had been stopped by order of Congress.[39]

The Clark amendment prompted Ford to propose a sweeping reform of the White House mechanism for dealing with intelligence gathering and oversight. He issued the first Executive Order dealing with intelligence on 18 February 1976. The order set up a new structure for the
control and direction of the American intelligence community. It directed that intelligence planning begin on the National Security Council
and that the DCI be responsible for the production of substantive national intelligence. The order also established the Committee on Foreign
Intelligence (CFI) and the Operations Advisory Group (OA) to serve as
checks on the autonomy of the CIA and to be staffed substantially with
executive office employees. Ford's order established a new body of executive intelligence oversight, the Intelligence Oversight Board (IOB),
made up of three private citizens to whom all elements of the intelligence community were required to report at least once each quarter.
The order also placed restrictions on physical and electronic surveillance
activities, experimentation, and assistance to law enforcement agencies.
And it contained the ironic but politically necessary command that "no
employee of the U.S. government shall engage in, or conspire to engage
in, political assassinations."[40]

Although not personally responsible for the CIA's drift into illegal-
ity, Ford missed a golden opportunity to reap political benefits from the
exposure of the agency's myriad sins. By stopping the Rockefeller Commission from publishing the assassination plots and by proving himself
incapable of stopping the Church committee from releasing that same

material, Ford allowed Congress to corner the post-Watergate market on morality. The Church committee secured the shift that had been taking place since 1973 as to whom the country saw as its moral leader. Unquestionably by 1976 that role had been taken away from the president and assigned to the Congress.

The Church committee also reinforced the shift of power away from the executive and onto Capitol Hill. With a more aggressive chair and with a greater sense of purpose than its counterpart in the House, the committee was no mere carnival sideshow. Despite his attempts, Ford could not deny the Church committee the documents that it requested; what the Rockefeller Commission had refused to do, the Church committee did with a vengeance. Ford could only sit and watch the inevitable. A strange combination of politics and public catharsis, the Church committee was a significant portent of the future. The Clark amendment had established congressional oversight of intelligence operations once and for all. That same congressional pressure would provide the most important element in the formulation and conduct of the administration's foreign policies.

8

★ ★ ★ ★ ★

"REASSESSMENT"

Few scholars are left who attempt to argue that Richard Nixon's foreign policy was anything less than revolutionary. Nixon was one of the first American leaders of either party to acknowledge that the Vietnam War had limited America's influence throughout the world and also among the first to recognize that the Soviet Union had become similarly restricted on the world stage, primarily because of its economic travails. Thus before the end of his first term of office, Nixon had succeeded in achieving a relaxation in U.S. relations with both the Soviet Union and the People's Republic of China and had succeeded in extricating the United States from Vietnam. Nixon's methodology in reaching those two goals can and should be debated; it most certainly was during the final months of the Watergate crisis. Nevertheless, he bequeathed to Ford a foreign policy that had begun a thorough reassessment of America's place in the world.

For the most part, Ford agreed with those changes. Had he had his way, détente would have been strengthened and devolution would have been completed. Yet just as with an economic or a social policy, Ford was unable to develop a foreign policy of his own. The War Powers Act had indicated a renewed congressional interest in overseeing the president as commander in chief; this attitude was demonstrated during the first crisis, domestic or foreign, that Ford faced as president—the Turkish invasion of Cyprus.

Cyprus had long been a pawn in Mediterranean politics. A small island located some fifty miles from the Turkish coast, Cyprus was inhabited by both Turks and Greeks. Since gaining his country's independence from Britain in 1957, Archbishop Makarios III had attempted to maintain a balance between the majority Greek population and the Turkish minority, which constituted one-fifth of the island's population. His efforts were opposed by Turkey, who, acting out of a centuries-old fear of a resurgent Greece in the Mediterranean, was wary that Makarios would seek union (*enosis*) with Greece to solve his problems. As a result, in March 1964 the Turks turned to the United Nations to mediate the crisis. Although a UN resolution guaranteed the integrity of Cyprus, Turkey periodically reaffirmed its right to intervene, thus prompting Greece to assert that any Turkish moves in Cyprus would bring retaliation.

The Nixon administration's hopes for stability in the region were dashed when on 15 June 1974 the Makarios government in Cyprus was overthrown by a group of Greek Cypriots led by Nikos Sampson and supported by the Greek military junta. Sampson immediately declared *enosis* between Cyprus and Greece. One month later, to the surprise of virtually no one, Turkey invaded Cyprus, using American-supplied North Atlantic Treaty Organization (NATO) weapons in their invasion. Kissinger managed to initiate peace talks at Geneva among the Greeks, the Turks, and the Cypriots, but they achieved nothing; four days after Ford took office, the talks broke down. Turkey then undertook a massive military move into the northern part of Cyprus, driving some 200,000 Cypriot refugees south. Blaming the United States for the Turkish invasion, on August 19 Greek Cypriots stormed the American embassy in Nicosia, killing American ambassador Rodger Davies in the attack.[1]

Faced with the possibility of a lengthy war that could weaken and perhaps destroy NATO, the Ford administration sided with Turkey. The relationship between the two nations had been on relatively solid ground since 1945. Turkey had allowed the United States to place its Jupiter missiles on its soil and had also allowed the presence of CIA listening posts and military bases along its border with the Soviet Union, bases from which U-2 reconnaissance flights had been launched. Many Americans, however, most notably Greek Americans, thought that the United States had sided with the wrong ally. Congress, sensing an opportunity to give the Ford administration a black eye in foreign policy before it was one month old, agreed. On September 24 the House voted overwhelmingly to forbid the use of any funds for military assistance to Turkey. Ford vetoed the measure on October 14, and the attempt to override failed by thirty votes. The bill was reintroduced the next day; Ford vetoed it again, referring in his veto message to the "dangers posed by legislative restrictions destroying our ability to assist the parties involved [in the dispute]." The House once again sustained the veto, but this time the override vote was closer—only sixteen votes short. Congress then presented Ford with a compromise measure: if Ford agreed to an embargo, he could delay its implementation until December 10. Despite Kissinger's objections, Ford signed the bill, and the White House heralded it as a moral victory. The embargo finally went into effect on 5 February 1975. Turkey reacted by closing all U.S. military and intelligence facilities and all but one NATO air base on their territory. It was a major defeat for Ford, and one that he was unable to reverse. Despite repeated attempts to cajole Congress, the embargo was only slightly modified and not fully repealed until three years later, during the Carter administration.

As the first foreign policy crisis after Nixon's resignation, the Cyprus affair represents an important turning point in the conduct of American foreign policy. For the first time in two decades, Congress had actually been the initiator of a foreign policy contrary to the desires of the White House. Coming as it did in the middle of the congressional elections of 1974, the crisis bolstered the faith the congressional Democrats had in their own foreign policy role as Ford lost the opening rounds with Congress over his policies toward the Soviet Union. The situation also testified to the decline of the influence of Henry Kissinger.

Henry Kissinger had emerged from Watergate with his reputation not only undamaged but enhanced. He was depicted in the press as the indispensable man, "Super-K," who had kept the nation's foreign policies intact while Watergate raged on. Aptly described by one Ford administration insider as "one of the most gifted men ever to serve his government, and not altogether eager to deny it,"[2] Kissinger, who was then serving in the dual capacity of secretary of state and national security adviser to the president, was the one Nixon holdover whose position was secure from the start. Ford had had little interest in or experience with foreign policy matters while in Congress. As vice president, he had been a member of Nixon's National Security Council; however, the vast majority of the international issues of the Nixon administration's final days had been handled quietly by Kissinger, involving neither Nixon nor other members of the administration. Kissinger expected that the situation would be much the same under Ford. As NSC deputy Joseph Sisco remembers, Kissinger thought that Ford "was a decent man, but he didn't give him very high grades intellectually. That was very clear."[3]

119

Kissinger's star dropped at exactly the same moment as Ford's, however. On 9 September 1974, the day after the announcement of the pardon, Kissinger walked into a congressional ambush. During testimony before the Senate Foreign Relations Committee, ostensibly to discuss détente, Frank Church assailed the Secretary over one of the more repugnant episodes of Nixon's administration: the complicity of the CIA, acting under orders from both Nixon and Kissinger, in attempting to bring down the elected Marxist government of Salvador Allende in Chile. Obviously working from information given during previous testimony before the committee, Church charged, "We . . . interfered for the purpose of bringing down that government, by an elaborate covert policy. . . . How can such a policy be squared with our traditional expression of the right of self-determination of other people?" Clearly caught off guard, Kissinger tried to extricate himself by claiming that "all of the matters to which you refer have been developed by well-established procedures in the government that have been consistently tightened, approved by the president and briefed to the appropriate committees." Church, obviously not convinced, replied "It is all the more appalling to me."[4]

The Chilean revelations punctured Kissinger's public-relations armor. Congressman Albert Quie of Minnesota called for Kissinger's resignation because of his "declining credibility."[5] Grumbling from within the White House, previously unheard of on issues of foreign policy, began. One of the transition team's recommendations had been to relieve Kissinger of his post at the NSC; that suggestion was now quietly reiterated by a number of Ford intimates.[6] Rumsfeld began to press Ford to see the matter from a political point of view, arguing that Kissinger's dominance over foreign policy made Ford look somewhat less than "presidential."[7] Kissinger had lost his invincibility; although he was able to convince Ford to follow his lead during the first few months, the president eventually accepted less and less of Kissinger's advice and went his own way.

Even under the best of circumstances, Kissinger would have had trouble selling détente on Capitol Hill during the Ford years. Nixon's policies had come under hard times, particularly since the Soviets had moved to support Egypt during the October 1973 Yom Kippur War with Israel, taking the world to the brink of nuclear war in the process. Inflationary troubles at home fueled the dislike for détente, since proposed grain sales to the Soviets would certainly push up the price of American wheat. Opponents of détente, then, included those conservatives who believed that Nixon had adopted a Yalta-like mentality, having given away too much to the Soviets and the Chinese and having received too little in return. But the opposition cut across both party and ideological lines: it included labor—traditionally anticommunist and virulently opposed to the free trade with the Soviets that Nixon and Kissinger had proposed—and a potpourri of liberal leaders who felt that the United States should deal only with nations that had committed themselves to supporting the basic human rights of their citizens. Even one of Ford's closest political friends, former Nixon secretary of defense Melvin Laird, spoke out against détente. In an article written for the July 1975 issue of *Reader's Digest*, Laird cautioned:

> Clearly, we must shed any lingering illusions we may have that détente means the Russians have abandoned their determination to undermine Western democracy and impose their system on the world. We must communicate to the Russians that the only alternative to *mutual* arms reduction is an American rearmament that would doom them to permanent military inferiority. We must show them that we will no longer tolerate the use of détente as a Russian one-way street.[8]

Perhaps most important, the antidétente forces also had a powerful ally within the administration in Secretary of Defense James Schlesinger. The former DCI had set himself as an opponent of any further détente with the Soviets during the last months of the Nixon administration. For example, Schlesinger told a group of newsmen in August 1973: "The Soviets . . . have a mailed fist. It is now encased in a velvet glove. We do not need a condition in which one discusses the beauty and texture of the velvet glove."[9] Ford had always disliked Schlesinger's imperious attitude and wanted to dismiss him from his cabinet in the early weeks of the administration. Yet firing Schlesinger would present a greater political problem than would keeping him—to dismiss him would paint him as a martyr and allow the antidétente forces to claim proof that the Ford administration had gone soft on communism. Schlesinger therefore was kept in the Ford administration, where he continued to preach vigilance in his congressional testimony, telling a House committee that "despite détente and its opportunities, the need for steadfastness is no less great than it was a decade or more ago."[10] He also continued his running feud with Kissinger, a struggle based as much on competing egos as it was on conflicting philosophies.

Schlesinger's ally and friend in the Senate was Henry "Scoop" Jackson of Washington. A Democrat with a hawkish record on defense issues (in 1963 he had refused to vote for Kennedy's Nuclear Test Ban Treaty until the administration added further "safeguards" for inspection and verification), Jackson had been a strong supporter of both

Johnson's and Nixon's Vietnam policy—so much so that when Jackson was up for reelection in 1970, Nixon pressured the Washington Republican party to run a weak candidate against him. Meanwhile, fueled by the passion of aide Richard Perle, an intense ideologue who had been christened the "Prince of Darkness" by opponents who had crossed swords with him on Capitol Hill, and by his own presidential ambitions, Jackson become one of the nation's leading critics of détente. Jackson centered his attack on the issue of the emigration of Soviet Jews. From many vantage points, the issue was a natural for Jackson. Perle was a steady advocate of developing a policy that would force Soviet Premier Leonid Brezhnev to moderate his emigration quotas. Moreover, as Jackson geared up for the 1976 campaign he was attentive to the value of Jewish financial support and to the number of Jewish voters in early primary states such as New York, Massachusetts, Florida, Illinois, and California.[11]

In fall 1972 Jackson proposed an amendment to the trade bill that contained the Most Favored Nation (MFN) clause for the USSR (Nixon and Brezhnev had already approved the trade agreement in Moscow— the House had passed the Nixon administration bill, but it had been stalled in the Senate for almost a year). That amendment linked a demand for freedom of emigration for Soviet Jews to the issue of improved trade between the nations; in order to keep their MFN status, the Soviets would have to promise unlimited Jewish emigration. Despite the election, Jackson got seventy-two Senate cosponsors from both sides of the aisle. Charles Vanik (D-Ohio) sponsored the bill in the House. Quite naturally, the Jackson-Vanik amendment infuriated the Soviets; from their view, it was an attempt by the U.S. Congress to meddle in the domestic policies of a sovereign nation. And they believed that they had been more than accommodating on the issue of Jewish emigration. In 1968 only 400 Jews had been given exit visas; in 1971 that number had reached 13,000, had jumped to 32,000 in 1972, and had peaked at 35,000 the next year.[12] Yet with their worsening economy, the Soviets could ill afford to jeopardize the possibility of achieving MFN status with the United States. Watergate bought time for both sides; as Congress became consumed with talk of impeachment, the fate of the trade bill remained unresolved as Ford took office.

Hoping to clear the issue from his desk before he had to meet with Brezhnev, Ford agreed to help push the negotiations on the trade bill. On 14 August 1974 Ford met with Soviet Foreign Minister Anatoly Dobrynin and convinced him that without more concessions from the Soviets on the issue of Jewish emigration, Jackson would successfully scuttle the trade bill. Dobrynin then agreed that the Soviets would up the number of exit visas to 55,000 per year as long as the administration promised not to put it on paper so that Jackson could use it. The next morning Ford reported the agreement to Abraham Ribicoff (D-Conn.) and Jacob Javits (R-N.Y.), telling them that if Jackson demanded that the deal be written down, it would, in Ford's words, "come unstuck."[13] On 20 September 1974 Ford met with Jackson and worked out a deal in which the Soviets would obtain an eighteen-month waiver on the Jackson-Vanik amendment.

One month later, however, Jackson went back on his word, writing Kissinger that the figure of sixty thousand was his "benchmark," and he expected it to be increased.[14] This shift further angered the Soviets, who had no intention of increasing the number of exit visas beyond the figure Dobrynin had already promised. The Soviets presented Kissinger with a formal letter of protest and warned that if the trade bill passed with Jackson-Vanik attached, they would ignore it. On 13 December 1974 the bill indeed was passed by a vote of 88 to 0. Ford was forced to sign the measure, despite the promise of Soviet displeasure, since a veto clearly would be overridden. Ford was livid over Jackson's betrayal, yet he understood the reason: "[Jackson] was about to launch his presidential campaign, and he was playing politics to the hilt."[15]

Jackson was not the only member of the Senate who was striking out against détente. During routine negotiations to extend the U.S. Export-Import Bank, Adlai Stevenson III of Illinois added an amendment allowing the president to lift the $300 million per year ceiling on credits to the USSR. Congressional approval would also be required, however, and Congress should take into account the emigration issue and Middle East arms-control talks. The amendment passed on 19 September, and weak economy or not, for the Soviets the Stevenson amendment was the last straw. One historian has called the passage of the Stevenson amendment a "watershed" in modern U.S.–Soviet relations.[16] The Soviets were disturbed that their concessions had been publicly repudiated; they were furious that their Import-Export Bank credits had been limited to $300 million. On 10 January 1975 the Soviets dismissed the October 1972 trade agreement between the two nations, a cornerstone of Nixon's plan for détente, thus making the congressional passage of the Trade Reform Act moot. Trade per capita between the two nations dropped, Jewish emigration fell from 35,000 in 1973 to 13,000 in 1975, and the rhetoric between the two nations became publicly bitter once again.[17]

Thus by fall 1974 relations with the Soviet Union were at their worst point since 1968. Congressional Democrats were winning the war against détente, and the Ford White House was unable to stem the tide. This was the backdrop for the November summit between Ford and Brezhnev as the two leaders took the next step in the Strategic Arms Limitations Treaty (SALT) talks to limit nuclear arms.

Negotiated by Nixon and Kissinger in 1972 and due to expire in October 1977, SALT I called for a simple freeze in the production of missiles. It had left the Soviets with a substantial superiority in Intercontinental Ballistic Missiles (ICBMs) and the United States with an equally substantial lead in missile systems with multiple warheads (MIRVs) and bombers. The Soviet ICBMs were bigger, land-based, and carried a greater throw weight (the capability to lift and carry a warhead) than did those of the United States. American missiles, most notably the Triad, were more mobile, faster, and smaller; they could also be launched from either bombers or submarines. Thus, negotiations to extend the life of SALT I centered on how best to go about limiting two defense systems—that were built upon completely different military hardware and that were invested by treaty with a symmetrical equality—in a way that would satisfy both sides that they were adequately protected.

Schlesinger spoke for the antidétente coalition when he argued that this was the moment to discard the idea of symmetrical equality and force the Soviets to limit their land-based missiles. He would accept nothing less than complete equality in terms of the number of missiles each side would possess in each classification. Jackson agreed, introducing an amendment requiring that all future agreements with the Soviets be based on numerical equality. Kissinger argued that to pursue such a harsh line could lead to Soviet withdrawal from the entire SALT process (a result that would have bothered few conservatives). Because Kissinger believed that it was not the weight of the missile that counted but the number of warheads that it would carry, he was content to allow the Soviets numerical superiority in ICBMs as long as the United States continued its superiority in MIRVs. Chancing a shrewd gamble, Ford resolved to let Brezhnev decide. When Kissinger flew to Moscow to begin the final preparations for the summit, he carried two proposals from Ford, one based on Schlesinger's plan for equal aggregates and one based on Kissinger's plan for symmetric equality. Brezhnev surprised Kissinger when he announced that he could go either way on the equal-aggregates issue. That was enough for Ford, who quickly set up a summit with his counterpart in the Soviet Far East.

Following a previously arranged trip to Tokyo, Ford flew to Vladivostok on 23 November 1974. A small port city in Siberia, Vladivostok housed the coastal headquarters of the Soviet Pacific Fleet. The negotiations were held at a military sanitarium outside Vladivostok called

Okeanskaya, a place that Ford observed looked like "an abandoned YMCA camp in the Catskills."[18] Ford and Brezhnev faced similar political problems in fall 1974: both men were dealing with depressed economies, both were being pressured from other arms of government to present a more strident foreign policy, both needed a treaty to shore up their sagging political fortunes. Ford got along well with Brezhnev, at least as well as had Nixon; several of Ford's staff noted the ease with which the two men gained rapport by bragging about their youthful athletic exploits.[19] Yet when the negotiations began, Brezhnev turned cold. He harshly demanded that Ford decide which plan he wanted— equality or symmetry. Leaving the meeting room for a consultation with his advisers, Ford took his staff into the subzero cold to conduct a last-minute poll on their views. It was a political decision, and everyone knew it. To choose equality would align Ford with Schlesinger, the Republican Right, and his congressional critics; to choose symmetry would place Ford in Kissinger's camp. Ford returned to the dacha and accepted the plan for equality.

At the end of two days of talks, the framework for the SALT II Treaty was agreed upon. Equal ceilings of 2,400 strategic delivery vehicles were permitted each side. The treaty also included other strategic delivery vehicles that might be deployed in the future, such as land-based ICBMs and bombers. Bomber armament was not restricted, except that ballistic missiles with a range of over 600 kilometers carried on aircraft had to be counted in the total of 2,400. Neither side could exceed a total of 1,320 MIRVs.[20]

It would seem that SALT II as drafted at Vladivostok would have satisfied both Schlesinger and Jackson, and the former grumbled his way to a public defense of the deal. Not so Jackson, who ignored the point that his demand for equality had been met and instead began to castigate the administration for what had been left out of the treaty. In figuring the numbers, Brezhnev had demanded that the Soviet medium-range bomber TU-22M, known to the United States as the Backfire, be excluded from the talley. Brezhnev vehemently argued that the Backfire could not reach American territory on a one-way mission without refueling and was therefore not subject to the limits of the treaty. Convinced that the Backfire was obsolete, Ford had no qualms about bargaining it away. Jackson, quietly supported by the Pentagon, was indignant, believing that Ford had allowed the Soviets to continue production of an intercontinental delivery system.

Jackson was equally indignant that an obsolete American weapon, the Tomahawk, had been bargained away. A cruise missile—engine driven, subsonic, limited to travel within the earth's atmosphere, and

125

with a wide margin of target error—the Tomahawk had long been passed over by American weapons planners in favor of ballistic missiles, which carried their nuclear payload at supersonic speeds to an unlimited array of targets. Kissinger saw the remaining American cruise arsenal as a good bargaining chip, since even these outdated missiles were supposed to be a decade ahead of Soviet cruise technology; thus he was willing to throw them into SALT II's scrap heap as a sop to the Soviets. The Tomahawk, then, was excluded from the aggregate total of 2,400 strategic delivery systems allowed to the Americans. An angry Jackson reinvoked images of Yalta, charging Ford with weakening America's defense by daring to consider the junking of any of its weapons systems.

Neither the issue of the Backfire nor the Tomahawk was resolved during the Ford presidency. With the quiet help of Schlesinger and the Pentagon, Jackson and other Senate opponents of the treaty were able to delay a Senate vote on the ratification of SALT II. As the election drew nearer, Ford spoke less and less about the treaty; during the campaign, one could hardly tell that a treaty was before the Senate. Although Ford claimed in a 1988 interview that the passage of SALT II would have been "guaranteed" in a second Ford administration, it did not happen in the first.[21]

As détente with the Soviet Union was being reassessed in the national debate, so too were American relations with Israel. When the Nixon administration came to an end, it was in the process of turning its Middle East policy from a disaster to a triumph. Nixon clearly saw the fine hand of the Soviet Union behind every action of Egypt, Syria, and the Palestine Liberation Organization (PLO); Arab violations of the truce following the 1967 Six Day War therefore could not be tolerated. Yet it is equally clear that Nixon found the Israelis to be an aggravating ally, intransigent in their demands and less reasonable in their view of the future of the Middle East than Nixon believed the new Egyptian president, Anwar Sadat, to be. Nixon thus pursued a policy that attempted to strike a balance of power in the Middle East, avoiding any plans or proposals that might polarize the two powers and perhaps lead to a showdown in the region between the United States and the Soviets. In short, Nixon's policy satisfied no one and angered the Israelis, who felt that they had been abandoned. When Egyptian and Syrian forces attacked Israel in October 1973, precipitating the Yom Kippur War, Nixon dragged his feet in sending help to the Israelis. Yet when Golda Meir's forces regrouped and surrounded the invaders, Nixon quickly intervened and forced Israel to accept a truce. The Israelis were angry, but the war had turned the Middle East into a foreign policy priority for Nixon. He used the postwar lull to initiate "step-by-step diplomacy"; agreements would be negotiated one at a time between each Arab nation and Israel as a prelude to a general peace in the region. After several months of shuttle diplomacy by Kissinger, agreements had been signed leading to the military disengagement of Egyptian and Israeli forces (the Sinai I Accord) and to the disengagement of Israeli and Syrian forces. Despite the initiation of a general peace conference in Geneva, however, Watergate interrupted the search for a region-wide peace treaty.

When Ford took over the White House, the next move in step-by-step diplomacy was the negotiation of an agreement between Israel and Jordan. But Ford had also inherited a new, untested Israeli government. Both Meir and her defense minister, Moshe Dayan, had stepped down in the wake of public disappointment over the result of the Yom Kippur War. They were replaced by Prime Minister Yitzhak Rabin, Foreign Minister Yigal Allon, and Defense Minister Shimon Peres. As one observer has noted, "Golda Meir may have been tough and difficult to deal with, but at least she was in control of the government. It was less clear that Rabin could guide the divided country through a complex set of negotiations."[22] As a governing troika, the new Israeli leadership not only was untested but they also bickered with each other. Rabin could promise only that new elections would be called before Israel would take any steps toward agreement with Jordan. After a meeting with Rabin in October 1974 Kissinger fumed to Joseph Sisco, the NSC's expert on the Middle East: "We are racking our brains to find some formula, and there sits a prime minister shivering in fear every time I mention the word Jordan. It's a lost cause."[23] On 10 September 1974 (two days after the pardon announcement), Rabin met with Ford in Washington. Ford later recalled that at the end of two days of talks, "we hadn't made much progress," and he asked Kissinger to set up an October trip to the Middle East.[24]

The stalling by the new Israeli government created a vacuum, and Yasir Arafat, chairman of the PLO, quickly stepped in to fill it. During the last week of October the leaders of the Arab states met in Rabat, Morocco. They announced that only the PLO—not Jordan—could negotiate with Israel on the future of the West Bank. Jordan's King Hussein, faced with virtual unanimity in favor of the measure, capitulated and joined in the consensus, thus ending, for all intents and purposes, any hopes of an immediate Jordanian-Israeli compact.[25]

Rather than abandoning the Middle East until after the congressional elections, Ford and Kissinger decided to turn their attention to the negotiations then under way between Egypt and Israel, but significant stumbling blocks stood in the way of a new Egyptian-Israeli accord—a Sinai II. Egypt wanted Israel to withdraw beyond the Mitla and Gidda passes and to give up their control over the Abu Rudeis and Ras Sudr oil fields. Israel's demands were more global. Not only did they refuse to give up the passes and the oil fields, but they also demanded that Egypt renounce its state of belligerency and required that any such agreement be of long duration. At the end of the second round of meetings, Kissinger proclaimed that he would go to the Middle East and that Israel would have to drop its demand for nonbelligerency.

In early February Kissinger began another round of shuttle diplomacy. He reported to Ford that Sadat was trying to be flexible but that the Israelis were intransigent. Sadat told Kissinger that he would agree to announce that the struggle between the two nations would not be solved by military means, that anti-Israeli propaganda would be stopped, and that the economic boycott would be relaxed. The Israelis, however, continued to demand an agreement of nonbelligerency, and they refused to consider abandoning either the passes or the oil fields until their demands were met. By March Kissinger had persuaded the two sides to subscribe in principle to a new agreement—Israeli forces would pull back about thirty-five miles from the eastern bank of the Suez Canal and the new dividing line between the two enemies would be in the vicinity of the strategic mountain passes of Gidi and Mitla in the Sinai desert. The Israelis would return the oil fields at Abu Rudeis on the Gulf of Suez, and the Egyptians would be able to use a road that linked those fields to the rest of the country. Yet even after the agreement had been met in principle, the Israelis continued to be intransigent, and there were signals suggesting that Rabin and his cabinet would reject the proposals crafted by his own negotiators. The stakes were high—a Sinai II Accord could be the means to snap the Ford administration out of its doldrums. Ford decided to up the ante.

On March 21, when Kissinger arrived in Tel Aviv, he learned that a letter from Ford had that day reached the prime minister. In it the president observed that "Kissinger has notified me of the upcoming suspension of his mission," and he stated his "profound disappointment over Israel's attitude in the course of the negotiations. . . . I have given instructions for a reassessment of United States policy in the region, including our relations with Israel." Such blunt language was virtually unheard of in diplomatic correspondence. And it backfired. Instead of caving in to Ford's threat, the Israelis stiffened their resolve. Reacting in kind, Sadat rejected all Israeli demands and refused to make a public statement of nonbelligerency.

For Kissinger, the disintegration of the Sinai II talks was a bitter blow. On March 23, he gave a tearful farewell at Ben-Gurion Airport and returned to Washington the next day. On his way home, seething with anger, he called Rabin a "small man," and back in Washington, he criticized the "lunacy" of Rabin's cabinet. Ford was even angrier; a golden opportunity had been lost, and he held Rabin personally responsible. Ford met with congressional leaders on March 23 to discuss the situation in the Middle East. When he emerged from the meeting, a grave Mike Mansfield told reporters that the administration was going to "reassess" its policies in the Middle East; Ford ordered Nessen to tell reporters that this observation was "correct."[26]

9

★ ★ ★ ★ ★

"THE RUNNING"

At the same time that Ford was struggling with détente and a Middle East reassessment, the final act had begun in the three-decade drama of America's commitment in Indochina. The Khmer Rouge and the North Vietnamese had begun operations to bring to pass what five previous American presidents had sworn to prevent—the fall of Indochina to the forces of communism. In the ultimate irony, both Cambodia and South Vietnam begged the United States—the nation that for many reasons had been incapable of winning a victory in Southeast Asia—for help in saving them from this final defeat. As it had been from the start, only one determination could save Cambodia and South Vietnam: the U.S. government would have to decide that they were worth saving.

Cambodia's Prince Norodom Sihanouk, a fairweather U.S. ally at best, had been overthrown in early March 1970 in a military coup led by his prime minister Lon Nol. Nol promptly asked the United States to help him rid his land of the North Vietnamese who had established military sanctuaries along his nation's eastern border. This was a fateful request; Nixon used it as his reason for the invasion of Cambodia in March 1970. The invasion did little to root out the North Vietnamese; protests at home, including the disaster at Kent State, forced Nixon to cut the operation short, withdrawing all troops from Cambodia at the end of June. Viet Cong and Cambodian Communist troops—the Khmer Rouge—turned on Nol and began a siege against his hapless government. The resulting civil war ushered in a period of immeasurable horror for the Cambodian people. Refugees poured over the border to South Vietnam; threatened from the North, the South Vietnamese threw them back. The atrocities inflicted upon the Cambodian people by the rapidly advancing Khmer Rouge were well known to the Nixon and the Ford administrations, who did little to stop them.

Although Cambodia had been abandoned, Nixon retained an interest in preserving South Vietnam. A peace agreement was signed on 23 January 1973 by the United States, North and South Vietnam, and the Viet Cong's Provisional Revolutionary Government. In its desire to extricate itself from Vietnam, the Nixon administration had accepted Hanoi's demands except for one—the regime of Nguyen Van Thieu was allowed to stay in power. No one believed that this situation would last. By March all U.S. forces had been withdrawn from South Vietnam, save a token force attached to the American embassy in Saigon.

In an effort to cajole Thieu into signing the cease-fire, Nixon promised him in writing, "You have my absolute assurance that if Hanoi fails to abide by the terms of this agreement it is my intention to take swift and severe retaliatory action."[1] In late 1972, with Nixon at the height of his popularity, it stands to reason that both Nixon and Thieu believed such a promise could be kept. As the full force of Watergate hit, however, the congressional reassertion of authority in the field of foreign affairs clearly would make it difficult, if not impossible, for a weakened Nixon to honor his promise. Nixon's practical problems were equally important as he had already squandered any goodwill on Capitol Hill that he would need for Congress to approve a recommitment of troops to Vietnam, even for a limited venture such as saving Saigon.

Nixon could not even promise that the United States would continue to bankroll the South Vietnamese effort to hang onto their country. Although Nixon fought to continue aid to Thieu at a pace approaching $500 million a year—the sum being provided at the time of the cease-fire—Congress refused to appropriate the funds. Kissinger requested $270 million to aid Cambodia, but there was little hope for the request. Congress approved the Case-Church bill on 4 June 1973, blocking funds for any further U.S. military involvement in Indochina. It was difficult to find any member on either side of the aisle who disagreed with the characteristically blunt assessment of Vermont's George Aiken: "As far as I'm concerned, I want to get the hell out."[2]

It is somewhat surprising, then, that one of Ford's first actions as president was to write Thieu on the day he took office that "the existing commitments this nation has made in the past are still valid and will be fully honored in my administration."[3] At this point Ford did not know about Nixon's secret promise to Thieu. Nevertheless, it is difficult to accept that Ford's letter was simply one of the many form letters that passed over his desk on that busy day, promising world leaders that U.S. policy would not suffer with the resignation of the president. As the former minority leader was well aware, despite his promise to Thieu, U.S. policy toward Vietnam had indeed changed in the year since the signing of the cease-fire. Only Congress could save Thieu, and its members showed no inclination to do so. In early September Congress voted to give Ford only $722 million of a requested $1 billion in aid, half of which comprised shipping costs. Ford immediately requested supplementary aid of $500 million, but that too came under immediate fire. Thus, any promises that the new administration might make to Thieu were, by virtue of the political situation, empty ones.

Still, the administration continued for the next several months to send signals that led Thieu to believe the president had control of the situation. Ford instructed Graham Martin, then serving as the American ambassador to South Vietnam, to promise Thieu that Ford would continue to fight for aid. This assurance, along with the guarantee of William Clements, deputy secretary of defense, during an August meeting with Thieu that "Congress will provide the money," gave Thieu a glimmer of hope in a desperate situation.[4] He wrote a second letter to Ford on 19 September 1974, beginning with the grim observation that "the prospects for the resumption of the talks between the two South Vietnamese parties are bleaker than ever, while the Communist generalized offensive continues unabated." Thieu then complained about the "utterly inadequate amount of military and economic aid which has been voted by the U.S. Congress" although he thanked Ford for his "efforts made on September 12 to persuade leaders of Congress to restore the cuts in aid funds." He then reminded Ford that South Vietnam had signed the 1973 peace treaty after promises of American aid and warned that he expected the United States to honor that commitment. Thieu also requested that the United States "show its support for the just cause of the Republic of Viet-Nam" by Ford's agreeing to meet with him.[5]

It took Ford three weeks to respond to Thieu. Sent on 24 October 1974 the reply once again completely misrepresented the political situation in Washington. Ford began by telling Thieu that "American policy toward Vietnam remains unchanged under this administration. We continue strongly to support your government's efforts to defend and to promote the independence and well-being of the South Vietnamese people." Claiming that he understood the "critical necessity of American military and economic aid for your country," Ford gave Thieu his "firm assurance that this administration will continue to make every effort to provide you the [financial] assistance you need." Once again, Ford had made promises that he was completely incapable of keeping. Claiming "prior commitments," he declined to meet with Thieu.[6]

This extraordinary correspondence shows beyond much doubt that until the end of 1974 Ford believed—or wanted Thieu to believe—that the United States would step in to save the South Vietnamese. Yet Ford knew full well that Congress would never allow that. It was Kissinger who initially had convinced Ford that such a policy was both feasible and necessary. There is no record—either archival or testimonial—that attests to Kissinger's arguing for any serious amounts of aid for Cambodia. As it had been from the start, the Cambodian situation was, in the words of journalist William Shawcross, a "sideshow." It was assumed by both Ford and Kissinger that the United States would soon have to abandon its embassy in Phnom Penh. For Kissinger, however, the situation in Saigon was quite another matter. At the time of the cease-fire he had believed that the North Vietnamese were exhausted and that the peace would hold. Yet he was soon forced to watch helplessly as a policy he had defended and a truce he had crafted went up in flames. As he faced the reality of the final fall of South Vietnam, and a concurrent loss of his prestige at home, Kissinger became obsessed with the need for the Ford administration to save Thieu. In an Oval Office meeting with the president, Scowcroft, and Martin, Kissinger fumed at Congress' decision to refuse Ford's request for $1 billion in aid, maintaining that "it is inconceivable we can spend $1 billion in Israel and not the same in Vietnam where many Americans have died."[7] It was also Kissinger who had drafted Ford's September 19 letter to Thieu that declined a meeting but promised support. Despite whatever qualms Ford may have had about the common sense of Kissinger's arguments, the only other option presented to him at the time—Schlesinger's argument that the president should pull all embassy personnel and U.S. forces out of Vietnam—was unacceptable. Lacking a viable alternative, Ford sided with Kissinger and continued the fight for aid to Thieu. The emptiness of that policy would be made apparent by the events of the new year.

On New Year's Day 1975 between eighty and one hundred Khmer Rouge battalions began their final siege on the Mekong Delta and Phnom Penh. All the main roads into Phnom Penh had been cut long before January, and the Khmer Rouge quickly consolidated their control of the Mekong River, the only other available lifeline to the capital. A

U.S. airlift tried to help the beleaguered city until the rainy season slowed down the offensive, but it was too little too late. By mid-March Lon Nol's army had been decimated; he had only about 60,000 remaining troops with which to keep the Khmer Rouge from overrunning Phnom Penh.[8] Meanwhile, the North Vietnamese began what would be their last offensive of the war: the city of Phuoc Long on the Cambodian border was overrun. Abandoning that city, Thieu moved to protect Ban Me Thout, a city located 150 miles northeast of Saigon and the next target of the advancing North Vietnamese.

The events of the first three months of 1975 changed Ford's outlook on the situation. Realizing that he would never get Congress to release the full $725 million that had been appropriated for Cambodia and Vietnam, Ford lowered his demands. On 28 January 1975 Ford asked Congress for $300 million in emergency military assistance for South Vietnam and $222 million in supplemental aid for Cambodia (Kissinger's State Department would not concur with the recommendation, preferring instead to remain "silent" on the issue).[9] Martin was furious, cabling his contact in the Defense Department that the excuse given—that $300 million was the "maximum that [Defense] said it could now substantiate"—was simply untrue.[10] It mattered little. Congress was simply not going to approve any action, financial or otherwise, that would prolong America's commitment to the war.

There could be no more hope for Cambodia or South Vietnam, a fact that Ford finally accepted. The evidence strongly suggests that in an attempt to cut his political losses, Ford constructed a policy that would pin the blame for the disaster on Congress' refusal to appropriate the necessary financial support. When the end came, it would be easy for Ford to argue that because Congress would not give him more money he could not adequately provide for Thieu. It is certainly possible to reach such a conclusion from Ford's decision to lower his aid request. Martin was right—$300 million was not enough, and everyone concerned knew that; however, Ford made it difficult for Congress to approve even that amount of money. He had attached to his request an insistence that Congress authorize $6 billion in reconstruction aid for South Vietnam over a three-year period.[11] This figure, as the administration must have known, was too high, and as such it jeopardized the administration's request for the $300 million.

Much too late Thieu realized that he had been lobbying the wrong branch of the U.S. government. Entertaining last-ditch hopes in February of convincing the members of a visiting congressional delegation to be generous with their aid, Thieu ordered his entire government to roll out the red carpet. Lavish banquets were thrown, and the delegates were squired virtually everywhere they wanted to go. Thieu even released dissidents who had been jailed for opposition to his regime on the demand of several of the delegates. Nevertheless, Thieu's request for more aid was given a cold rebuff.[12]

Quite aware that Thieu would receive no further help from the Americans, Hanoi moved swiftly to finish the kill. The entire world was stunned by how fast the end came. The final battle for South Vietnam—the Ho Chi Minh Campaign—began on 10 March 1975 when the North Vietnamese attacked Ban Me Thout. The city fell in only two days, the South Vietnamese withdrawing in panic. Two retreating infantry divisions were ambushed and annihilated in Phu Bon province. Saigon was clearly the next target, so Thieu ordered his troops to abandon the northern and the central provinces and drive to protect Saigon. The strategy was called *dau be, dit to*—lighten the top, keep the bottom. Ambassador Martin continued his encouraging reports to Washington in an attempt to convince both administration and Congress that Thieu knew what he was doing. He did not. *Dit to* simply made the path south easier for the North Vietnamese. Learning that the South Vietnamese army had abandoned them, the entire population of Hue and nearby Danang evacuated their cities, massing at the Danang airfield to catch a flight out. Ten days after the fall of Ban Me Thout, both Hue and Danang had fallen. On the same day that Ban Me Thout fell, Congress rejected Ford's request for $300 million in supplemental funds.

Ford was in Palm Springs on a golfing holiday when Danang fell—pictures of him playing golf were interspersed on the nightly news with pictures of the horrors of war. Although this presented a public relations quandary, Ford could do no more in Washington than he could in Palm Springs; indeed, he may have wished to do no more. Yet the fall of Danang only increased the calls for support for Saigon. Martin and other observers, reliving the 1960s, continued to argue that if only more aid was forthcoming, the South Vietnamese army could set up a redoubt around Saigon. Kissinger supported Martin, strenuously opposing any withdrawal, which would lead to a panic. But Ford's military advisers, including Schlesinger, told Ford that the capital city could not hold.[13] Ford now disagreed with both sets of advisers; he knew that Saigon was doomed, but he continued to be opposed to a precipitate withdrawal. It was in the context of this debate that Ford received Thieu's last effort. He wrote Ford on March 25, begging the president to "take the two following necessary actions: to order a brief but intensive B-52 air strike against the enemy's concentration of forces and logistic bases within South Vietnam, and to urgently provide us with necessary means to contain and repel the offensive."[14]

Thieu's final letter moved Ford to order Gen. Fred C. Weyland, the army chief of staff, to go to Vietnam to assess the situation. Weyland's report of his trip, given to Ford in Palm Springs on 4 April 1975, supported Kissinger's argument. Weyland concluded that the current military situation was "critical" and that South Vietnam was "on the brink of a total military defeat." He recommended that $722 million in aid immediately be appropriated. Weyland also supported Thieu's request for American military intervention, noting that "South Vietnamese military leaders at all levels have repeatedly cited the importance of B-52 attacks to the conduct of a successful defense against superior enemy forces and there is sound military justification for such a point of view." Weyland concluded, "What is at stake in Vietnam now is America's credibility as an ally. We must not abandon our goal of a free and independent South Vietnam."[15]

Weyland was followed into Ford's office by David Hume Kennerly, who presented a different kind of report. As Ford's White House photographer, Kennerly had established himself as a brash alternative voice to the rather staid advice that Ford usually received. Young, preferring jeans to suits, and showing irreverence for virtually all authority, Kennerly offered a bluntness and caustic wit that Ford appreciated. Moreover, Kennerly's Pulitzer Prize–winning photographs of Vietnam for *Time* magazine formed solid credentials for assessing the situation. When Kennerly showed Ford the photos he had taken during his trip with Weyland, photos that made the devastation of South Vietnam and Cambodia even clearer than had the press reports, Ford was taken aback. Kennerly then gave his recommendation to the president in his customary style: "Mr. President, Vietnam has no more than a month left, and anyone who tells you different is bullshitting."[16]

The prospect of renewing the bombing of the North was absurd. Congress would never stand for it, Ford was personally against it, it was legally indefensible (Ford himself had helped shepherd through the 1973 bill outlawing any further U.S. military commitment), and the president risked an outpouring of protest that could easily eclipse the reaction to Nixon's decision to invade Cambodia. Despite support for Weyland's position from Al Haig, then serving as head of NATO, Ford rejected the proposal to redeploy American B-52s. Sensing that Ford could not be swayed, Kissinger fell into line and supported the decision; however, he argued that one last attempt be made on Capitol

Hill. Ford agreed, and on 10 April 1975 the president went before a joint session of Congress to ask for the $722 million in aid for the South Vietnamese that Weyland had recommended and another $250 million for humanitarian aid. There was no applause when the president made his pitch. During the talk, two of the Watergate babies, Toby Moffett of Connecticut and George Miller of California, got up and walked out of the chamber.

Ford's speech stunned one of Thieu's lieutenants, who heard the talk broadcast in Saigon on the following morning. He concluded that Ford had finally abandoned South Vietnam and was "setting up a request and giving Congress a way to turn him down. He was putting the blame for Vietnam's fall on Congress' shoulders."[17] Congress certainly fulfilled that role; during an April 14 meeting with the Senate Foreign Relations Committee, during which Ford made a rather weak case for his aid request, Jacob Javits responded, "I will give you large sums for evacuation, but not one nickel for military aid for Thieu."[18]

Yet plans for evacuations had barely started. Ambassador Martin had begun to shred documents and to send home nonessential personnel, but he continued to be optimistic about the time that South Vietnam had left and refused to accede that a complete evacuation was yet necessary. As the military situation worsened, the White House finally pressured Martin to move. Kissinger cabled Martin on April 18 that after a "very sober" NSC meeting, the evacuation schedule had to be speeded up; he also promised to send Martin anything he needed to make the operation a success. In the margin of the order a sarcastic aide penned, "One Magic Wand."[19]

As the administration agonized over the fate of South Vietnam, Cambodia crumbled. Lon Nol had stepped down on April 1, replaced by an acting president, Saukham Khoy. That afternoon Khmer Rouge forces broke through the government's last defenses on the Mekong River. Khoy cabled the White House: "I appeal to you to convey to the American legislators not to deny these vital resources to us."[20] Unlike Thieu, who received a visit from Weyland after making his last-ditch request, Khoy did not receive even a response from the White House. As Ford spoke to Congress on April 10 to request more aid for South Vietnam, he read Khoy's letter but did not renew his call for aid: "In January, I requested food and ammunition for the brave Cambodians. I regret to say that as of this evening, it may be too late."

The next day, with Khmer Rouge troops poised for a full-scale attack on the southeastern part of Phnom Penh, the United States began its evacuation plan, code-named Operation EAGLE PULL. In a little over two hours, American helicopters flew 276 persons, including Khoy and eighty-two Americans, out of the capital as Khmer Rouge forces stormed into the city. The U.S. ambassador offered to take Khoy's successor, Sirik Matak, but the Cambodian leader was defiant: "I cannot, alas, leave in such a cowardly fashion. I have only committed this mistake of believing in you, the Americans."[21] Matak would be captured, tortured, and then beheaded by the Khmer Rouge.

The victorious Khmer Rouge renamed the country Democratic Kampuchea and declared the "Year Zero." So began the period called the "Purification of the City." Phnom Penh and other neighboring cities were emptied; those of the three million who inhabited the city who could not keep up the pace of the forced exodus—women and children not excluded—were shot. Hospitals were emptied, foreigners rounded up, and executions begun. It is impossible to know the number of people who died in the "killing fields" of the Pol Pot regime; suffice it to say that historians are comparing it to the Holocaust during World War II.

Yet even on the day that Cambodia fell, the focus of a White House meeting was South Vietnam. Schlesinger claimed that intelligence reports did "not anticipate a direct attack on Saigon" because of the heavy cost in North Vietnamese lives and because the North wanted to be able to claim that the united people of Vietnam, rather than an invading army from the North, were responsible for the final expulsion of the Americans. Ford blamed Congress, fuming that it had "shown no sign of cooperation in a meaningful way" and closed the meeting by cautioning his aides not to talk about evacuation as it was "a code word in [South Vietnam] which could lead to panic and chaos. We hope for the best, we have contingency plans for the worst."[22]

One of those contingency plans had to do with Thieu himself. There is some evidence from an interview that Martin gave to *Newsweek* correspondents in 1985 that the administration was considering supporting a military coup against Thieu's government and that Martin had warned Thieu about the imminent danger to his life.[23] Thieu's vice president, Nguyen Cao Ky, supports this assessment, remembering that "maybe one week before the end Martin came to my house and told me I would take over from Thieu. We talked about who to bring into the new government."[24] The day after Martin claimed that he had talked to Thieu, 21 April 1975, Thieu resigned as president of South Vietnam.

The time had come for Ford to speak to the nation. As he had done when he announced his amnesty program, the president chose to give his speech on Vietnam in the heart of opposition territory—on a college campus. Ford had already scheduled a speech at Tulane University for April 23, two days after Thieu's resignation. The operative line was Ford's proclamation that "today, America can regain the sense of pride that existed before Vietnam. But it cannot be achieved by refighting a war that is finished as far as America is concerned." America would not intervene; Saigon and Phnom Penh would fall.

The Tulane speech also represents a significant break between Ford and Kissinger over foreign policy. On the return flight, when asked if Kissinger had played any role in drafting the speech, Ford replied with a gruff no.[25] Milton Friedman, who had written the speech for Ford, remembered that it was standard practice to send speeches having to do with foreign policy to Kissinger for approval. But Kissinger did not see a draft of the Tulane speech; he had, instead, signed off on a speech that Ford had given that same afternoon at the Navy League in New Orleans, thinking *it* was the Tulane speech. In short, when Kissinger finally saw a copy of the speech on the ticker, it was too late to stop Ford from delivering it.[26] Hartmann remembers that the next morning a furious Kissinger vented his anger during a meeting with Ford, but to no avail.[27]

During a meeting on the economy on 28 April 1975, Brent Scowcroft entered the room and handed Ford a note. The president took a long time to read it and whispered to Scowcroft, "If they're attacking, we have to respond." Scowcroft started to leave, but Ford interjected, "Do we have the resources to make an impact?" Scowcroft answered, "Yes, sir," and Ford responded, "OK."[28] The North Vietnamese had begun a rocket attack on the Saigon airport, and two American Marines had been killed. Ford assembled his National Security Council and orders were given to begin the heliborne evacuation of the city.

The next morning Armed Forces Radio began playing "White Christmas," and the announcer proclaimed that the temperature was "one hundred and five degrees in Saigon and rising"—the prearranged signal to begin the evacuation. Thirty-four helicopters launched from aircraft carriers in the South China Sea and 750 combat troops were used to evacuate the city. The operation was code-named FREQUENT WIND; it was more appropriately labeled by the Vietnamese, who called it "The Running."[29] As the gunfire from the advancing North Vietnamese troops grew closer, panic set in. Earlier in the month, Martin had promised Kissinger that he would be able to evacuate the entire embassy in one helicopter lift; but thousands of Vietnamese were storming the embassy, claiming to have ties to American citizens or soldiers and screaming to be taken along. Scenes would be broadcast on the nightly news of embassy personnel using clubs and their fists to beat away people from the already dangerously overloaded helicopters. In Washington, Scowcroft was in charge of the operation, making sure that Martin got the extra flights he was demanding. Martin kept the helicopters flying and evacuated as many people as he could. After nineteen hours of crisis, at 7:46 P.M. Washington time, 29 April 1975, the last helicopter lifted off from the roof of the American embassy. Some 1,400 Americans and 5,600 Vietnamese had been evacuated. Others had escaped by other means—6,000 by barge convoy down the Mekong River.[30] The next day South Vietnam surrendered, and Saigon was immediately renamed Ho Chi Minh City; the Ho Chi Minh Campaign had taken only fifty-five days.

Ford was certainly correct when he admitted to the cabinet that "we came out of a very difficult situation better than we had any right to expect."[31] For his part, Kissinger was incensed; the chaotic evacuation only proved in his mind that he had been right all along. To Rumsfeld, Kissinger quipped, "I'm the only secretary of state who has lost two countries in three weeks."[32] To the press, he was more solemnly critical of his president's policy: "One lesson we must learn from this experience is that we must be very careful in the commitments we make, but that we should scrupulously honor those commitments that we make."[33] Kissinger was virtually alone in his despair over Vietnam. Most members of the administration, believing that they had left the issue behind them in time for the presidential election, agreed with the Ford aide who, on the plane to Washington after the Tulane speech, raised his glass with a toast: "Fuck the war."[34]

10

★★★★★

"LET'S LOOK FEROCIOUS"

At 3:10 A.M. on Monday, 12 May 1975, the Cambodian Khmer Rouge government fired upon the American merchant ship *Mayaguez*, then sailing in the Gulf of Siam; Cambodian sailors boarded the ship and took its crew prisoner. When captured, the *Mayaguez* was headed from Hong Kong to U.S. bases in Sattahip, Thailand and was carrying a load of commercial Department of Defense cargo, including spare parts and supplies but not arms.[1] Nevertheless, Cambodia defended the action, claiming that the *Mayaguez* had strayed outside international waters and had, in fact, trespassed on Cambodian territory. At the time of her capture, the *Mayaguez* was about seven miles from Poulo Wai, an island claimed by both South Vietnam and Cambodia; however, as a matter of policy, the United States recognized an international limit of only three miles.

This was not the first hostile action of the new Khmer Rouge government in the weeks following American withdrawal from Cambodia and Vietnam. Ten days prior to the *Mayaguez* incident, they had seized and released several Thai fishing boats; eight days earlier, they had fired on a South Korean ship and unsuccessfully attempted to board her; six days before, several South Vietnamese craft had been confiscated, and five days before, a Panamanian ship had been stopped and detained for thirty-six hours.[2] Nor was it the first seizure of an American commercial vessel. Over the preceding twenty-three years, Ecuador had seized twenty-three vessels and had beaten and shot at numerous American crews. Rather than react in a hostile fashion, previous administrations had paid fines to secure the release of the ships.[3]

When the *Mayaguez* was captured, however, it was only thirteen days after Ford's Tulane speech proclaiming the end of the Vietnam debacle, only two months after the collapse of peace talks in the Middle East and the beginning of reassessment, and the New York City fiscal crisis was white hot. The Ford White House was at the nadir of its fortunes, and from the opening moments of the *Mayaguez* crisis, both Ford and his team sensed that the plight of the captured crew could be turned in their favor. They had a duty to take steps to retrieve the hostages, and they did so. But the *Mayaguez* crisis offered a timely opportunity: the Ford administration could use the situation to prove that America—and Ford—was still tough.

After the Khmer Rouge opened fire, the *Mayaguez* sent a distress call via Indonesia, and the Pentagon's National Military Command Center (NMCC) was alerted at 5:12 A.M. Ford was advised of the capture during his regular intelligence briefing that morning by his assistant national security adviser, Brent Scowcroft. At this point, the whereabouts of the *Mayaguez* were unknown, but it was believed to be headed for Kompong Som, a mainland port sixty-eight miles northeast of Poulo Wai. Ford was then briefed by Henry Kissinger, and the president called a meeting of the National Security Council for noon.

That first meeting set the tone for the entire crisis. First, it was assumed—with little hard intelligence to back it up at that point—that the ship was headed for Kompong Som. This thought evoked memories of the 1968 seizure of the USS *Pueblo* by the North Koreans and the incapability of the Johnson administration to free the captured crew for over a year. Evidence also suggests that the Ford White House believed that their actions were being watched closely by North Korea hoping for another sign of U.S. weakness in Southeast Asia to use as a pretense for launching a second invasion of South Korea.[4] As a result of these assumptions, one insider remembered, "there wasn't a dove in the place."[5] Negotiating with the Khmer Rouge, with whom the United States had yet to establish formal diplomatic relations, was never a serious option. Ford remembered Kissinger saying, "At some point, the United States must draw the line. This is not our idea of the best such situation. It is not our choice. But we must act upon it now, and act firmly."[6] Ford ordered the carrier USS *Coral Sea* to the site, dispatched a strong diplomatic protest note, ordered photo reconnaissance and the assembly of an amphibious task force, and issued a public demand for

the return of the vessel and crew.[7] At 1:50 P.M. Nessen released a statement regarding the *Mayaguez*, telling the press that the president "con-
siders this seizure an act of piracy."

Despite numerous chronologies available covering the three days of
crisis over the *Mayaguez*, the memories of the participants differ over the
order of events and over the timing of specific decisions. On one point,
however, their recollections are unanimous—Ford's behavior was calm
and rational throughout the crisis and his demeanor spread to his team.
Most observers who were in the Situation Room at the time agree with
the assessment of White House photographer David Hume Kennerly:
"I'll tell you, if ever a man was in control of the situation, he was it. [It]
firmly established him in my mind as the President of the United
States."[8]

Throughout the rest of May 12 rescue plans were developed and
staffed out to various White House personnel. These strategies included
the seizing of the ship itself as early as the morning of May 14 and the
storming of Koh Tang Island the next day to retrieve the crew. Several of
these strategies went beyond rescue, however, and proposed ways to
punish the Cambodians for their action. These moves included the
bombing of the Cambodian warships that had been involved in the seizing of the *Mayaguez* and the bombing of additional targets of military
significance in Cambodia.[9] Clearly, the White House saw in the seizure
of the *Mayaguez* both a crisis and an opportunity—they had to get the
crew back, but they would use the incident to look tough.

At 9:43 P.M. a navy reconnaissance plane reported that the *Mayaguez*
had weighed anchor and appeared headed for Kompong Som. The
crew of the P-3 plane estimated that it would take the ship six hours to
reach the mainland (later it was learned that the stalling tactics of the
Mayaguez's captain, Charles T. Miller, were responsible for the slow
speed); Scowcroft informed the president and then returned to his office. As the *Mayaguez* moved closer to the mainland, Scowcroft dismissed any hopes of intercepting and boarding the ship. The possibility
of the crew's becoming *Pueblo*-like hostages seemed more real with every passing minute, and Scowcroft's next move was to judge whether
aircraft could be used to keep the *Mayaguez* from reaching the mainland.
He asked Maj. Gen. John A. Wickham, Schlesinger's military assistant,
to offer an assessment. At 1:00 A.M. Wickham reported that Thai-based
F-4 fighters could quickly reach the ship and fire across its bow.[10] At 2:23
A.M. Scowcroft called Ford, told him that the ship was "underway and it
is fifteen minutes out of Kompong Som," offered the assessment that "I

don't think there is any chance of intercepting them now," and recommended that the fighters try to stop the ship from reaching the mainland. Ford gave the order to proceed, concluding, "It doesn't seem to me there is any other alternative, Brent. But dammit, they hadn't better sink it now! . . . That would be the ultimate in stupidity."[11] Yet almost as soon as Ford had given this order, the *Mayaguez* was reported to have changed its course from Kompong Som and toward the Cambodian mainland, anchoring off Koh Tang, an island immediately offshore. As a warning for the ship to stay there, A-7 aircraft fired into the water near the *Mayaguez*. But by 7:15 A.M., the *Mayaguez*'s crew was confirmed to have been transferred to the island of Koh Tang.

With the anchoring of the *Mayaguez* at Koh Tang Island, the basic assumption under which the White House had been working—that the Cambodians were planning to take their hostages to the mainland— could easily have been called into question. Several observers in the White House began to wonder if the Khmer Rouge had control of the situation; several more began to speculate that the Cambodians did not want the crew to be brought ashore lest their captors risk the sting of American retaliation. But intelligence was unsure about how many of the crew actually had been taken off the boat and transferred to the island. Ford therefore continued to believe that the ultimate goal of the Khmer Rouge was to move the crew to the mainland, and he focused on preventing that from happening. At 5:52 A.M. Ford remembers that Schlesinger called him: "We talked for more than an hour." They discussed the parallel of the *Pueblo*, and Ford ordered Schlesinger "to make sure that no Cambodian vessels moved between Koh Tang and the mainland."[12]

As the second meeting of the NSC began at 10:22 the following morning, no one knew exactly how many of the crew had been removed to the island. Nevertheless, the assumption continued to be made, more on the gut feeling of those present than on any hard evidence, that the crew's captors were planning to take them to the mainland. In a memo to White House Counsel Philip Buchen summarizing the meeting, Jack Marsh, presidential counselor for defense and national security, remembered Ford's marching orders: "At about 11:30 A.M., the president issued instructions that U.S. forces would interdict all craft moving to and from the island immediately in order to prevent the Americans from being taken to the mainland." Even though the Thais were strongly protesting any use of their bases for a retaliation against Cambodia, Ford ordered a battalion of 1,100 Marines airlifted from Okinawa to Thailand and ordered the carrier USS *Hancock* to sail with an amphibious assault unit from the Philippines. It was also decided that at 7:00 P.M. a helicopter assault would be made on the *May-aguez* to retrieve control of the ship.[13] In the process of preparing the assault, eighteen air police and five crewmen died in a crash in Thailand.

At 8:10 P.M., the Cambodians moved. In spite of warning fire, three Cambodian patrol boats had tried to leave Koh Tang, apparently headed toward the mainland port of Kompong Som. Recently declassified memoranda of conversations between Ford and Scowcroft allow us to piece together the next two hours of the crisis with some precision. Scowcroft informed the president that one of the patrol boats had been sunk and that another had returned to Koh Tang; however, the third was continuing at full speed toward the mainland. Neither man was sure whether the boat contained any of the crew of the *Mayaguez*; nevertheless, they did not hesitate:

> Scowcroft: If they can't stop it any other way, we have no choice but to destroy it.
> Ford: I think we have no choice. . . . If we don't do it, it is an indication of some considerable weakness.
> Scowcroft: No question about it.
> Ford: I think we should just give it to them.
> Scowcroft: To show them we mean business.
> Ford: I am glad they got the first two. I think we ought to take action on the third one.[14]

Five minutes later Scowcroft called General Wickham, telling him of Ford's order to destroy the boat. Wickham responded, "We may lose the thing here in the next few minutes."[15]

Over an hour later Wickham reported to Scowcroft with new information that changed everything. One of the pilots who had been dispatched to destroy the patrol boat reported seeing a group that looked like Caucasians huddled on its bow. Wickham sought presidential approval to disable the boat by hitting it in the rear. Scowcroft believed that they had already secured such approval, but Wickham, noting that the original order had been to destroy, not disable, interjected, "Well, now we have a question as to the identity of the people on the bow. Do we want to stop them and possibly sink the boat? Why don't you run it past the president?"[16] Scowcroft immediately called Ford, who changed his initial order and instructed the pilot to do his best to stop the craft without sinking it.[17] Despite constant harassment from U.S. airplanes, however, the patrol boat made it to the mainland.

At a meeting of the NSC at 10:40 P.M., Kissinger again was insistent in his call for force; Schlesinger, citing the dangers inherent in such a mission, was much less so. Not surprisingly, Ford sided with Kissinger and ordered the NSC to plan military moves the next day. The attack would include a landing on Koh Tang, the recovery of the ship, and air attacks on the mainland so that Koh Tang would not be reinforced.[18]

Throughout the following day, May 14, armed forces moved into position for the strikes. The main assault force would number 175 Marines. At 3:52 P.M. the NSC met for a fourth time. The plans for the strike force were reviewed, and Ford entertained any final thoughts on their use. There was little debate over the plan to board and search the *Mayaguez*; there was, however, a great deal of debate over whether the mainland should be bombed. Rockefeller and Kissinger supported the measure; Schlesinger and the Joint Chiefs continued to argue against it. Once again Ford chose a punitive response. At about 4:45 P.M., Ford approved the plan. It was to be the first navy boarding operation since 1826 and the first use of U.S. military power since the end of the Vietnam war.[19]

At 6:30 P.M., Ford briefed the bipartisan congressional leadership. Speaker of the House Carl Albert (D-Okla.) wanted to know if Americans might be on the boats that were to be destroyed; Ford answered, "There is no way of knowing." Senate Minority Leader Mike Mansfield (D-Mont.) asked, "Why are we going into the mainland of Asia again when we practically have the boat in our custody?" Ford answered, "There are aircraft and boats in the area. The operation is designed to prevent those forces from interfering with our operations." Mansfield then asked if there was any hard evidence that the Americans were on the mainland; Ford replied, "We are not sure where they are." Albert informed Ford that there were "charges on the floor . . . that you have violated the law." Ford replied testily, "I have a right to protect American citizens." Robert Byrd (D-W.Va.) then asked why the leadership had not been consulted before the decision to strike. Ford's response may well have signaled his disgust with the new political order that demanded the president to make a full accounting of his national security actions to Capitol Hill: "It is my constitutional responsibility to command the forces and to protect Americans. It was my judgement, based on the advice of the JCS [Joint Chiefs of Staff], that this was the prudent course of action. Had we put the Marine's lives in jeopardy by doing too little, I would have been negligent. It is better to do too much than too little."[20]

At 7:09 P.M., one-and-one-half hours after the decision was made at the fourth NSC meeting, U.S. Marines landed on Koh Tang Island. Told by intelligence reports that the island was protected by no more than twenty irregulars and their families, the Marines encountered heavy groundfire from between 150 and 200 dug-in Cambodian troops. Numerically superior and well-disciplined, the Cambodians held their fire until the Marines were at point-blank range. In the first hour, fifteen Marines were killed, and eight helicopters—one of which carried all the radios for the command—had been shot down; only one hundred Marines actually landed on the island. One general noted, "We were lucky all of the Marines did not get killed." Indeed, Cambodian resistance continued for several hours after the White House declared the landing a "success."[21]

As the landing on Koh Tang began, however, Scowcroft received a summary of a statement read over a Cambodian radio station, broadcast one hour earlier, that pronounced their willingness to return the ship. This news caused a momentary flash of doubt in Ford's mind over whether to go ahead with the air strikes on the mainland; however, Kissinger talked him into staying the course.[22] At approximately 9:00 P.M. the first strike against Kompong Som was made. Ten minutes after the air strikes had begun, the USS *Holt* pulled alongside the *Mayaguez*; forty-eight Marines armed with riot gas boarded the vessel, only to find that the crew was not aboard.

Now faced with a possible losing venture on Koh Tang Island, a missing crew, and a bombing raid on the mainland that might at that moment be killing both Cambodians and the *Mayaguez's* crew, the White House took a step back. With no formal diplomatic channel available to get a message to the Cambodians, the administration improvised. At 9:24 P.M. Ron Nessen read a statement to the press announcing that a rescue operation had begun and that the United States would cease its military operation when the Cambodians announced the complete and unconditional release of the crew. Reporters were told to file their stories quickly. The White House was gambling that the Khmer Rouge was monitoring the international news wires.

It may well have been a good bet. One hour later a navy reconnaissance pilot saw thirty Caucasians waving white flags on a small fishing vessel; within minutes the crew of the *Mayaguez*, released by their Cambodian captors, safely boarded the USS *Wilson*. The bombing of the mainland, however, went on until approximately midnight, and, had Ford had his way, it would have gone on longer. The final air strike ordered by the president was never carried out; Ford continues to believe that Schlesinger, who had argued the most passionately against the attack, personally held up his order.[23]

Ron Nessen voiced the feeling of the administration when he told the press, "All's well that ends well."[24] The press and the administration presented the crisis as an example of strong presidential decisionmaking that had led to a victory of the United States over an aggressor nation. It was easy to convince the press of the idea of a military success; the crew, after all, had been retrieved, unlike the men on the *Pueblo*. Sensing the potential usefulness of the crisis, White House staffers had kept verbatim—to the *minute*—records of presidential decisionmaking during the crisis. These chronologies were released to the press immediately after the emergency had abated.

Yet this victory clearly had to be in the eyes of the beholder. The crew had been retrieved but at a cost of more lives than the number of the crew itself. Moreover, a General Accounting Office (GAO) report that followed the crisis concluded that it was the People's Republic of China that had helped to secure the release of the crew by putting pressure on the Cambodians.[25] As for Ford's decisionmaking, the available chronologies are so contradictory that they offer little more than evidence of White House concern with Ford's image: they were positioning the outcome of the crisis even before it was over. Indeed, the published memories of the participants are so completely at odds with the archival record that one must call into question the intent of those writers.

Newly declassified documents present a different picture of the Ford administration during the *Mayaguez* incident (see notes). Rejecting any idea of negotiation, the administration steered toward a plan that was less a rescue operation than a punitive mission. The bombing of the Cambodian mainland comes dangerously close to being irresponsible. Never completely sure of the whereabouts of the crew but faced with evidence that they might have been moved to the mainland (the "Caucasians on the bow" report), Ford nevertheless ordered the bombing, an action taken despite the possibility that the crew might be lost in the process. When the Marines finally evacuated, they returned empty-handed since the hostages had been moved before the operation began. It can be argued that Ford threw caution to the wind when he agreed to a plan to retrieve the crew of the *Mayaguez*—a plan that was a punitive operation born of a political need.

More important, however, the crisis offered an opportunity for Ford to look presidential. In many instances throughout the crisis, the White House participants showed that they agreed with Kissinger's advice given early in the emergency: "Let's look ferocious."[26] Ford also seized the opportunity to grasp the national security agenda from Congress by not consulting it about the administration's course of action as the War Powers Act demanded. Rather, Congress was informed about the decision to make the air strikes two hours after Ford had given the order to proceed.

All told, it was the biggest political victory of the Ford presidency. Virtually overnight Ford's ratings went up eleven points in the polls.[27] Despite having been completely ignored in the planning of the mission, Congress was overwhelmingly positive in its response; most of the replies echoed that of Jack Edwards (D-Ala.): "I am very proud of our country and our president today."[28] Within the space of three days the Ford presidency had received a shot of adrenalin. Yet if the incident was a victory, it was one of crisis management rather than of substantive policy implementation. The same problems persisted in the making of long-term foreign policy in the second half of 1975 that had plagued the administration in the first half.

Throughout the summer of 1975 the split widened between Ford and the coalition against détente. In mid-June AFL-CIO president George Meany invited Ford to a banquet at the Washington Hilton to be held on June 30, honoring Soviet dissident and author Aleksandr Solzhenitsyn.[29] A week after he received the invitation, two charter members of the coalition, Senators Strom Thurmond (R-S.C.) and Jesse Helms (R-N.C.) informed the president that the Senate had proclaimed Solzhenitsyn an honorary citizen of the United States; they hoped that Ford would find time to meet with the writer sometime on June 30.[30] Once again the president had been backed into a political corner by his party's conservative wing. Arguing that Ford should do nothing more to anger the Right, Jack Marsh advised Ford to attend the dinner. Kissinger, on the other hand, argued against it, fearing that the Soviets would be further angered if Ford met with so famous a political dissident and anxious that the dinner would feature anti-Soviet rhetoric. Kissinger suggested that Ford instead invite Solzhenitsyn to the White House for a brief meeting.[31]

Ford was indignant that he had been put in so transparently political a predicament over an issue that stood to alienate the Soviets further, especially since he would be leaving for his second summit with Brezhnev in a matter of days. He also personally disliked the irascible Solzhenitsyn, whom he called a "goddamned horse's ass."[32] Taking the hard road, Ford turned down both the dinner invitation and the proposed visit, claiming a tight schedule before leaving for the summit. His refusal was immediately leaked to the press, and Helms and Thurmond issued a public invitation for Ford to receive Solzhenitsyn on July 4, a date they must have known to be impossible given Ford's highly publicized speaking tour that day in several different cities celebrating the American Bicentennial. Seething, Ford told his advisers that he refused to meet with Solzhenitsyn for "cosmetic" reasons.[33] He turned down this second offer but issued to Solzhenitsyn an open invitation to visit the White House after the Helsinki summit had been completed. The visit, however, was no longer important—the confrontation had been the issue. Ford remembered that "as soon as I issued the invitation, everyone seemed to lose interest in arranging the meeting. Helms never pushed it again, and Solzhenitsyn himself was reported to be too busy to come to Washington."[34]

As he struggled with the Solzhenitsyn affair, Ford prepared for his second and final meeting with Brezhnev. Seeking economic ties to the West and military security in their Eastern European satellites, the Soviets had been pushing for a conference to discuss the boundaries of Eastern Europe for over a decade. Recognizing that a significant part of the Soviet agenda was achieving formal acceptance of their occupation of the Eastern European satellites, the West had balked at such a conference until the early 1970s, when détente made it possible. The Conference on Security and Cooperation in Europe (CSCE) had thus begun in Geneva in spring 1973. The Soviets used the meetings to work toward a European settlement and an economic agreement with the West. Given the political climate surrounding the Jackson-Vanik amendment, however, they were also forced to address the issue of human rights. This element slowed down the process, but by summer 1975 the conference had prepared an agreement, the "Final Act." It called for the peaceful settlement of disputes, greater economic and scientific cooperation, and a freer movement of peoples, ideas, and information among the thirty-three signatories. It also confirmed the post–World War II borders of Eastern Europe as permanent, and it called for the nonintervention of any nation in the internal affairs of another. Although the Final Act contained a provision that allowed for these frontiers to be changed "by peaceful means and by agreement," the Republican Right immediately attacked the agreement as a sellout.

Once again Ford was caught between the Right and détente. Kissinger was adamant that Ford attend the conference. In a briefing paper written for the president, Kissinger argued that "the United States has participated in CSCE with restraint" and that its intentions were lofty: "to maintain Alliance cohesion; to insist that the CSCE's declarations are political, not legal; and to seek such possibilities of easing tension between East and West as might be possible." Most important, Kissinger reported, "The CSCE results are not wholly what the Soviets wanted. The documents are not legally binding. . . . Our rights to Berlin have been preserved. *The Soviets did not get an agreement to a post-CSCE European Security Arrangement designed to undermine NATO. . . . Beyond that, the philosophy which permeates most of the*

CSCE's declarations is that of the West's open societies."[35] The Republican Right, once again invoking images of Yalta, argued that the Final Act sold the peoples of Eastern Europe into a permanently servile status. Scoop Jackson publicly called upon the president not to go to Helsinki, and various ethnic groups promised that they would not support Ford in the upcoming election should he attend. Ford, however, believed that the potential gains from the trip outweighed the drawbacks. It offered him the opportunity to meet with Brezhnev again, to defuse the Backfire controversy, and to get a SALT II treaty that the Congress would accept. It did not happen.

Ford met twice with Brezhnev on July 30; both times it was clear that the early amicability between the two leaders had vanished. The events of the past eight months had left a bitterness in Brezhnev that was exacerbated by his failing health. A heated argument between Ford and Brezhnev began over American interference in the Middle East and then shifted to the issue of the Backfire. Ford based his new objections on new intelligence reports about the bomber's capabilities; Brezhnev snapped, "Our figures are right. We know what the plane can do. Your figures are wrong." A second meeting, immediately following the conclusion of the conference, also yielded little.[36] The exchange ended any hope of getting a SALT II treaty before the American presidential election.

Ford's speech to the closing meeting of the assembly on 1 August 1975 confirmed the severity of the differences between the two superpowers. Trying to send both Brezhnev and the Republican Right a message, Ford spoke slowly and with conviction:

> To my country, these principles are not clichés or empty phrases. We take this work and these words very seriously. We will spare no effort to ease tensions and to solve problems between us, but it is important that you realize the deep devotion of the American people and their government to human rights and fundamental freedoms and thus to the pledges that this conference has made regarding the freer movement of people, ideas, and information.

The Right immediately skewered the Helsinki Accord as a sellout to the Soviets. Reagan announced that he was "against it, and I think all Americans should be against it."[37] To make matters worse, Ford had gained nothing from his support of the accord: SALT II was lost, and Brezhnev had become intractable. Détente was dead, and from Ford's point of view it had died in vain.

Badly needing a foreign relations victory before the upcoming election, the administration began to evaluate its Middle East reassessment.

Lasting only three bitter months, Ford's policy changes had been an angry response to what the administration perceived as Israeli intransigence in the Middle East peace process. Negotiations on Israel's request for F-15 fighter planes were suspended, a shipment of missiles was indefinitely delayed, and scheduled visits by Israeli diplomats were canceled. In fact, Ford was so angry at the scuttling of Sinai II that he wanted to ensure that Rabin understood his reaction personally. On 27 March 1975 Ford met with Max Fisher, a Detroit businessman and chairman of the Jewish Agency for Israel who had served as an adviser to Nixon on Jewish matters and was a good friend of Ford's. Fisher's biographer reports that Ford told Fisher that he held the Israelis responsible for the breakdown of the talks, and, quoting Ford, that "Rabin and Allon misled us into thinking they would make the deal. I never would've sent [Kissinger] if I didn't think we had an agreement. The Israelis took advantage of us." Fisher agreed to go to Israel to assess the situation. When he arrived, Meir told him that the rift was not the fault of the Israelis but a result of Kissinger's leaks to the press. Rabin told Fisher that he too was upset about Ford's impression that the Israelis has deliberately misled him.[38]

Ford's demand for a reassessment had long since turned into a strategic blunder. Just as they had done when faced with Ford's threatening note of 21 March 1975, the Israelis again refused to budge. Moreover, they had been joined by the American Jewish Community, who held Ford and Kissinger accountable for deserting an ally. Most of the Jewish community's wrath was heaped on Kissinger, and much of it came from the direction of Capitol Hill. The American Israeli Political Action Committee (AIPAC) had been buttonholing congressmen, who in the midst of withdrawal from Vietnam and the increasing revelations about Kissinger's role in Watergate-related transgressions were more than happy to see the secretary of state fall from grace. Spurred on by AIPAC, which was particularly vile in its characterizations of Kissinger, seventy-five senators sent Ford a letter in May urging him to be "responsive" to Israel's request for $2.59 billion in aid and to support Israel's demand for "defensible" frontiers. Ford was angered by this latest intrusion of Congress into the diplomatic process: "It really bugged me. The senators claimed the letter was 'spontaneous,' but there was no doubt in my mind that it was inspired by Israel."[39]

Facing the worst barrage of criticism in his public career, Kissinger was forced to back down. He told Ford he was concerned that Sadat would give up on the process and be driven into the arms of a more radical Middle Eastern leader, such as Muammar Qaddafi.[40] In April Kissinger met with a bipartisan foreign policy group, including George

Ball, McGeorge Bundy, Cyrus Vance, William Scranton, and George Shultz; they recommended an end to the step-by-step process and a return to the more comprehensive idea of a Geneva Conference that would include both the Palestinians and the Soviets. Yet Ford was still angry. Early in May he announced that he would go to the Middle East to meet with Sadat; *then* he would meet with Rabin.

After a stopover at the NATO summit, Ford held three meetings with Sadat in Salzburg on June 1. The Egyptian president struck Ford as a reasonable man who was angry over his treatment by the Soviets and open to a rapprochement with the United States. Sadat suggested that the way to Sinai II might be through a proposal for the creation of a Sinai buffer zone around the Gidi and Mitla passes, monitored by U.S. civilians. The next week, during a visit to Washington, Ford and Kissinger suggested the idea of the buffer zone to Rabin without telling the prime minister that it was Sadat's idea. Rabin expressed interest, and when his cabinet agreed that it was an acceptable place to begin, Kissinger began a round of shuttle negotiations.

Yet Israel's resistance to American interference had not abated. When he arrived in Israel, Kissinger's hotel was surrounded by mobs shouting "Jew boy! Jew boy, go home!"—an epithet Nixon had used on the Watergate tapes to describe Kissinger.[41] In private negotiations, Rabin upped the ante, pressing the United States for more arms than the $1.5 billion that Ford had previously promised to provide. Desperately needing a foreign policy victory, Ford agreed.

In separate ceremonies on September 4, Egypt and Israel signed the second Sinai Accord. Israel conceded two strategic Sinai passes and returned the Abu Rudeis oil fields, and Egypt granted nonmilitary Israeli cargo passage through the reopened Suez Canal. The buffer zone between the two armies, policed by some 150 civilians, was proclaimed. Both sides agreed not to resort to military action. In a secret side agreement with Israel, Ford promised not to negotiate with the Palestine Liberation Organization (PLO) as long as it refused to accept Israel's right to exist and also guaranteed weapons supplies for Israel as well as oil, if necessary.[42] Even so, Israel refused to ratify the agreement formally until the U.S. Congress had acted. In exasperation, Ford told a meeting of the bipartisan congressional leadership: "They are not the easiest people to deal with."[43]

11

★★★★★

"I DIDN'T TAKE REAGAN
SERIOUSLY"

By the end of 1974, Ronald Reagan was privately asserting that Ford was a "caretaker" who had been "in Congress too long."[1] Still, even though virtually every leader who colored himself a conservative had been begging Reagan to run, he was wary. It took the intercession of John Sears, a former Nixon campaign strategist who quit the White House after John Mitchell had bugged his phone, to convince Reagan that Ford's base of support within the party was weak enough that Reagan could win the nomination. Sears's connections to the eastern media and party leaders were strong and his confidence was infectious—Reagan made him his campaign manager. Sears's strategy for the primary campaigns was, in retrospect, the only strategy available to the Reagan camp—Reagan had to win in the early primaries and win big, thus forcing Ford to drop out of the race.

Throughout the second half of 1975, Reagan hammered at two themes. First, he positioned himself as the true heir to Republican conservatism. Second, he presented himself as an outsider who could attack the entrenched powers of Washington and win. When he voiced these ideas in generalities, as he most often did, Reagan was a particularly effective stump speaker; however, when he tried to articulate a specific program he often got himself into trouble. The most publicized example of this foible occurred during a 26 September 1975 speech at the Executive Club of Chicago, in which Reagan proposed "nothing less than a systematic transfer of authority and resources to the states" that would "reduce the outlay of the federal government by more than $90 billion, using the spending levels of fiscal 1975. With such a savings, it would be possible to balance the federal budget, make an initial $5 billion payment on the national debt and cut the federal personal income burden of every American to an average of 23 percent."[2]

Reagan's formula was little short of ridiculous. A Ford researcher quickly pointed out that federal cutbacks of the scope that Reagan proposed would cause such high unemployment that the results could be disastrous. The press soon zeroed in on the revelation that the plan could not be put into effect without raising taxes—and New Hampshire, home of the first primary, was one of the few states that had no sales or state income taxes. Reagan had overextended himself, promising a level of federal intervention into the economic sphere that far surpassed any of the plans put forth by the Democratic administrations that he was fond of bashing. Reagan had carelessly fallen into one of the most deadly traps in any political campaign—he had made promises to the voters that he could not keep.

Gerald Ford would have us believe that one reason his opponent did so well in the 1976 primary season was because of just such gaffes: "I didn't take Reagan seriously."[3] Precisely the opposite is true. The White House was worried about Reagan from the start, but the early steps they took to deal with his challenge made their situation even worse.

Ford made his first move toward preparing himself for a Reagan challenge in mid-June, when it was announced that Howard H. "Bo" Callaway would serve as the head of the President Ford Committee (PFC). A southern conservative who had bolted from the Democratic party to support Barry Goldwater for the presidency in 1964, Callaway was the first Republican congressman from Georgia since Reconstruction. Nixon had appointed him secretary of the army in 1973, and Callaway had worked hard at winning back those conservatives who had been bruised by détente. On the surface, Callaway's appointment seemed like a strategic stroke of genius; however, the *New York Times* was quick to quote a Callaway acquaintance who called him "plastic" and a "segregationist."[4] This criticism seemed to catch the White House completely off guard. One staffer volunteered, "If this is the case, it may be prudent early on to determine if Bo is or has been a member of a country club or similar social group which has a racial clause or covenant in its membership rules. This applies for any real estate holdings which he has or may have had."[5] No such problem cropped up, but Callaway caused a bigger stir when he confided to the press that Rockefeller was the "number one problem" standing in the way of Ford's reelection. Staff Secretary Jerry Jones would soon write to Rumsfeld that "the Reagan supporters are very happy each time Bo opens his mouth."[6]

However impolitic his statement to the press, Callaway was right—Rockefeller was a problem. Many Ford staffers were openly lobbying for his removal from the ticket; ostensibly, they reasoned that his presence on the ticket would hurt Ford with conservatives as he faced the Reagan challenge in the primaries. Despite later protests to the contrary, Callaway pressed the hardest for Rockefeller's removal. In the PFC's first "Weekly Report," sent to Ford and to other key White House staffers, Callaway was characteristically blunt:

> Rockefeller's spot on the ticket is probably the most important issue in the campaign, in so far as Reagan and the convention is [sic] concerned. Many in the Reagan camp feel that their biggest opportunity at the convention is to keep Rockefeller off the ticket. If they think they can do this by influencing the President now, they are likely to be Ford delegates; if they feel the President's mind is made up and they can influence only on the convention floor, they are likely to be Reagan delegates. We need to continue to emphasize that this is an open question, so that we can get Ford support, both from those who support Rockefeller and those who don't. Rockefeller and I are in agreement on this subject.[7]

There is some polling data available that suggests Callaway's concern was valid; there is as much data and testimony suggesting that Rockefeller would have held together the party's moderates during the fall election better than any of the others who were being touted for his job. Nevertheless, Rockefeller was furious. He complained to Ford about Callaway and privately told everyone who would listen that he believed Rumsfeld was behind Callaway's actions (Rumsfeld's response to this was direct: "I didn't have a goddamn thing to do with it, and everyone knows it").[8] Yet throughout the summer and early fall of 1975, Rockefeller was publicly dutiful. The entire political world was shocked, then, when on November 3 Rockefeller announced that he was withdrawing from the ticket.

In a 1988 interview Ford continued to argue that Rockefeller withdrew from the ticket of his own volition and that he was not asked to withdraw by the president or by anyone else.[9] Yet virtually no one, either inside or outside the administration, agrees with Ford. Hartmann, who was one of Rockefeller's most vocal advocates within the administration as well as one of Ford's greatest defenders, is unequivocal: "[Rockefeller took] himself off the ticket at Ford's personal request."[10]

159

David Hume Kennerly, who was in the Oval Office when Rockefeller arrived to submit his letter of withdrawal to Ford, laughed when asked the same question: "Of course he was pushed! . . . How could you read it any other way?"[11]

Throughout the rest of the campaign, Rockefeller was one of Ford's most vocal supporters. He made appearances in almost every primary state, was instrumental in delivering the New York delegation to Ford only weeks before the convention, and was a force on the floor of the convention in Kansas City when the Reagan forces made their final try for the nomination. He responded to the endless questioning of the press about whether he was forced off the ticket by saying that it was a choice he had made on his own because he "didn't want to cause [Ford] any problem."[12] Rockefeller's private thoughts were quite different, however, as he revealed in 1977 to Trevor Armbrister, background researcher for Ford's memoirs:

> Well, if you want to set the record straight, and [Ford] may not want to say this . . . I have never told anybody this except you, but you are writing this book and it is his book. . . . He asked me to do it . . . to withdraw as vice president. . . . [He said] I would hurt him in getting the nomination. . . . But you see he never really understood that I was only there to help him and the country.[13]

On the same day that Rockefeller declared his withdrawal from the ticket, Ford added to the tumult by announcing the resignation of several other cabinet-level officers. James Schlesinger had irritated Ford from the beginning of the administration. Although Kissinger's efforts to court a favorable press were ignored by Ford, Schlesinger's attempts to do the same were not. An early story that he had placed U.S. forces on alert prior to Nixon's resignation—a story that other officials in the Pentagon vehemently denied—had angered Ford. The announcement from the Pentagon that the crew of the *Mayaguez* had been recovered—in direct defiance of Ford's orders that all news come out of the White House—further infuriated the president. The last straw was the propagation of rumors that Schlesinger was privately aiding the Reagan camp.

Yet Schlesinger was the darling of the Right because of his opposition to détente, an irony since in fact he was less a hawk than either Ford or Kissinger. He had argued for a quicker pullout from South Vietnam, and he had counseled caution during the *Mayaguez* crisis, perhaps to the point of canceling the fourth air strike on Kompong Som. Nevertheless, firing Schlesinger would be a gunshot across the bow of the

Reagan ship. If Schlesinger was to go, steps must be taken to lessen the blow to the conservatives.

One of the greatest myths about the Ford presidency is that Kissinger controlled foreign policy. As had Nixon before him, Ford used Kissinger as his chief negotiator, but neither president followed Kissinger's advice blindly. Indeed, for Ford, quite the opposite was true since Kissinger's influence had been on the wane since the beginning of the administration. Yet despite the constant calls from the Right for Kissinger's dismissal, Ford never seriously entertained the idea. Yet the president had never liked Kissinger's holding dual positions as national security adviser and secretary of state. Throughout the travails of Vladivostok, Vietnam, the Middle East, and Helsinki, Ford had not wished to demote Kissinger. But with the administration's foreign policy under fire and the election season only months away, Kissinger had become more vulnerable.

On Sunday, 2 November 1975, Ford called in Schlesinger and Director of Central Intelligence William Colby—whose job had been in jeopardy since his testimony to the Church and Rockefeller committees—and asked for their resignations. Colby was replaced by George Bush, then ambassador to the People's Republic of China; Schlesinger was replaced as secretary of defense by Donald Rumsfeld. Rumsfeld was replaced as staff coordinator by his assistant, Richard Cheney. Later that day, Ford informed Kissinger that he was relieving him of his duty as head of the National Security Council. To replace him, Ford promoted Brent Scowcroft, the Kissinger assistant who, in Ford's eyes, had distinguished himself during the evacuation of Saigon and the *Mayaguez* incident. Ford also took the opportunity to remove the ailing Rogers Morton as commerce secretary, replacing him with Elliot Richardson, Nixon's former attorney general and one of the favorites of the party's moderate wing.

The White House slant on what the press quickly dubbed the "Sunday Morning Massacre" was simple: criticism from Reagan to the contrary, Ford was making a difficult presidential decision. Few journalists accepted this view. Nevertheless, most observers agreed with the *New York Times*, which concluded that it was "highly doubtful" that Ford had made any political gains from these maneuvers.[14] Conservatives protested that Schlesinger had been sacrificed simply because of his convictions. As for Kissinger's demotion, Reagan was crystal clear: "I am not appeased."[15] Yet the biggest surprise for the White House was the vehemence of the criticism over the removal of Rockefeller. Bo Callaway's judgment that "having the issue of Governor Rockefeller out of the way is very helpful to the campaign" was definitely not the case.[16] In a backlash that no one expected, many Republican moderates accused Ford of disloyalty. It was relatively easy, then, for Reagan to concentrate on Ford's motives, charging that the president was desperate and would do anything to get elected—even sacrifice his own vice president and cabinet.

If, as many of Ford's advisers have attested since that point, the events of late October were an attempt to counter Reagan with the picture of a decisive president, it failed. In fact, Reagan recognized that the negative reaction against Ford provided the perfect time to enter the race formally. Reagan called Ford at the White House on November 19 to tell him that he was announcing the next day that he would run for the Republican nomination. In the course of that strained conversation, Reagan argued that his challenge would not be divisive. Ford disagreed, musing in his memoirs: "How can you challenge an incumbent president of your own party and *not* be divisive?"[17] Ford had reason to worry: Reagan was about 12 percentage points ahead in the polls.

Prior to the cabinet shake-up, the Ford campaign had been inefficient and slow to respond to the flourishing Reagan challenge. Having had no experience in running a national campaign, Callaway was behind schedule in mobilizing the state organizations, and his inefficiency and brusque manner had led to the resignation of several top-level campaign staffers. But the White House had heard a clarion call in the reaction to the cabinet shake-up and in Reagan's formal announcement. Despite attempts by Hartmann to reestablish his role as Ford's chief campaign adviser, Richard Cheney quickly emerged as the White House liaison for the President Ford Committee. The thirty-eight-year-old Cheney had worked for Wisconsin governor Warren Knowles and Wisconsin congressman William Steiger before being brought into the Nixon administration by Rumsfeld in 1969. For the next six years he served as a Rumsfeld protégé in the executive branch (his Secret Service code name was, appropriately, "Backseat"). After Rumsfeld was assigned to NATO, Cheney took a position as a partner in an investment advisory firm; when Rumsfeld returned to the White House in fall 1974, he brought along Cheney as his deputy. Then Rumsfeld went to the Pentagon, and Cheney was promoted to chief of staff; as the campaign began, Cheney was in the process of smoothing out many of the turf battles that Haig and Rumsfeld had been unable to settle.

One of Cheney's roles was to serve as White House liaison to the PFC. Cheney generally ignored Callaway and instead dealt with his assistant, Stuart Spencer, who had worked for Rockefeller in 1964 and

Reagan in 1966 and 1970, leaving the Reagan team in 1975. Having joined the California for Ford organization in May 1975, he was brought into the national organization by Callaway in July.[18] By October Spencer was attending weekly meetings with Ford and Cheney, and by the end of the year, Callaway had been completely moved aside. The following March, dogged by allegations that he had used his influence improperly as army secretary to gain permission to build a ski area on what was then government land, Callaway resigned; he was replaced by Rogers Morton, largely a pro forma appointment. It was Cheney, Spencer, and pollster Robert Teeter of Michigan, another alumnus of the Nixon campaign organization, who developed the strategy for the early primary races.

Their strategy went against the advice of Hartmann, who argued that Ford needed to emphasize those aspects of his personality that had been loved before the pardon, during the honeymoon month—the "nice guy" image. Spencer, Teeter, and Cheney argued that Ford had to continue his attempt, begun with the cabinet shake-up, to create a new image in the public mind—that of a decisive president. A mobile television unit was set up outside the White House, and Ford began to polish his performances before a videocamera. New York advertising executive Peter Dailey, who had worked for Nixon in 1972 and would coordinate Reagan's advertising in 1980, was brought into the campaign. He emphasized the use of still montage ads showing Ford at work, looking "presidential."

In New Hampshire, Spencer combined Dailey's presidential spots with other ads that attacked Reagan's $90 billion speech, a tactic particularly fruitful in a state with no sales tax. As a result and despite his huge lead, Reagan was on the defensive throughout the New Hampshire campaign. Even Nixon's announcement one month before the primary that he was going to visit China as a private citizen failed to rekindle the memory of the pardon that Ford's handlers feared it would (a front-page editorial in the ultraconservative *Manchester Union-Leader* was headlined, "Let the Red Chinese Keep Him").[19] Meanwhile, John Sears made his first strategic mistake of the campaign. Despite tracking polls showing that Reagan was clearly losing ground, Sears arranged for Reagan to travel to Illinois during the weekend before the New Hampshire primary, a decision that Reagan believes made the difference in the voting.[20]

On February 24, Ford beat Reagan in New Hampshire with 51 percent of the vote. Although it was a virtual tie, with Ford winning by only 1,317 votes out of 108,000 cast, it was nevertheless a come-from-behind victory in a state that Reagan should have won. Yet Reagan was in it to stay. After a March 10 discussion with several Reagan supporters, a White House staffer wrote in a memo that "a conservative Republican, who is usually a reliable source, said that he was with the Reagan people last night and found no sentiment whatsoever for reducing their efforts, much less thought of dropping out of the race. Source advised me that Reagan will be stepping up efforts in both Illinois and North Carolina . . . rather than discuss their own programs, they will attack us."[21]

What they began to attack was détente. Reagan saw the issue as tailor-made for his campaign against the Washington establishment. Using Henry Kissinger as a foil, he could attack the Ford administration without attacking Ford and gain political capital with the right wing of the party. Reagan tried to use the issue in Florida, where polls showed that the state's large Hispanic and over-sixty-five population seemed receptive to such a message. Repeatedly, Reagan charged that "Henry Kissinger's recent stewardship of U.S. foreign policy has coincided precisely with the loss of U.S. military supremacy."[22] But Ford negated the foreign policy issue in Florida by using the incumbency with great skill, promising a $33 million missile contract to Orlando and an $18 million transit system to Miami.[23] Reagan's campaign was finished when he told a Daytona Beach audience that the government should invest Social Security money into the stock market, a plan Ford attacked as a foolish risk in a mass-mailing that promised he would not try to amend Social Security. On the strength of the senior-citizens' support, Ford won the primary on March 9 with 53 percent of the vote.

Reagan did not back off from the attack, however. As his staggering campaign turned its attention to the now critical North Carolina primary, he instead co-opted an issue that would become the turning point in the campaign: the debate over the ownership of the Panama Canal.

The Hay-Bunau Varilla Treaty of 1903 allowed for the construction of a canal through the Isthmus of Panama and gave the United States perpetual authority over the ten-mile-wide territory through which the canal was to run. During the seventy years since the signing of the treaty, Panamanian resentment against Americans had run deep. In December 1963 tempers had reached such a fever pitch that the Johnson administration banned the flying of American flags in the Canal Zone. That order was ignored in January 1965 by a group of American high school students, and the subsequent rioting spurred Johnson to send in troops. Before it was over, four American soldiers and twenty Panamanians had died, and many more had been injured.

In the aftermath of the rioting, both countries agreed to reconsider the 1903 treaty. Negotiations lasted until summer 1967, when the Johnson administration announced that it had concluded three new treaties. His conduct of the Vietnam War had lost Johnson any control of Congress, however, and the treaties were never submitted to the Hill. The situation was further complicated in 1968 when Gen. Omar Torrijos, who had been linked to Castro, came to power in a coup that overthrew Panama's elected government. Torrijos quickly became a favorite target of conservatives in Congress who, in the wake of Vietnam, denounced any steps that would lessen American power in its own hemisphere. Senators Strom Thurmond and John McClellan sponsored a resolution in March 1974 that opposed any termination of U.S. sovereignty in the Canal Zone. Thirty-six senators joined in the signing of the resolution, four names over the necessary number to defeat any treaty.

Kissinger had long argued that the United States had little to gain and everything to lose if it stayed in Panama. The unstable political situation could easily get worse if rioting began anew in the Canal Zone or if Torrijos suddenly turned to Moscow. Kissinger also privately feared that if the United States did not renegotiate the treaty, it could get involved in another guerrilla war, worse even than Vietnam.[24] Thus Kissinger and Panamanian Foreign Minister Juan A. Tack signed an Agreement on Principles in February 1974 that was to provide the basis for a new treaty. Negotiations began immediately, but twenty months later Ford's special emissary to the talks, Ellsworth Bunker, became so frustrated that he publicly admitted, "Significant conceptual problems are still not resolved." Ford searched for a compromise, and on 18 August 1975 he sent modified instructions to his negotiating team, ordering them to "make efforts to obtain a right in principle for the United States to participate in Canal defense, including a limited military pressure in Panama, following the expiration of the treaty period applicable to defense."[25] This effort did little to quiet conservatives, who agreed with Republican congressman Robert Bauman of Maryland that the Canal Zone "is as much a part of the United States as Talbot County."[26]

Jesse Helms, who was running Reagan's campaign in his home state, told Sears that the Panama Canal issue would run well in North Carolina. Reagan hit it with a vengeance, accusing Ford of backing down to Panamanian "blackmail." It was not long before a Reagan line guaranteed applause: "When it comes to the Canal, we built it, we paid for it, it's ours and we should tell Torrijos and Company that we are going to keep it!" Ford's team, believing that Reagan had been defeated for good in Florida, was slow to pick up the danger of the Panama issue. When they finally did, Ford's responses were weak as he proclaimed that the United States would "never give up" its operational and defense rights to the Canal and that Reagan's claims were "irresponsible."[27] The issue led to Reagan's startling victory in North Carolina on March 23, when he captured 52 percent of the vote and twenty-eight of the available fifty-four delegates. It was only the third time in American history that a challenger had defeated an incumbent president in a primary state.

The Reagan campaign had been rejuvenated. To keep his momentum alive, Reagan decided to abandon the upcoming Wisconsin primary and buy a nationwide television address on 31 March 1975.[28] In it, he stressed the outsider theme that had been central to his campaign from the beginning, noting, "For most of his adult life [Ford] has been part of the Washington establishment. Most of my adult life has been spent outside of government." But his sharpest barbs were saved for Ford's foreign policy:

> "Wandering without aim" describes U.S. foreign policy. Angola is a case in point. We gave just enough support to one side to fight and die but too little to give them a chance of winning. Now we're disliked by the winner, distrusted by the loser, and viewed by the world as weak and unsure. . . . Is this why Mr. Ford refused to invite Alexander Solzhenitsyn to the White House? Or why Mr. Ford traveled halfway around the world to sign the Helsinki Pact, putting our stamp of approval on Russia's enslavement of the captive nations?

As a result of the broadcast, money began to flow in, and several congressmen who had previously been on the fence decided to support Reagan publicly.

Meanwhile, Ford's campaign was deteriorating. The Callaway resignation preceded the North Carolina defeat by only a matter of days; the press was quick to characterize the president's campaign as a rudderless ship. Trouble followed on the diplomatic front. On March 22 a nationally syndicated newspaper column quoted from a December 1975 address given by State Department Counselor Helmut Sonnenfeldt to American diplomats in London, in which Sonnenfeldt supposedly advocated a "permanent organic union" between the Soviet Union and Eastern Europe. As it turned out, Sonnenfeldt had not said that, but the reaction was sharp from all quarters. Romania attacked the statement as a sign of the "collusion" between the USSR and the United States; the Yugoslavs believed that the statement was directed largely at them, regarding it as a form of pressure adopted by the United States in response to their nonaligned policies. Reagan charged in a television address that in effect Sonnenfeldt had proposed that "captive nations

should give up any claim to national sovereignty . . . [and] simply become a part of the Soviet Union" and used what was now christened as
the Sonnenfeldt Doctrine as further proof that the Ford administration
had gone soft on communism.[29]

Press Secretary Ron Nessen's attempt to stop the bleeding boomeranged. On April 17, Nessen braved the hooting crowd and appeared as
the host of NBC's "Saturday Night Live." He took part in skits about
Ford's intelligence and physical coordination and even persuaded Ford
to make three taped appearances on the show. The press had a field
day, and Nessen was criticized from every angle—from making an inappropriate appearance to being a lousy comic.[30] *Washington Post* columnist
Bill Gould quoted a reader: "If Ford had agreed to Nessen's appearance,
I don't see how I can vote for a man who could be so dumb."[31] In his
book on *Humor and the Presidency*, Ford was cautious in his evaluation of
the event: "Tactically, it was probably a mistake. . . . Even if we did
make an error, I believe it is always better to err on the side of more exposure and access rather than less." One staff member was blunter in
his assessment: Ford was "pissed."[32]

John Connally, former governor of Texas and Nixon's secretary of
the treasury, told Ford point blank that he had no chance at all of winning Texas. Reagan's huge lead in the state was based largely on the
strength of his foreign policy message. Texas' voting law, which allowed
party crossover for any candidate, also favored Reagan—conservative
Democrats could avoid more liberal candidates in their own party and
vote for him. Ford meanwhile had opened another foreign policy door
for Reagan by allowing Kissinger to fly to South Africa to try to deal
with the issue of apartheid, a pivotal decision in a state where the racial
issue was still so volatile. The May 1 primary brought a record turnout
as 100,000 Texas Democrats voted for Reagan, giving him a clean sweep
of all ninety-six delegates. Three days later Reagan won primaries in Alabama, Georgia, and Indiana. Reagan went on to an impressive win in
Nebraska on May 11, while Ford won in West Virginia, where he had
hardly campaigned. Ford also won big victories in Michigan and Maryland on May 18, but Reagan was still ahead in delegates (by Ford's
count at this point, 528 to 479 with six primaries left).[33] Rogers Morton,
now the official chairman of the President Ford Committee, was asked if
he was planning a change in strategy; he quipped, "I'm not going to re-
arrange the furniture on the deck of the *Titanic*."[34]

Yet as the Ford campaign readied itself for the final primary show-
downs in California, Ohio, and New Jersey on June 8, a major change in
strategy was indeed being planned. Reagan's victories caused some observers in the Ford White House to question Dailey's original advertis-

ing campaign, based on positioning Ford as presidential. Several of Ford's younger advisers, including White House photographer David Hume Kennerly and speechwriter Don Penny, argued that a change was necessary. They persuaded Ford to fire Dailey and to turn to James Jordan, head of Batten, Barton, Dursten and Osborne, Inc, (BBD&O) in New York. Jordan produced campaign commercials that came to be known as "slice of life ads," in which he used professional actors to play Ford supporters who talked about issues such as high prices. According to Kennerly, "It was an attempt to try to shake loose a kind of a constipated organization and make them do something."[35] The ads were terrible; the actors looked stilted and phony as they read their lines. The commercials were soon canceled, Dailey was restored to the campaign, and Penny and Kennerly were temporarily personae non grata among the campaign staff.[36]

Jordan's advertisements certainly did not help the situation in California, but the campaign was lost there already. Despite a ferocious attack from Spencer, who zeroed in on a statement Reagan made in an Ohio debate that he would commit U.S. troops to Rhodesia if the African nation asked for them ("When you vote Tuesday, remember: Governor Ronald Reagan couldn't start a war. President Ronald Reagan could"), Ford made little headway. Reagan won California as expected, but Ford won New Jersey and Ohio. The situation was tenuous, and the nomination could now go either way. It is in this light that many observers have interpreted the last foreign policy crisis of the Ford administration; indeed, many question whether the evacuation from Lebanon was even a true crisis.

By 1975 the Palestinian population in Lebanon—enlarged by the refugees flowing in after Israel's conquest of the West Bank in the 1967 Six Day War and from the 1970 Jordanian Civil War—numbered around 350,000. They could easily be considered an army in exile, fronted by the Palestine Liberation Organization and increasingly in control of the city of Beirut. The Palestinians had begun retributive raids into Israel by 1970, and the Israelis had responded in kind. The Lebanese could not control the Palestinian presence, nor could they play a mediative role in the conflict between the PLO and the Israelis. Lebanese Muslims tended to support the Palestinians, seeing them as part of a pan-Arab cause against the Israelis. Opposing the Muslim and Palestinian guerrillas were the Christian Maronites who made up the Phalange, a group who balked at the Palestinian presence in their homeland, arguing that the Palestinians had strangled democracy in their country. The Phalange had allied themselves with the Israelis. The scene was perfectly set for slaughter.

It began on 13 April 1975, when the Phalange stopped a bus loaded with twenty-seven Palestinians and killed everyone on board. What would become known as the Lebanese Civil War had begun, and it quickly threatened to take on an international dimension. Supporting the Phalange, Israel began air raids on Palestinian refugee camps in Lebanon; backing the PLO, the Syrians supported raids into Israel. The attacks soon turned into a bloodbath. In December 1975, on a day that Lebanese remember as Black Saturday, four Christians were found shot to death in East Beirut. Reports suggest that a Christian leader, Bashir Gemayel, gave orders to kill forty Muslims in retaliation. Christian roadblocks were set up, and as Muslims stopped to pay their tolls, they were taken from their cars and hacked to death by hooded men with knives.

Ford hoped that the United States would be able to remain neutral in the crisis until after the election. But by early January the Christians had made advances and the PLO had entered the war in earnest. West Beirut, which the PLO controlled, was a city in chaos, and Palestinians were beginning to fire upon other Palestinians. In early June, ostensibly to stabilize the situation, the Syrians entered Lebanon in force to save the Christian Maronites, but their presence did little to help, and much to increase, the mobocracy in Beirut. On June 16 U.S. Ambassador Francis E. Melloy, his economic aide, Robert O. Waring, and their driver disappeared in Beirut. They were found dead—without their shoes or socks—on a beach near Beirut. Immediately, attention shifted to the fourteen hundred Americans living in Lebanon. With a speed unprecedented among Ford's advisers, the decision was made to evacuate the U.S. nationals by sea.

Whether the Americans in Lebanon were in any real danger remains a question. Indeed, despite the deaths of Melloy and Waring, many of those directly affected by the crisis said that their lives were never threatened and that they wanted to stay—only 116 Americans and 147 third-country nationals chose to be evacuated. Nevertheless, the administration soon shifted into crisis mode. Unlike during the *Mayaguez* crisis, when Nessen kept the press at bay, the evacuation of Lebanon was deliberately made into a media event. On June 20 television crews were invited to film an embassy official as he opened a garage door; inside were two American Marines, bearing, as the official told the camera, the bodies of Melloy and his aides. In the background, an unidentified aide yelled, "Come on. Let's not waste time. Let's go."[37] Later that day a navy landing craft evacuated the 263 Americans and Europeans from Lebanon. The only shots heard were those from PLO guards who fired into the air to keep journalists away. Indeed, the Palestinians, perhaps hoping to ingratiate themselves to the United States, helped the Americans leave.[38]

The timing of the evacuation was missed by no one. Reagan was quick to charge Ford with manufacturing a crisis for his own political gain, but Reagan was not the only critic. The British embassy privately made it clear that it deplored Ford's actions and attributed them to being part of his election campaign.[39] If favorable publicity was Ford's goal for the evacuation, however, no independent source has come forth to confirm that motive. At any rate, the long-range impact of the crisis was negligible. The primary election campaign had shifted into its final phase—one that Ford would control.

As the primaries came to a close and state conventions began their work to choose the remaining delegates, Ford was 170 votes short of the nomination and Reagan 270 short. Convinced that Reagan would be no more than a minor irritant, the Ford campaign had done a terrible job of laying the groundwork for a blitz on the state conventions. Yet it was the sort of campaigning—barnstorming from convention to convention, speaking with individual delegates rather than making public speeches in front of huge crowds—that Ford did best. As minority leader and as vice president, Ford had run this type of campaign for two decades as he crisscrossed the country campaigning for congressional candidates. For this election Ford combined his love of close-range campaigning with a skillful use of the incumbency. Delegates were invited to the White House, patronage jobs were dangled everywhere, and Ford offered every state convention a marquee speaker: the president of the United States. This blitz kept Reagan from taking control of the process. By the end of the last state convention, Ford had closed the gap and was reported as having 1,102 first-ballot delegates—28 shy of the nomination. Reagan had 1,063, short 67 votes, and 94 delegates were still reported as uncommitted.

John Sears later reminisced about those final weeks of the campaign: "The incumbent could offer them anything. And he could do it. So we were in a position where if we just stayed and did nothing, we were gonna be beaten."[40] Sears took a gamble unprecedented in American political history and persuaded Reagan to announce his running mate before the convention had even assembled in Kansas City. Despite Reagan's having gone on record with his statement, "I do not believe you choose someone of an opposite philosophy in hopes he'll get you some votes you can't get for yourself," that was precisely the strategy that Sears had come to believe was Reagan's last chance for victory.[41] Sears had been beating the bushes for a liberal Republican who would consent to run with Reagan and, without securing Reagan's approval for the venture, had sounded out Richard Schweicker. The Pennsylvania senator would certainly appeal to liberal Republicans. He had been given an 89 percent approval rating from the liberal Americans for Democratic Action and was the only senator to receive a 100 percent rating from the AFL-CIO's Committee on Public Education (COPE); conversely, the Americans for Conservative Action gave him a rating of 8 percent.[42] Schweicker would later say that his decision to join Reagan "was not so much based on differences of philosophy, but more out of belief that Ford could not win" and that he thought "it was necessary for the future of the Republican party to unite the Eastern and the Western wings."[43] For his part, Reagan was primarily interested in capturing the huge Pennsylvania delegation. Thus, on July 26 Reagan announced one of the oddest political combinations in recent history: he would pair himself with "a man of independent thought and action" who "has not become a captive of what I call 'the Washington buddy system.'"[44]

The announcement elicited a combination of incredulity and derision. Conveniently forgetting their criticism of Ford at the time of the Rockefeller withdrawal, many conservatives charged Reagan with selling out. But even more important, Schweicker could not swing Pennsylvania to Reagan. Congressman John Heinz of Pennsylvania, a Ford supporter, told Jack Marsh not to worry too much about Schweicker "because he is not too much 'on the in' with the hard core, regular Republicans in Pennsylvania."[45] Heinz's assessment certainly turned out to be true; six previously uncommitted Pennsylvania delegates immediately declared for Ford, and the Pennsylvania delegation eventually gave Ford 93 of its 103 votes. Reagan found he had cast aside much of his conservative base and gained nothing in return. Ford thus entered the Kansas City convention with enough delegates to win on the first ballot.

Sears had one last trick up his sleeve. Speaking before the rules committee on Monday, August 9, he proposed that the party require that every nominee disclose his running mate before the convention began. Sears tried to position the amendment, Rule 16C, as a grand reform, but it was pure politics; Ford supporters called it the "misery loves company" amendment. Ford was in control of the rules committee, and Sears's Rule 16C was defeated as expected. As Sears prepared to challenge the committee's ruling on the convention floor, however, his proposal almost caught on. In the forty-eight hours before the convention formally opened, Ford's short list for vice president had leaked out, and, as was expected in a tight race, it was a rather long list. Reagan forces wailed that Ford was planning on choosing a liberal Republican to balance his ticket—just as Reagan had done but more openly. Rule 16C was thus touted as a way to open the process of choosing the party's vice-presidential candidate. Most of the drama was provided by the Mississippi delegation. Controlled by state party chairman Clarke Reed, a publicity hound who had been holding back his decision until he could tell which man would win, he finally threw the state to Ford. Rule 16C was defeated on the floor of the convention by a vote of 1,180 to 1,069. The true depth of Reagan's support was exposed, and Ford was nominated that same night, winning by 1,187 to 1,070. Carrying out a prearranged finale, Ford walked over to Reagan's hotel, and the two men emerged for the traditional unity photos.

In the 16 September 1976 *New York Review of Books*, Garry Wills called the convention challenge the "dumb-out at the O–K Corral" but then made the salient comment that Reagan had "humiliated Ford without defeating him."[46] Reagan, however, did win two important victories at the convention. First, he won the platform. The Morality in Foreign Policy plank commended Solzhenitsyn, criticized the Helsinki agreement, and promised a foreign policy "in which secret agreements, hidden from our people, will have no part." Kissinger and Rockefeller were vehemently opposed and adamant to remove it; Cheney and Nessen argued that given the nonbinding nature of party platforms, it was a concession that Ford could afford to make. Ford was angry but ordered that the plank be supported. It passed, as did a Reagan-sponsored plank calling for a constitutional amendment banning abortion.

Second, Reagan ended up winning the vice-presidential sweepstakes even without being chosen to run with Ford (the record is still unclear as to whether he would have accepted had he been asked). When Ford began discussions on the choice of his running mate, the specter of Ronald Reagan and his numerous supporters hung over the room. In the early morning hours after the night of the nomination, Ford met in his hotel suite with several of his aides, and four names were discussed as finalists. Anne Armstrong, former cochair of the Republican National Committee (RNC), the first woman to be named counselor to the president, a member of Ford's Council on Wage and Price Stability, and ambassador to England, came breathlessly close to being named the first woman on a national party ticket. Also considered were Assistant Attorney General William Ruckelshaus and Sen. Howard Baker of Tennessee. Ford let it be known that during their unity meeting, Reagan had responded favorably to Kansas senator Robert Dole. The meeting broke up without a decision, and a second meeting was scheduled for the following morning. At that meeting, after a brief discussion, Ford announced, "It's Dole."[47]

Ford later explained his choice by pointing out that Ruckelshaus had never won a statewide race, Armstrong would be too chancy, and Baker had no base of support in the Northeast. Dole, on the other hand, with whom he felt comfortable, would help in the Midwest with voters angered by the grain embargo.[48] Yet it is now clear that in the intervening hours after the first meeting, pressure was brought to bear on Ford by the Reagan forces to make Dole his choice. A movement had cropped up to nominate Reagan for vice president from the convention floor regardless of Ford's choice. Rockefeller remembers that "Clark[e] Reed got ahold of Cheney to tell him that the Southern delegates would drop Reagan as a vice-presidential candidate if Ford took Dole."[49] This circumstance is confirmed by a recently released set of handwritten notes from Ron Nessen, dated 15 August 1976: "Ford leaning to Ruckelshaus as late as 5[:00] A.M. As a result of a series of calls from Southerners, Ford turned to Dole."[50]

Ford's acceptance speech to the convention was not the usual anticlimax, delivered by a candidate who had spent three days in town being crowned rather than nominated. Ford needed to win back Reagan delegates and to send a message to the country that despite trailing by twenty points in the polls he still intended to fight and win. The speech needed to be the best that Ford had ever delivered, and it was.

Speaking more forcefully than ever before, Ford proclaimed: "We concede not a single state, we concede not a single vote." Observing that he was the first incumbent president since Eisenhower "who can tell the American people America is at peace," he received the first of several standing ovations. Yet the line that brought the delegates to their feet and kept them there had been kept secret until moments before the speech: "I'm ready and eager to go before the American people and debate the real issues face to face with Jimmy Carter." The response was immediate; the delegates jumped from their chairs and launched into a demonstration of several minutes' duration, chanting "We want Ford." Ford's voice grew even stronger after this moment, and the audience continued to interrupt him with standing ovations. As he concluded, he predicted that at the polls the American people would say, "Jerry, you've done a good job, keep right on doing it."[51]

12

★★★★★

"THE NO-CAMPAIGN CAMPAIGN"

Former Georgia governor Jimmy Carter had appeared as a contestant on the TV show "What's My Line" in early 1975. None of the panelists could guess who he was or what he did.[1] Ford himself viewed Carter as a "flash in the pan," and he had trouble believing that the Democrats "were about to rest their hopes on an outsider with little more going for him than a winning smile."[2] Yet in fall 1976 this talented man, a complex combination of virtue and political ambition, would face off against Ford for the presidency. And in August Carter held a twenty-point lead in the polls.

In many important ways, Jimmy Carter had run the same type of campaign in the primaries as Ronald Reagan had. He presented himself as the consummate outsider ("I haven't been part of the Washington scene"), a Georgia farmer who refused to accede to the power of the eastern Democratic bosses and whose acceptance of the work ethic would quickly turn this lack of national experience to the nation's advantage. Carter also hammered at the postpardon Ford presidency, attacking Ford's foreign policy with vigor (criticizing Helsinki: "We ratified the Russian takeover of Eastern Europe").[3]

Carter's departure from Reagan's tactics, and from those of most presidential contenders of the postwar period, was in his conscious positioning of himself as a Wilsonian moralist. His favorite definition of politics was drawn from theologian Reinhold Niebuhr: "The sad duty of politics is to establish justice in a sinful world."[4] Carter parlayed this view of the politician as defender of the faith into a decided political asset in the post-Watergate political climate. His approach is captured at its simplest in his most famous speech line, repeated over and over throughout both the primaries and the fall campaign, "I'm Jimmy Carter and I'm running for president. I will never lie to you." More important, Carter consciously positioned Republicans as casual watchdogs of the Republic, whose morals could be called into question. His acceptance speech at the Democratic convention clearly stated this theme:

> Each time our nation has made a serious mistake, the American people have been excluded from the process. The tragedy of Vietnam and Cambodia, the disgrace of Watergate, and the embarrassment of the CIA revelations could have been avoided if our government had simply reflected the . . . high moral character of the American people.[5]

Far from being coy or retiring about his values, Carter placed them on the table for all to see. He planned to corner the market on morality and beat the Republicans senseless with it.

There were certainly weaknesses in the Carter juggernaut. Despite Carter's attempt to keep it hidden from view, reporters on the campaign trail had seen many examples of his inflexibility, his rigorous discipline in pursuit of a goal, and his willingness to change his mind on a policy position for political gain. Yet Ford was not the best candidate to exploit these flaws. Spencer and Cheney recognized that a key component of any successful strategy must be an attempt to use the incumbency to make Carter look unpresidential. White House staffer Michael Raoul-Duval centered a June memo on this theme, arguing that after the convention Ford should announce that he needed to stay in Washington to attend to the job of being president. Duval dubbed his strategy the "no-campaign campaign."[6] Still, Ford had almost lost the nomination by running a primary campaign that positioned him as presidential while Reagan reminded audiences that Ford, not he, was a member of Washington's power elite. Ford's handlers were also aware that his own shifting positions on issues throughout his presidency would be attacked by Carter.

Yet any thoughts of developing a Harry Truman "give-'em-hell" type of campaign for Ford ran into opposition. When Ford finally hit the campaign trail in the primaries, he had been unable to convey his natural personal charm to large audiences, and his stiff speaking style suffered by comparison to the more folksy, comfortable Reagan—it would compare poorly to Carter as well. Thus the argument that ran through the White House for the immediate two weeks after the convention was the same one that had persisted before the primaries—should Ford campaign on the stump and flaunt his "nice guy" image or should he stay in Washington and campaign for president by being president?

In the days following the convention, Cheney and Spencer had developed an outline of a strategy plan for the fall campaign. Their framework was refined by pollster Bob Teeter and James Baker III, a former undersecretary of commerce who had replaced the ailing Rogers Morton as chairman of the President Ford Committee. The final plan, a 120-page, spiral-bound memorandum with appendixes, was presented to Ford by Cheney and Spencer some two weeks after the convention. It was based on one simple assumption, earthily articulated by Spencer as he began their meeting: "Mister President, as a campaigner, you're no fucking good."[7] As if that were not straightforward enough, the memorandum itself began with the blunt but truthful observation, "If past is indeed prologue, you will lose on November 2nd." They reasoned that although Teeter's polls showed that Ford was perceived as "honest and decent . . . you are not now perceived as being a strong, decisive leader by anywhere near a majority of the American people." A frontal attack on Carter was, in their opinion, the best strategy. Carter's campaigns needed to be exposed as "very slick, media-oriented," and Carter should be positioned as "a candidate that takes positions based on polls, not principles." But they cautioned that Ford would not be the best person to lead that attack. In fact, they envisioned a campaign where Ford would be "an active candidate, and yet be perceived as a working president." The strategy, then, was threefold. There would be a new advertising campaign that would emphasize Ford's human side. As had been the case in almost every successful presidential election, the vice-presidential candidate would go on the attack, and Dole would aim his barbs at Carter's weak spots—duplicity and questionable trustworthiness. Finally, Ford would stay above the fray in Washington as long as possible, continuing in his efforts to be seen as a high-profile president, thus getting his actions on the nightly news.[8]

Ford's advertising was clearly the most successful component of this campaign strategy. Dissatisfied with a perceived inertia in a key area of the campaign, Spencer had replaced ad executive Peter Dailey with New York executives Douglas Bailey and John Deardorff. The two men had distinguished themselves in 1974 with an apparent minor political miracle—their ad campaign was directly responsible for getting James Rhodes, best known for calling in the National Guard on the demonstrators at Kent State University, reelected as governor of Ohio.

Bailey and Deardorff had long been advocates of giving the Ford campaign a more informal style. Their early ads emphasized Ford's qualifications—"Without seeking the presidency, Gerald Ford has been preparing for it a lifetime"—but showed him in shirtsleeves. There were also spots showing Ford with his family—"Sometimes a man's family can say a lot about the man."[9] Carter countered with ads designed to show him as more presidential—wearing business suits and reading formally worded scripts in which he commented on the issues. But Bailey and Deardorff stuck with their plan—indeed, Ford's ads became more personable in orientation as Carter's became more presidential—and to the end they continually tested better than Carter's ads.[10] Indeed, many observers argue that in any other election year Ford's advertising would have made the difference. But in 1976 new finance laws had taken effect, and both parties, for all intents and purposes, were running their campaigns on an equal footing. The total amount of money that both could raise, including matching money, was $13.3 million, and both candidates received $21.8 million in federal funds. It was the first time in modern memory that the Republicans did not have a sizable advantage in terms of fund-raising.[11]

Dole's contribution to the campaign was not as positive. Elected to the Senate in 1968 and serving as Republican National Committee chairman in 1971–72, Dole had developed a reputation as an irascible maverick (in 1974 when he was asked if he wanted Nixon to come to Kansas to campaign for him, he said that he would settle for a flyover).[12] Despite a speaking style that was perfectly suited for being Ford's hatchet man, Dole did not relish having to play this role in his first national campaign. He began the campaign as a one-man truth squad, following Carter around the country and speaking in the same town immediately after Carter had left. Yet his influence was immediately hampered by charges in the press that a lobbyist for the Gulf Oil Corporation had made an illegal corporate contribution to Dole's 1973 reelection campaign. ABC News ran a story reporting the rumor that Reagan had called Ford and asked him to replace Dole because of the allegations. Nessen later learned that "the so-called Reagan conversation was a story planted by a publicist working on the Carter-Mondale campaign."[13] Nevertheless, the damage had been done. Dole sputtered for the rest of the campaign, becoming more of a hindrance than a help to Ford's chances. Larry Speakes, then serving as Dole's press secretary, remembered that Dole was so bitter that he refused to prepare for his October debate against Democratic vice-presidential candidate Walter Mondale.[14] This lack of preparation probably contributed to his famous slip—his charge that "if we added up the killed and wounded in Democrat wars in this century, it would be about 1.6 million Americans, enough to fill the city of Detroit." Most people shared the reaction of *Washington Post* reporter Jules Witcover: "In his big moment in the living rooms of America . . . [Dole] had lived up to his earlier billing: dark, brooding, sarcastic, even mean. I confess that as I sat at my typewriter . . . I thought of Richard Nixon."[15]

The third phase of the campaign, that of consigning Ford to Washington, never really happened. Although Ford started out the month of September making a major television splash by signing bills at the White House, such images went for nought. The ghosts of Watergate soon conspired again to tarnish the image of Gerald Ford.

Carter had been so successful in the primaries in part because a Watergate-weary nation was searching for an honest man to lead them. Ford *seemed* to be that man, but Carter *said* he was that man. The events of early September brought the credibility of both candidates into serious question, however, and effectively stopped the discussion of significant issues for the rest of the campaign. A serious chink in Carter's armor appeared when he admitted in the pages of *Playboy* that he "looked on a lot of women with lust" and had "committed adultery in my heart many times." He also used the terms "screw" and "shack up" when responding to questions probing his views on premarital sexual relations. The reaction was sharp—even Carter's own pastor admitted, "I do wish he would have used different words"—and it began a September slump for Carter as his twenty-point lead shrunk to twelve.[16] Yet Ford was not able to deliver a knockout blow. Throughout September, as Carter hammered away at the legacy of the "Nixon and Ford administrations," Ford was busy running a defensive campaign; he was forced to deal with charges that reminded the nation of the depths of resentment over official malfeasance that Watergate had left behind.

The first charge to surface seemed trivial enough. Early in September the *New York Times* reported that FBI director Clarence Kelley had had a Bureau carpenter install a window sash in his home and that he had not paid the fee of $335. The White House initiated an investigation of the matter and found that Kelley had received numerous gifts from the FBI executive conference on occasions such as wedding anniversaries and Christmas. These items had been purchased with money pooled together from voluntary donations; the most expensive of them was a chair, purchased for $105 by sixteen members of the executive conference at a cost of $6.56 apiece. As for the window, the investigation found that Kelley was in the process of reimbursing the government.[17] Nevertheless, Carter pounced: "When [the American people] see the head of the FBI break a law and keep his job, it tells everybody crime must be okay." Ford thrust with the information that Kelley's wife was dying of cancer at the time; Carter parried by responding that Kelley's impending remarriage suggested that his remorse was thin.

The next incident involved William Whyte, vice president of U.S. Steel, director of the second transition team, and Ford's close friend. In September the *New York Times* reported that Whyte, along with other corporate friends, had financed several pleasure trips for Ford while he was minority leader. The story charged that Whyte had paid for Ford's room during golfing weekends at the Pine Valley Country Club near Clementon, New Jersey, in 1964 and 1971; Whyte said that he personally had paid only for Ford's caddy and greens fees.[18] This development was more serious than Kelley's foolishness. As described by the *Detroit Free Press* at the height of the flap, "Indeed, there is no evidence that any of Ford's golfing partners have received specific favors. . . . But that isn't the only issue. For whether [they] have sought it or not, they do have a very 'special privilege' that others lack—access to the president." One consumer-group lobbyist complained, "Even if Ford is not guilty of a conflict of interests playing golf with corporate executives, he is displaying an identity of interests, which is not healthy for the country."[19] Ford protested that these were "personal friends" and that he could easily separate their friendship from their business roles. But with U.S. Steel in the courts facing severe antitrust problems, the issue lingered.

Even more serious was the recurrence of an allegation that had dogged Ford during his vice-presidential confirmation hearings. He was alleged to have received contributions from the Marine Engineers Beneficial Association (MEBA) in his congressional campaigns, which he had not disclosed as mandated by federal law. Ford was not helped by MEBA's rather unsavory reputation at the time. In 1965 its president, Jesse Calhoon, had been arrested and released on charges of assaulting a union official (during negotiations, he reportedly jumped on top of the table and kicked his opponent in the face).[20] The fact that Carter had been endorsed by MEBA and that it had contributed more to Carter's campaign than had any other union was largely missed.[21] Although correspondence and financial records in Ford's papers bear out his contention that "during my years in the House, I had received MEBA's financial support, and I had disclosed every contribution," there is no way to verify Ford's claim that his veto of a cargo preference bill so infuriated Calhoon that the labor leader went to the papers and concocted a story that Ford had accepted cash payment from the union.[22]

The story nevertheless made its way to the FBI. Director Kelley dutifully turned it over to Attorney General Edward Levi, who felt that he had no choice but to refer the matter to Charles F. C. Ruff, the new Watergate special prosecutor. Ruff sent investigators to Grand Rapids with subpoenas for the Kent County Republican Committee's records from 1964 and also subpoenaed MEBA's records. When the investigations were revealed in the press, Ford was caught in a dilemma. He could not interfere with the special prosecutor, lest he risk charges of Nixonian tampering with the Justice Department; he could only announce that he had full confidence in Ruff—and wait.

These crises buzzed like gnats around Ford's head as he prepared for his first debate with Carter, scheduled for September 26 in Philadelphia's Walnut Theater. The American public had last been treated to presidential debates in 1960, and the Kennedy-Nixon confrontation had long since become legendary; Kennedy's style had slaughtered Nixon's substance. If the past offered any precedent, Ford was destined to have trouble with any live television appearance; his rather wooden speaking style had long been a concern of his campaign handlers. Ford was also preoccupied with the countless number of stories that had come out over the past month—on the morning of the first debate, the *New York Times* ran a front-page story on the MEBA investigation.

Yet Carter helped Ford out by not remembering his history. Carter prepped as had Nixon in 1960, by isolating himself from his advisers and poring over briefing books. Ford prepped as had Kennedy; his aides rehearsed him in a mock studio set up in the White House and worked with him not so much on his answers as on how he looked delivering those answers. It worked. Overprepared, looking somewhat dazed, Carter admitted later that he was in awe of being on the same stage as the president. As a result, and just as the Ford advisers had hoped, he acted with an uncharacteristic deference to Ford. From start to finish, Carter was clearly on the defensive. The major theme of the questioning was the economy. Ford argued that "in the last twenty-four months, we've turned the economy around and we've brought inflation down to under 6 percent." He also focused on the theme of a $10 billion tax cut, which he had promised along with a balanced budget. Carter, on the other hand, was unable to explain his projection of a $60 billion surplus by 1981. Nor could he explain a September 20 Associated Press interview in which he had predicted that he would have to raise taxes on middle-income taxpayers. He countered with the promise that "I would never do anything that would increase the taxes for those who work for a living or who are presently required to list all their income,"

181

a statement that Ford correctly pointed out to be a complete contradiction of his earlier position. And Ford struck out at Carter's stand against the Washington establishment: "The anti-Washington feeling, in my opinion, ought to be focused on the Congress of the United States."[23]

The first debate also provided a memorable technical glitch. With the candidates well into a spirited discussion of the abuses within the intelligence community, the sound went out. For twenty-seven minutes, the two men refused to move or even to address each other (Ford speechwriter Bob Orben later reflected that the two men looked like two fellows in a tailor shop waiting for their pants to be given back).[24] But the problem did little to spoil Ford's best performance of the fall campaign. Immediately after the telecast, the Roper poll declared that 39 percent of the viewers thought Ford had won, 31 percent thought Carter had won, and 30 percent thought it was a draw. The advantage was enough to give a serious boost to the Ford campaign; the next day's polls showed that Carter's twelve-point lead had been cut to eight.

Rejuvenated, Ford resolved to rid himself of the MEBA investigation. Convinced that Ruff was playing politics and deliberately dragging his feet on the case, Ford called his good friend, Washington lawyer Edward Bennett Williams, for help. Williams suggested that Ford call a press conference and essentially say that "justice delayed is justice denied. That'll get Ruff off his ass." It worked. Ford met the press on September 30 and emphatically denied that he had misused any campaign funds. Campaigning in Boston, Carter said that he accepted Ford's statement, and as far as he was concerned, the matter was closed. Ruff wrote Buchen on October 13 that his investigation "is now complete, and the evidence developed has disclosed no violation of law on the part of President Ford. The matter has therefore been closed." The next day the Watergate Special Prosecution Force released a statement that agreed with Ruff's.[25]

The exoneration offered Ford little comfort, however, as he was forced to deal with new allegations. Ironically, the progenitor of the crisis was Nixon's Watergate cover-up czar, White House Counsel John Dean. During the last week of September, the *Washington Post* had printed advance excerpts from Dean's upcoming book, *Blind Ambition*, which charged that as minority leader Ford had moved to squelch the Patman committee's investigation into Watergate. The story had a direct Watergate ring to it, and charges that Ford had been an agent of the cover-up began to surface. Carter jumped on the Dean revelations with a vengeance. On the day that the story appeared, while in Evansville,

Indiana, at a rally for Indiana Democratic candidates, Carter declared: "Richard Nixon was bad enough. It's been worse the past two years."[26] Both Congresswoman Elizabeth Holtzman (D-N.Y.) and Congressman John Conyers (D-Mich.) wrote letters to Special Prosecutor Ruff demanding that he investigate. Perhaps tired of chasing Ford-related issues, Ruff refused, claiming that the case fell under the jurisdiction of the Department of Justice. Not surprisingly, Levi undertook a three-week investigation and announced that he had come up with nothing.

Dean was also responsible for a story that led to one of the worst fears of any incumbent's campaign manager—the firing of a cabinet member in mid-campaign. Flying back from the Kansas City convention, Secretary of Agriculture Earl Butz was sitting with singer Pat Boone and Dean, who was covering the convention for *Rolling Stone*. After a few drinks, Butz began to tell off-color jokes to his captive audience, one of which disparaged blacks. Boone later was forced to confirm the story for the *New Times*, and Dean reported the joke in *Rolling Stone*, attributing it to an unnamed cabinet member. About a week later Butz learned that the *New York Times* was going to name him as that cabinet member. Ford met with Butz on Friday October 1, and reportedly gave him a "severe reprimand." Later that Friday the *New York Times* ran the story, and Butz personally called the three television networks and read an apology. Nevertheless, calls for Butz's resignation appeared from virtually every quarter. On Monday morning Butz met with Ford; around noon, with tears in his eyes, he went before the press and resigned.[27] Ford's assessment of Dean was entirely predictable: "a low-down, no-good, son of a bitch. A sniveling bastard."[28]

Carter once again seized the moral high ground, raging that "the spirit of this country has been damaged by Richard Nixon and Gerald Ford. We don't like their betrayal of what our country is, and we don't like their vision of what this country ought to be."[29] Yet Carter had problems of his own. Despite Dean's reporting, the gap between the two combatants had stayed about the same; Ford now had about eight points to make up in approximately four weeks. The second debate, held on October 6 at San Francisco's Palace of Fine Arts Theater, was critical. And the theme of the debate was foreign policy—a subject in which the incumbent is usually better informed but also the area that had almost lost Ford the nomination to the Reagan conservatives.

This time Carter left nothing to chance. He went through rehearsal sessions with his advisers and vowed to go on the attack to reverse the overwhelming feeling after the first debate that he had been too solicitous. He did so early in the debate by borrowing one of Reagan's most effective lines—"As far as foreign policy goes, Mr. Kissinger has been the president of this country"—and he charged that Ford "has been in office two years and there has been absolutely no progress made toward a new SALT agreement." Ford countered by pointing out that Carter's proposed $15 billion in defense cuts would hurt the country's security. Carter rebutted the charge: "As a matter of fact, I have never advocated a cut of $15 billion in our defense budget," a statement that was simply untrue.[30] To that point, the match was dead even. It fell to Max Frankel of the *New York Times* to detonate the debate. His question to Ford was lengthy, dealing with the issue of the captive nations of Eastern Europe: "They used to brag, back in Khruschev's day, that because of their greater patience and because of our greed for business deals, they would sooner or later get the better of us. Is it possible that, despite some setbacks in the Middle East, they've proved their point?"

Frankel's question was far from unexpected. Scowcroft had prepared an answer to any question about Helsinki or the Sonnenfeldt Doctrine, and Ford had underlined this passage as he read through his briefing book.[31] The night before the debate, Ford had gone through a three-hour rehearsal with his aides. When Scowcroft asked whether Helsinki and the Sonnenfeldt Doctrine represented a "change in U.S. policy toward acquiescence in Soviet domination of Eastern Europe," Ford's reply had been forceful, clear, and on point with the prepared answer in his briefing book:

> Not at all. The policy of this government at the present time is to recognize the independence, the sovereignty, and the autonomy of all Eastern European Countries. This has been the policy of the United States since after World War II. . . . The President of the United States believes that those countries are independent and sovereign. And we feel that all other Eastern European nations and Baltic nation countries are in the same category. The so-called Sonnenfeldt Doctrine never did exist. And I can assure you that we do not *recognize* any sphere of influence by any power in Europe at the present time.[32]

Ford's response to Frankel, however, was a disaster. It was a long, rambling answer, which purported to list his accomplishments in negotiations with the Soviet Union. Then Ford mangled the last line of his prepared answer:

> There is no Soviet domination of Eastern Europe, and there never will be under a Ford administration. The United States does not concede

that those countries [of Eastern Europe] are under the domination of the Soviet Union.

Moderator Pauline Frederick began to announce that it was Carter's turn to rebut. But Frankel, looking slightly confused, asked for a follow-up: "Did I understand you to say, sir, that the Russians are not using Eastern Europe as their own sphere of influence and occupying most of the countries there and making sure with their troops that it is a communist zone, whereas on our side of the line the Italians and the French are still flirting with the possibility of Communism?" Frankel had given Ford a chance to retract his gaffe or to worsen the wound. Ford made it worse:

> I don't believe, Mr. Frankel, that the Yugoslavians consider themselves dominated by the Soviet Union. I don't believe that the Rumanians consider themselves dominated by the Soviet Union. I don't believe that the Poles consider themselves dominated by the Soviet Union. And the United States does not concede that those countries are under the domination of the Soviet Union.

Carter was quick to point out the extent of Ford's political blunder: "I'd like to see Mr. Ford convince Polish-Americans and Hungarian-Americans in this country that those countries don't live under the domination of the Soviet Union."

It is easy to see what the president meant—if one substitutes the words "a part of" for the words "dominated by," Ford not only would have been correct, but he also would have been true to the spirit of his policy pronouncements on Eastern Europe made throughout his presidency. Yet those individuals on the Ford team who later accused the press of inflating a minor mistake into a major crisis missed the point. It was a minor mistake—until the follow-up. Ford had the opportunity at that point to catch himself, recall the passage in the briefing book, and fix the error. Instead, Ford repeated his error, and more vigorously than in his initial answer. The follow-up made a bad situation worse, crystallizing the issue in the minds of the viewer.

It was a catastrophe, and Ford's staff knew it. Spencer remembered that when Ford made his slip, the usually taciturn Scowcroft turned to him and said, "You've got a problem." Missing the import of Ford's mistake, Spencer asked why. Scowcroft then told Spencer how many Soviet divisions were at that moment in Poland, and Spencer felt chilled.[33] Immediately after the debate, Scowcroft and Cheney held a press conference, and to the very first question, "Are there Soviet troops in Poland?" Scowcroft simply replied, "Yes."[34] This exchange certainly was not enough to stem the tide; before the evening was over, surveys showed that Ford had lost the debate by an overwhelming forty-five points. The next day Cheney went into Ford's compartment on Air Force One and told him that he needed to issue a clarification. Ford refused.

The damage was being compounded with every passing minute. Spencer joined Cheney in Ford's compartment, and together they convinced Ford that at least he had to address the issue in that afternoon's speech at the University of Southern California. Ford agreed, but incredibly his speech kept the matter open as he observed that "last night in the debate, I spoke of America's firm support for the aspiration of independence of the nations of Eastern Europe. The United States has never conceded—and will never concede—their domination by the Soviet Union." The next day Ford went through another speech without putting the matter to rest, telling a breakfast meeting of San Fernando Valley businessmen that Poles "don't believe that they are going to be forever dominated—*if they are*—by the Soviet Union. They believe in the independence of their great country." Furious, Spencer and Cheney demanded that Ford extricate himself from the situation. When he did so at the Glendale City Hall, he was less than contrite ("I was perhaps not as precise as I should have been. I recognize there are Soviet divisions in Poland. I regret it. And I am very proud of the courageous attitude of the Polish people who want freedom. . . . It *was* a misunderstanding"). The White House did not issue an official clarification until October 12—six days after the San Francisco debate.

Frustrated, more angry with the press than with himself, Ford refused either to apologize for or even to clarify a remark that made perfect sense to him. It was the error of a tired politician, behind in the polls, who had reacted carelessly. It did little to help combat the image of Ford as not up to the job, and it stoked the fires of those critics who questioned his intelligence. Immediately after the second debate, the Gallup poll showed a surge for Carter—widening his lead for the first time since mid-July. Two days before the final debate Carter was holding onto a six-point lead, forty-seven to forty-one, with 12 percent of the electorate still undecided.[35] The third debate, held in Williamsburg, Virginia, on October 21, was a tame affair, with neither candidate wanting to make a mistake nor saying much of substance.

Exhausted, with his voice failing him, Ford crisscrossed the country, hammering at a theme that in retrospect probably should have been heavily incorporated into the campaign—he repeated his promise to cut taxes. The response to this guarantee was strong, and it became the theme of Ford's final advertising blitz. But the general state of the economy deflated any chance that the tax issue would close the gap; on October 28 the Commerce Department released its index of leading economic indicators, showing that the economy had declined for the second straight month.[36]

It was the lowest voter turnout since 1948—only 54 percent of all eligible Americans voted.[37] The low turnout favored Carter and contributed to the closeness of the results. Carter won 49.9 percent of the vote to Ford's 47.9 percent. In the electoral college, Carter's margin was even narrower—the closest since 1916—297 votes to 241. If only 8,000 voters in Hawaii and Ohio had gone for Ford, he would have won.

In an election this close—only four others had been as close or closer—there can be no one reason for the result. Many people blamed the pardon even though it was hardly discussed during the fall campaign. Others focused on a related issue, supported by Carter, that he was elected because of a "deep desire among the people for open government, based on a new and fresh commitment to changing some of the Washington habits which had made it possible for the American people to be misled."[38] Some blamed Dole; others blamed the bumbler image (the *Manchester Union Leader*'s headline the day after the election ran: "Shifty Beats Stupid"); still others blamed the Reagan challenge for taxing the party's resources in a divisive primary and allowing Carter to get a head start.[39] Perhaps the least convincing reason was offered by those who argued that the country believed that "it was time for a change": the country believes that each time an incumbent is defeated.

Gerald Ford lost the 1976 election because of poor strategy decisions. He greatly underestimated Ronald Reagan, and as a result the campaign for the nomination was closer than it should have been. The primary campaign not only taxed the financial and physical resources of the Ford camp, but it also forced them to recognize the depth of Reagan's support at the convention—they did so by acceding to Reagan's preference for vice president, a choice that did little to help Ford in the fall campaign. In that campaign, Ford proved himself the equal—some would say the superior—of Carter as a campaigner, and he was able to rise above the allegations of wrongdoing both in his political past and in his administration. Yet the Poland gaffe was an important mistake, not because a human being slipped up on national television but because the president of the United States refused for three days to acknowledge that he had made a mistake. Nevertheless, the election could easily have gone either way, and most observers agree that the announcement of the economic slowdown just days before the vote was

187

the turning point for Carter. In retrospect, if Ford had continually reminded the public of his commitment to a tax cut instead of waiting until the last days of the campaign to concentrate on the issue, the result of the presidential election of 1976 might have been different.

13

★ ★ ★ ★ ★

"IF I'M REMEMBERED, IT WILL PROBABLY BE FOR HEALING THE LAND"

During the first week of July 1976, America celebrated the bicentennial of its Declaration of Independence from the British Empire. "Heritage USA" had been planned for over four years, and the nation was ready for a party. Hoopla and hype mixed with patriotic introspection— Philadelphia's Memorial Hall was home both to the memories of 1776 and the world's largest birthday cake, on display and covered with gaudy red, white, and blue icing. Millions of tourists packed into New York City on the Fourth of July to witness the breathtaking sight of 325 sailing ships from thirty nations moving into New York Harbor; they also bought millions of dollars of Bicentennial paraphernalia both from hucksters and mainstream merchandisers. Few complaints were raised, little analysis offered. In many ways, the Bicentennial was, in the words of the director of the New York State Bicentennial Commission, "a kind of catharsis . . . a way of clearing the American soul in a very positive way." Many observers believed that the experience of the Bicentennial demonstrated that America had indeed been healed from the wounds of the previous decade and agreed with *Time* magazine when it observed that "after thirteen consecutive years of assassinations, race riots, youth rebellion, Viet Nam, political scandal, presidential collapse, energy crisis, and recession, the nation's mood seems optimistic again."[1]

Gerald Ford believed that his administration was largely responsible for the nation's new mood. He recalled that Fourth of July for the

189

group of scholars and reporters assembled at Hofstra University in April 1989 to study his presidency:

> What I remember most about the super Fourth of July was the sight of Americans hugging each other and shouting for joy. I can still see those seas of smiling faces with thousands of flags waving friendly greetings. . . . I can still hear the Liberty Bell toll, echoed by church bells across this beautiful land. It was a long day, and just before my head hit the pillow that night, I said to myself, "Well, Jerry, I guess we've healed America. We haven't done so badly, whatever the verdict in November."[2]

This view does not represent an isolated instance in Ford's own assessment of his presidency. He labeled his tenure as *A Time to Heal*, and he continued to tell interviewers into the 1990s, as he did the *Harvard Business Review* in 1987, "If I'm remembered, it will probably be for healing the land."[3]

Historians have generally accepted this assessment, pronouncing the Ford tenure as a caretaker administration, ignoring any in-depth assessment of his policies, and proclaiming his legacy a healing of the nation. Yet the nation's optimism about its future in 1976 may or may not represent any true change from the tumult caused by Vietnam and Watergate. In 1974 Ford inherited a nation looking for the stability in policy that Nixon had not provided and for a renewed faith in the basic honesty of its president. A thorough assessment of his legacy therefore must consider both these aspects.

Historians and political scientists alike have found it difficult to assess the policies of the Ford administration in part because it had trouble articulating its agenda for the American people—a long-range plan showing the direction in which the administration hoped to take the nation. George Bush, who had the same problem as president, in 1988 would call it the "vision thing." There was no campaign for a "New Deal" or a "New Frontier" coming from the Ford White House, and Ford claims that he never saw such an approach as a high priority: "If 'vision' is to be defined as inspirational rhetoric describing how this or that new government program will better the human condition in the next sixty days, then I'll have to confess I didn't have it."[4] This attitude has led most observers to conclude that the administration had no agenda for its policy and to agree with the assessment of administration critic Adlai Stevenson III: "[Ford had] no strong views of where the country should be going, no strong understanding of history and the world."⁵

This criticism seems to be valid. The administration originally did not have an agenda mainly because there was little time to think of one. The three-month transition period between presidencies is the period when a president-elect can best develop an agenda for his administration; for all intents and purposes, Ford had no transition period at all. Yet Ford was in office for twenty-nine months; there was certainly an opportunity for the administration to articulate a long-range plan, a sense of direction for the nation. Several of Ford's advisers tried to cajole him into developing such a plan, but the president was simply not interested. In 1975 Robert Goldwin, a special consultant to the president with responsibility for seeking ideas from scholars outside the administration, became particularly concerned with this issue. Goldwin and Dick Cheney met with Ford in the Oval Office to try to encourage him to articulate his vision for the country. The meeting went downhill after Ford's response to their first question, "What do you wish to be identified with?" He answered, "I like people."⁶

Historians may well hold Ford accountable for not providing the nation with a vision for its future. Yet it must be noted that no one in August 1974 expected Ford to have an agenda or cared very much if he did. As *Time* magazine's Hugh Sidey put it in his perceptive study of the first months of the Ford administration, "While no one claimed that Ford would provide brilliance or vision, the hope that his soundness would compensate for his failings grew to enormous proportions."⁷ Clearly, the nation wanted tranquillity and stability, not imagination. Yet as the Ford administration pursued its policies, it provided anything but equilibrium. Ford's attempt to exorcise the ghosts of Watergate by pardoning Nixon backfired badly, and both the decision itself and the manner in which it was decided shadowed the rest of his presidency. Flip-flops in economic policy, a social policy with little cohesion, and a worsening in détente—all were caused in equal measures by political policymaking with a Democratic Congress and by a desire to appease the Republican Right, and they led to a feeling that the administration had no rudder.

On one point, however, Ford was firm. He refused to accept passively the shift in the balance of powers caused by Vietnam and Watergate. Ford's casual attitude toward the trappings of the presidency—his penchant for retrieving his own newspaper and his request that the military band replace "Hail to the Chief" with the "Michigan Fight Song"—garnered a lot of press and was a large factor in the affection that America developed for its inherited president. Ford's was no Whig presidency, however, and he refused to accede to the demands of the Democratic Congress after the Power Earthquake of 1973–74. He used the veto more liberally than any of his predecessors in an attempt to affect legislation. Ford also refused to accept congressional oversight as an accomplished fact, rejecting the idea that Congress controlled the fate of South Vietnam until it was too late to save the American government from the humiliation of the Running, committing the CIA to Angola even in the midst of a congressional investigation into the intelligence community, and completely shutting the Congress out of the *Mayaguez* operation.

Although Ford never articulated it, the administration apparently had an agenda—a continuation of the policies that had been followed by the moderate wing of the Republican party since World War II—a conservative approach to economic and social policy and a cautiously internationalist approach to foreign policy. Yet that agenda was sacrificed to politics, and the cost was a legacy of instability in the policy arena. Ultimately, there is room for criticism of the motives behind and the decisions of the Ford administration's policymaking. Yet few analysts have availed themselves of the opportunity to criticize, because it has been assumed that the Ford administration largely healed the breach of faith between the president and the American people. Clearly, Ford was more successful in this regard than he was at setting a coherent policy agenda. Gerald Ford made the nation feel better about itself. His midwestern simplicity and his transparent humanity—even to the point of falling down a flight of stairs every now and again—endeared him to the American people. Yet it was his basic honesty and relative candor that provided the greatest service to the nation. The nation's experience with Nixon required that Article 2 of the Constitution be rethought—moral leadership had now become an unwritten part of the job description for the presidency. Ford proved that a president could provide that quality again. In his first press conference, Ford responded to a question about setting up a code of ethics for the executive branch tersely, "The code of ethics that will be followed will be the example that I set." And Gerald Ford clearly set an example. He reset the nation's ethical compass and put the ship of state on a course that avoided disaster.

Although Ford's fundamental decency restored much of the luster to a badly tarnished presidency, one should not conclude that at the end of his tenure the nation had fully regained trust in its government. As future developments would demonstrate, it had not, and it was the pardon that kept Ford from completely healing this breach of faith. It spotlighted his past relationship with Nixon, provided Nixon with an avenue of escape from any act of contrition, and revealed Ford's penchant for secretive decisionmaking that roughly paralleled that of his predecessor. By granting a pardon on Nixon's terms, Ford had wasted a golden opportunity begun in his honeymoon month to erase the breach of faith. Thus, even though the pardon was not an overt issue in the 1976 campaign, it perpetuated a political climate in which an unknown candidate, with no other assets save his promise to eliminate all vestiges of past Republican misdeeds from Washington, could become a viable candidate. Ford's own miscalculations of strategy lost him a close election, but the pardon made Jimmy Carter's victory possible.

The leadership of the Ford administration, then, presents a paradox. Nixon bequeathed to Ford a situation that all but made it impossible for Ford to establish a "Ford presidency" before he took the reins of power. The pardon caused this situation to be even more constricting, and the Democratic Congress and the political demands of the Reagan challenge made effective policy leadership a virtual impossibility. Ford was reduced to dealing with policy matters on a case-by-case basis, a position that challenged his abilities as a political leader. The policy crises of his administration demonstrate that in the political areas of command and persuasion, the Ford administration was not as strong as its immediate predecessors. Yet as a moral leader, Ford surpassed the examples of every president since 1960. He had healed the scars of the spirit caused by Watergate and Vietnam, and the nation was stronger in 1976 than it had been in 1974. When I asked Ford how he wanted to be remembered as president, he replied without hesitation: "I want to be remembered as a . . . nice person, who worked at the job, and who left the White House in better shape than when I took it over."[8] This legacy will remain, as it should, Gerald Ford's greatest gift to the American people.

NOTES

All public statements made by either Richard Nixon or Gerald Ford while president can be found in Richard M. Nixon, *Public Papers of the Presidents of the United States: Richard Nixon, 1969–1974*, 6 vols. (Washington, D.C.: U.S. Government Printing Office, 1971–75), and Gerald R. Ford, *Public Papers of the Presidents of the United States: Gerald R. Ford, 1974–1976*, 6 vols. (Washington, D.C.: U.S. Government Printing Office, 1975–79). Thus speeches and proclamations by these two presidents are uncited in this book unless a videotape of a specific speech, usually made by the White House Communications Agency, was consulted.

ACRONYMS AND SHORT TITLES

[declassified] Document was declassified by a government agency at the request of the author.
Ford CP Gerald R. Ford Congressional Papers, Gerald R. Ford Library (GFL)
Ford PP Gerald R. Ford Presidential Papers, GFL
Ford VP Gerald R. Ford Vice-Presidential Papers, GFL
GFL Gerald R. Ford Presidential Library, Ann Arbor, Michigan
NP Richard M. Nixon Presidential Materials Project, National Archives
NYT *New York Times*
RAC Rockefeller Archives Center, Tarrytown, New York
WHCF White House Central Files

PREFACE

1. Arnold Abrams, "Ford Remembered for Healing America," *Newsday*, 9 Apr. 1989, p. 21.

CHAPTER ONE. "THANK GOD, IT WORKED"

1. Gerald R. Ford, *A Time to Heal: The Autobiography of Gerald R. Ford* (New York: Harper and Row, 1979), p. 422, and James Cannon, *Time and Chance: Gerald Ford's Appointment with Destiny* (New York: Harper Collins, 1994), p. 9.

2. Arthur G. Brown interview (1980), GFL Oral History, p. 4.

3. Ford, *A Time to Heal*, p. 53.

4. William A. Syers, "The Political Beginnings of Gerald R. Ford: Anti-Bossism, Internationalism, and the Congressional Campaign of 1948," *Presidential Studies Quarterly* 20 (Winter 1990): 127–42.

5. Hedrick Smith, *The Power Game: How Washington Works* (New York: Random House, 1988).

6. Fawn Brodie, *Richard Nixon: The Shaping of His Character* (New York: W. W. Norton, 1981), p. 276; comments of Robert P. Griffin in *The Ford Presidency: Twenty-two Intimate Perspectives of Gerald R. Ford*, ed. Kenneth Thompson (Lanham, Md.: University Press of America, 1988), p. 5; Stephen E. Ambrose, *Nixon: The Education of a Politician* (New York: Simon and Schuster, 1987), pp. 553–54; Ford, *A Time to Heal*, pp. 72–73.

7. Ford, *A Time to Heal*, p. 84.

8. Ibid., pp. 85–86.

9. John Ehrlichman, *Witness to Power: The Nixon Years* (New York: Pocket Books, 1982), p. 172.

10. Ford, *A Time to Heal*, p. 88.

11. Jan Aaron, *Gerald Ford: President of Destiny* (New York: Fleet Press, 1975), p. 70, and Stanley Kutler, *The Wars of Watergate: The Last Crisis of Richard Nixon* (New York: Alfred A. Knopf, 1990), p. 420.

12. *NYT*, 24 May 1969, 30 May 1969; "Role of Vice-President Designate Gerald R. Ford in the Attempt to Impeach Associate Supreme Court Justice William O. Douglas," Library of Congress, Legislative Reference Service (1973), p. 3.

13. Ehrlichman notes of meeting with the president, 9 Oct. 1969, NP, Special Files, Ehrlichman, box 9. These notes corroborate Ehrlichman's memory of the meeting in Ehrlichman, *Witness to Power*, p. 101.

14. Robert T. Hartmann, interview with author, 27 July 1988.

15. Robert Hartmann, *Palace Politics: An Insider's Account of the Ford Years* (New York: McGraw-Hill, 1980), pp. 67–68.

16. Ford, *A Time to Heal*, p. 93.

17. William Safire, *Before the Fall: An Inside View of the Pre-Watergate White House* (Garden City, N.Y.: Doubleday, 1975), p. 269.

18. Ehrlichman notes of meeting with the president, 16 Apr. 1970, NP, Special Files, Ehrlichman, box 9.

19. Brown to Patman, 31 Aug. 1972, in *Hearings on Presidential Campaign Activities*, vol. 5 (Washington, D.C.: U.S. Government Printing Office, 1973), pp. 2188–90.

20. Marjorie Boyd, "The Watergate Story: Why Congress Didn't Investigate until After the Election," *Washington Monthly*, Apr. 1973, p. 38.

21. Recording and transcript of conversation (conversation no. 779-002) in NP. John Dean comments on this discussion, with remarkable accuracy according to the tape, in *Blind Ambition* (New York: Simon and Schuster, 1976), pp. 138–39.

22. Draft, 27 Sept. 1972; letter, 28 Sept. 1972, Ford CP, General Correspondence, box A169, folder 14 (emphasis mine).

23. U.S. Congress, House, Committee on the Judiciary, *Nomination of Gerald R. Ford to be the Vice President of the United States* (Washington, D.C.: U.S. Government Printing Office, 1973), pp. 157–58.

24. *Washington Post*, 4 Oct. 1972, p. 1.

25. Stephen E. Ambrose, *Nixon: Ruin and Recovery, 1973–1990* (New York: Simon and Schuster, 1991), pp. 238–39, and Lester A. Sobel, ed., *Presidential Succession: Ford, Rockefeller, and the 25th Amendment* (New York: Facts on File, 1975), p. 42.

26. Richard M. Nixon, *The Memoirs of Richard Nixon* (New York: Grosset and Dunlap, 1978), pp. 925–26. Many of these recommendations can be found in NP, WHCF, Subject Files, EX FG 38/A, appointment of U.S. vice president (2 folders).

27. Ford, *A Time to Heal*, p. 109.

28. See U.S. Congress, House, *Nomination of Gerald R. Ford*, and U.S. Congress, Senate, Committee on the Rules and Administration, 93d Congress, *Nomination of Gerald R. Ford of Michigan to be President of the United States* (Washington, D.C.: U.S. Government Printing Office, 1973).

29. Gerald R. Ford, "The Rule of Law: Equal Justice for All," *Vital Speeches*, 15 Dec. 1973, p. 149.

30. Hartmann, *Palace Politics*, p. 121.

31. Ford, *A Time to Heal*, p. 116.

32. *NYT, The End of a Presidency* (New York: Bantam Books, 1974), p. 250.

33. Bob Woodward and Carl Bernstein, *The Final Days* (New York: Simon and Schuster, 1976), pp. 333–34.

34. Ford, *A Time to Heal*, pp. 14–15.

35. Sobel, ed., *Presidential Succession*, p. 198.

36. Ford, *A Time to Heal*, p. 17.

37. Ford VP, John O. Marsh Files, Subject Files, box 59, last cabinet meeting folder.

38. Ford, *A Time to Heal*, pp. 21–22.

39. Ibid., pp. 27–30.

40. Nixon, *Memoirs*, pp. 1078–79.

41. Ford, *A Time to Heal*, p. 30.

42. Ibid., pp. 39.

43. Hugh Sidey and Fred Ward, *Portrait of a President* (New York: Harper and Row, 1975), p. 14.

CHAPTER TWO. TRANSITION

1. Theodore H. White, *Breach of Faith: The Fall of Richard Nixon* (New York: Atheneum, 1975).

2. Richard Reeves, *A Ford, Not a Lincoln* (New York: Harcourt Brace Jovanovich, 1975), pp. 47–48.

3. Gerald Ford, *A Time to Heal: The Autobiography of Gerald R. Ford* (New York: Harper and Row, 1979), p. 118.

4. Robert Hartmann interview, 3 May 1985, William Syers Papers, GFL, box 1.

5. *Wall Street Journal*, 10 July 1974.

6. Philip W. Buchen, interview with author, 15 July 1988.

7. Dom Bonafede, "White House Report: Ford and Staff Tend to Business . . . and Wait," *National Journal Reports*, 10 Aug. 1974, p. 1180.

8. Eric F. Goldman, *The Tragedy of Lyndon Johnson* (New York: Dell, 1968), p. 119.

9. Alexander M. Haig, Jr., *Inner Circles: How America Changed the World* (New York: Warner Books, 1992), p. 510.

10. Agenda and note, 25 July 1974, in Ford VP, L. William Seidman Files, box 108.

11. Buchen, interview with author, 15 July 1988.

12. James M. Naughton, "The Change in Presidents: Plans Began Months Ago," *NYT*, 26 Aug. 1974, p. 24.

13. Brian Lamb, interview with author, 7 Aug. 1990.

14. "The First Week," ca. 8 Aug. 1974, Ford PP, Philip Buchen Files, box 62, transition folder no. 1.

15. Lamb, interview with author, 7 Aug. 1990.

16. Buchen, interview with author, 15 July 1988.

17. Ford, *A Time to Heal*, pp. 24–26; Naughton, "Change in Presidents," p. 24; A. James Reichley, *Conservatives in an Age of Change: The Nixon and Ford Administrations* (Washington, D.C.: Brookings Institution, 1981), p. 290; Bob Woodward and Carl Bernstein, *The Final Days* (New York: Simon and Schuster, 1976), pp. 400–401.

18. Memorandum for the vice president, 8 Aug. 1974, Ford PP, Buchen Files, box 62, transition folder no. 1.

19. Ford, *A Time to Heal*, pp. 38–39.

20. Buchen, interview with author, 15 July 1988.

21. Ron Nessen, *It Sure Looks Different from the Inside* (Chicago: Playboy Press, 1978), p. 31.

22. Jerry Jones interview, 17 Dec. 1976, James Hyde and Stephen J. Wayne Oral History Collection, GFL, box 1.

23. Roger B. Porter, *Presidential Decision Making: The Economic Policy Board* (Cambridge: Harvard University Press, 1980), p. 67n.

24. Philip Buchen interview, 13 Mar. 1985, Syers Papers, GFL, box 1.

25. Ford, *A Time to Heal*, p. 148.

26. Robert Hartmann, *Palace Politics: An Insider's Account of the Ford Years*, (New York: McGraw-Hill, 1980), p. 220.

27. Gerald R. Ford, interview with author, 1 Sept. 1988.

28. See memo, "Five Areas of Restructure in the White House," Scranton to transition group, 13 Aug. 1974, Scranton Papers, Composite General Accessions, GFL.

29. D. Bonafede, "White House Report: Ford Reverses Trend in Strengthening Cabinet Role," *National Journal Reports*, 3 May 1975, pp. 652, 655.

30. Shirley Anne Warshaw, "Cabinet Government in the Modern Presidency," in *The Presidency in Transition*, ed. James P. Pfiffner and R. Gordon Hoxie (New York: Center for the Study of the Presidency, 1989), pp. 138-40.

31. William Safire, *Before the Fall* (New York: Belmont Tower Books, 1975), p. 498.

32. Rockefeller interview with Trevor Armbrister, 21 Oct. 1977, James Cannon Papers, GFL, box 35.

33. Bob Woodward and Walter Pincus, "The Bumpy Years of Bush: From UN Ambassador to CIA Head," *Washington Post National Weekly Edition*, 29 Aug.-4 Sept. 1988, pp. 12-13, 8.

34. *Newsweek*, 18 Aug. 1974; Michael Turner, *The Vice President as Policy Maker: Rockefeller in the Ford White House* (Westport, Conn.: Greenwood Press, 1982), p. 28; Fitzhugh Green, *George Bush: An Intimate Portrait* (New York: Hippocrene Books, 1989), p. 136; Bob Woodward and Walter Pincus, "Bush and the Politics of Who You Know," *Washington Post National Weekly Review*, 22-28 Aug. 1988, p. 15.

35. Rockefeller interview with Trevor Armbrister, 21 Oct. 1977.

36. Sam Roberts interview on "Midday," RAC, videotape no. 116.

37. Ford, *A Time to Heal*, p. 145.

38. Pat Buchanan, on "The Conservatives," Jan. 1987, Public Broadcasting System.

39. Nelson Rockefeller, on "Meet the Press" 15 June 1975 (NBC) RAC, videotape no. 75.

40. Lester A. Sobel, ed., *Presidential Succession: Ford, Rockefeller, and the 25th Amendment* (New York: Facts on File, 1975), p. 209.

41. Turner, *Vice President as Policy Maker*, pp. 38-39.

42. Reeves, *A Ford, Not a Lincoln*, p. 147.

43. Sobel, ed., *Presidential Succession*, p. 213.

44. Joseph Persico, *The Imperial Rockefeller: A Biography of Nelson A. Rockefeller* (New York: Simon and Schuster, 1982), p. 249.

45. *U.S. News and World Report*, 19 Aug. 1974, pp. 11, 17.

46. *Washington Post*, 14 Aug. 1974.

47. *Newsweek*, 19 Aug. 1974, p. 27.

48. "A Pitch for Privacy," *Washington Post*, 28 Apr. 1991, p. F5.

49. David Hume Kennerly, *Shooter* (New York: Newsweek Books, 1979), p. 117.

50. Nessen to Rumsfeld, 14 May 1975, Ron Nessen Papers, box 132, White House memoranda, Rumsfeld folder.

51. Ford, *A Time to Heal*, p. 65.

52. Myra Gutlin, *The President's Partner: The First Lady in the Twentieth Century* (New York: Greenwood Press, 1989), p. 132.

53. Transcript, "60 Minutes," Sunday 10 Aug. 1975, in vertical file [Betty Ford, 1975] GFL. See also "Woman of the Year," *Newsweek*, 29 Dec. 1975, p. 19, and Eliot Fremont Smith, "Reporting (Gasp!) What Betty Ford Said," *Columbia Journalism Review* (Nov.–Dec. 1975): 15–17.

54. Gutlin, *President's Partner*, p. 132.

55. Paul F. Boller, Jr., *Presidential Wives: An Anecdotal History* (New York: Oxford University Press, 1988), p. 417, and Betty Ford, *The Times Of My Life* (New York: Harper and Row, 1978), p. 225.

56. Boller, Jr., *Presidential Wives*, p. 426.

57. Jerald terHorst, telephone interview with author, 26 Aug. 1988; comments of Jerald F. terHorst in *The Ford Presidency: Twenty-two Intimate Perspectives of Gerald R. Ford*, ed. Kenneth Thompson (Lanham, Md.: University Press of America, 1988), p. 213; Ford, *A Time to Heal*, pp. 156–57.

CHAPTER THREE. "FOR GOD'S SAKE, ENOUGH IS ENOUGH"

1. Lawrence Baskir and William A. Strauss, *Chance and Circumstance: The Draft, the War, and the Vietnam Generation* (New York: Vintage Books, 1978), p. 244.

2. Price to Ehrlichman, 25 July 1972; Ehrlichman to Nixon, 26 July 1972, NP, White House Special Files, President's Office Files (President's Handwriting File), box 18, dated folder.

3. Baskir and Strauss, *Chance and Circumstance*, p. 209.

4. Ibid.

5. Ford to unidentified correspondent, 11 Mar. 1974, Ford VP, Issues File, box 10.

6. Timmons to Haig, 16 Aug. 1974, Ford PP, Alexander Haig Files, White House staff memoranda, box 2, Timmons folder.

7. Myra MacPherson, *Long Time Passing: Vietnam and the Haunted Generation* (New York: New American Library, 1984), p. 410.

8. Dept. of Defense, *After-Action Report: Implementation of President's Clemency Program*, 2 vols. (Oct. 1975), appendixes A and B, and *Presidential Clemency Board: Report to the President*, (Washington, D.C.: U.S. Government Printing Office, 1975), p. xi.

9. Goodell to Ford, 25 Nov. 1974, Ford PP, WHCF, FG 6-28, Executive, box 67.

10. *Clemency Board: Report to the President*, p. xiii.

11. Alexander M. Haig, Jr., *Inner Circles: How America Changed the World,* (New York: Warner Books, 1992), p. 513.

12. Ibid., p. 480.

13. Ibid.

14. Gerald R. Ford, *A Time to Heal: The Autobiography of Gerald R. Ford,* (New York: Harper and Row, 1979), pp. 1–3; Haig, *Inner Circles,* pp. 480–81; Robert Hartmann, *Palace Politics: An Insider's Account of the Ford Years* (New York: McGraw-Hill, 1980), pp. 125–28; Bob Woodward and Carl Bernstein, *The Final Days* (New York: Simon and Schuster, 1976), p. 322.

15. Ford, *A Time to Heal,* p. 3.

16. Ibid., p. 4 (emphasis Ford's).

17. Haig, *Inner Circles,* pp. 481–83.

18. Seymour Hersh, "The Pardon: Nixon, Ford, Haig and the Transfer of Power," *Atlantic,* Aug. 1983, p. 61.

19. Hartmann, *Palace Politics,* p. 131.

20. Ford, *A Time to Heal,* p. 6.

21. Ibid., pp. 9–10.

22. Ibid., p. 13, and Hartmann, *Palace Politics,* pp. 137–38.

23. Quoted in Clark R. Mollenhoff, *The Man Who Pardoned Nixon* (New York: St. Martin's Press, 1976), p. 92.

24. Quoted in Robert Sam Anson, *Exile: The Unquiet Oblivion of Richard M. Nixon* (New York: Simon and Schuster, 1984), p. 42.

25. Garment memo, Buchen Files, Subject, GFL, box 32, Nixon pardon, general folder.

26. Anson, *Exile,* p. 44, and James Doyle, *Not above the Law: The Battles of Watergate Prosecutors Cox and Jaworski* (New York: William Morrow and Company, 1977), p. 364.

27. Philip W. Buchen, interview with author, 15 July 1988.

28. Nessen to Cheney and Marsh, 30 Jan. 1976, Nessen Papers box 127, Cheney folder no. 1.

29. White House Communications Agency videotape, Ford press conference, 28 Aug. 1974, GFL, No. F42.

30. Ford, *A Time to Heal,* p. 159.

31. Ford, *A Time to Heal,* p. 162.

32. Anson, *Exile,* pp. 46–48; Ford, *A Time to Heal,* pp. 160–64; Haig, *Inner Circles,* p. 513; Hartmann, *Palace Politics,* pp. 257–59, 261.

33. *NYT,* 18 Aug. 1974, p. A1.

34. Anson, *Exile,* p. 31.

35. Becker to Buchen, 29 Aug. 1974, Ford PP, Buchen Files, Subject, box 29, Nixon Papers, Counsel's Office memoranda folder.

36. Ford, *A Time to Heal,* p. 164.

37. Stephen E. Ambrose, *Nixon: Ruin and Recovery, 1973–1990* (New York: Simon and Schuster, 1991), pp. 457–58; Anson, *Exile,* p. 51; Ford, *A Time to Heal,* p. 165; Hartmann, *Palace Politics,* p. 248.

38. Quoted in Ambrose, *Nixon: Ruin and Recovery,* p. 458.

39. Becker Memorandum for the file, 13 Sept. 1974, Benton Becker Papers,

GFL, box 2, memorandum folder. Becker informed the author as to the translation of the code name "the Bird" in a telephone interview, 9 June 1992 (emphasis mine).

40. Becker memorandum for the file, 13 Sept. 1974, Becker Papers, box 2, memorandum folder.

41. The deal was spelled out, and agreed to by Nixon, in Nixon to Arthur Sampson (chairman, General Services Administration), 6 Sept. 1974, Ford PP, Buchen Files, Subject, box 28, Nixon Papers agreement folder.

42. Those four drafts, with Becker's handwritten comments, are found in Becker Papers, box 2, Nixon pardon–acceptance folder. See also Becker memorandum for the file, 27 Sept. 1974, Becker Papers, box 2, memorandum folder.

43. Anson, *Exile*, p. 55, and Ambrose, *Nixon: Ruin and Recovery*, p. 460.

44. Ruth to Jaworski, 3 Sept. 1974, Ford PP, Buchen Files, Subject, box 32, pardon–general folder, and Leon Jaworski, *The Right and the Power* (New York: Pocket Books, 1977), p. 292.

45. Jaworski, *Right and the Power*, pp. 290–92, 295.

46. Press conference quoted in Jaworski, *Right and the Power*, p. 296.

47. Richard Ben-Veniste and George Frampton, Jr., *Stonewall: The Real Story of the Watergate Prosecution* (New York: Simon and Schuster, 1977), p. 307.

48. Buchen, interview with author, 15 July 1988.

49. White House Communications Agency videotape, GFL, Ford pardon announcement, 28 Aug. 1974, no. F53.

50. Transcript of press conference, 8 Sept. 1974, Ford PP, WHCF, Jl-1-Nixon Executive, box 4, dated folder.

CHAPTER FOUR. "DOESN'T HE HAVE ANY SENSE
OF TIMING?"

1. *U.S. District Court for the Southern District of Alabama, Watts v. Albert, Ford, and Haig* [Civil Action File no. 74-401-H], in Ford PP, Buchen Files, box 46, president-lawsuits folder.

2. Robert Hartmann, *Palace Politics: An Insider's Account of the Ford Years* (New York: McGraw-Hill, 1980), pp. 216–17.

3. Timmons to Haig, 10 Sept. 1974, Ford PP, Haig Files, White House memoranda, box 2, Timmons folder.

4. Hugh Sidey and Fred Ward, *Portrait of a President* (New York: Harper and Row, 1975), p. 74.

5. Korologos to president, 10 Sept. 1974, Ford PP, WHCF, Jl-1-Nixon Executive, box 4, dated folder.

6. John R. Coyne, Jr., *Fall In and Cheer: A Thoughtful, Often Irreverent View of American Politics* (Garden City, N.Y.: Doubleday and Company, 1979), p. 93.

7. John E. Yang, "How the Watergate Class of '74 Played Kings of the Hill," *Washington Post National Weekly Edition*, 22–28 June 1992, p. 12.

8. H.R. 1367, 16 Sept. 1974; H.R. 1370, 17 Sept. 1974; copies in Ford PP, WHCF, Jl-1-Nixon Executive, box 4, dated folder.

9. Hungate to Ford, 17 Sept. 1974, Ford PP, WHCF, Jl-1-Nixon Executive, box 4, dated folder.

10. Videotapes of Ford testimony, RAC, videotapes no. 76 and no. 77.

11. Yang, "Class of '74," p. 12.

12. Hedrick Smith, *Power Game: How Washington Works* (New York: Random House, 1988), pp. 20–21.

13. Lou Cannon, *Reagan* (New York: G. P. Putnam's Sons, 1982), p. 206.

14. Theodore H. White, *America in Search of Itself: The Making of the President, 1956–1980* (New York: Harper and Row, 1982), p. 242.

15. Ronald Reagan, *An American Life: The Autobiography* (New York: Simon and Schuster, 1990), p. 142.

16. Hartmann, *Palace Politics*, p. 336.

17. Jerald terHorst, telephone interview with author, 26 Aug. 1988.

18. Gerald R. Ford, *A Time to Heal: The Autobiography of Gerald R. Ford* (New York: Harper and Row, 1979), p. 175.

19. Copy in terHorst folder, GFL, Vertical File.

20. *NYT*, 9 Sept. 1974, p. A34.

21. *Time*, 16 Sept. 1974, p. 10.

22. Doug Hill and Jeff Weingrad, *Saturday Night* (New York: Vintage Books, 1987), p. 75.

23. Richard Reeves, "Jerry Ford and His Flying Circus: A Presidential Diary," *New York*, 25 Nov. 1974, pp. 42–46.

24. Richard Reeves, *A Ford, Not a Lincoln* (New York: Harcourt Brace Jovanovich, 1975), p. 26.

25. Ford, *A Time to Heal*, p. 289.

26. Gerald R. Ford, *Humor and the Presidency* (New York: Arbor House, 1987), p. 48.

27. Andrew Radolf, "Trivial Images and the Presidency: Former Presidents Carter and Ford Assess the Press," *Editor and Publisher*, 28 Jan. 1989, p. 7.

28. Smith, *Power Game*, p. 427.

29. James Naughton, "Nessen's Problem," (unlabelled clipping, GFL Vertical File).

30. John J. Casserly, *The Ford White House: The Diary of a Speechwriter* (Boulder: Colorado Associated University Press, 1977), p. 17.

31. William Slater, "The White House Press Corps during the Ford Administration" (Ph.D.diss., Stanford University,1976), p. 88.

32. *Detroit Free Press*, 27 June 1975, p. 1, and "Nessen's Complaint," *Newsweek*, 7 July 1975, p. 43.

33. Slater, "White House Press Corps during the Ford Administration," pp. 85–86, 88.

34. See David Gelman, "Nessen's Report Card," *Newsweek*, 12 Jan. 1976, pp. 52–53, and Dom Bonafede, "White House Report: Nessen Still Seeks 'Separate Peace' with the Press," *National Journal*, 11 Oct. 1975, pp. 1409–16.

35. Ford, *A Time to Heal*, p. 187.

36. John Hersey, "The President," *New York Times Magazine*, 20 Apr. 1975, p. 38.

37. Reeves, *A Ford, Not a Lincoln*, p. 126.

38. Roger B. Porter, *Presidential Decision Making: The Economic Policy Board* (Cambridge, Eng.: Cambridge University Press, 1980), p. 11.

39. Hartmann, *Palace Politics*, p. 282, and Ron Nessen, *It Sure Looks Different from the Inside* (Chicago: Playboy Press, 1978), p. 150.

40. A. James Reichley interview with William Simon, A. James Reichley Papers, GFL, box 2.

41. Reichley interview with Nelson Rockefeller, Reichley Papers, box 2.

42. Reichley Interview with Donald Rumsfeld, Reichley Papers, box 1.

CHAPTER FIVE. STAGFLATION

1. John Robert Greene, *The Limits of Power: The Nixon and Ford Administrations* (Bloomington: Indiana University Press, 1992), pp. 69–77.

2. Greenspan to Ford, 19 Sept. 1974, U.S. Council of Economic Advisors Records, GFL, Alan Greenspan Files, box 1, dated folder; Seevers to Ford, 21 Nov. 1974, U.S. Council of Economic Advisors Records, GFL, Alan Greenspan Files, box 1, dated folder; Gerald R. Ford, *A Time to Heal: The Autobiography of Gerald R. Ford* (New York: Harper and Row, 1979), p. 125.

3. David Howard Davis, "Energy Policy in the Ford Administration," in *The Politics of Policy Making in America: Five Case Studies*, ed. David A. Caputo (San Francisco: W. H. Freeman and Company, 1977), p. 40.

4. Greenspan to Ford, 6 Sept. 1974, U.S. Council of Economic Advisors Records, GFL, Alan Greenspan Files, box 1, dated folder; Richard Reeves, *A Ford, Not a Lincoln* (New York: Harcourt Brace Jovanovich, 1975), p. 153; Greenspan to Ford, 17 Sept. 1974, U.S. Council of Economic Advisors Records, GFL, Alan Greenspan Files, box 1, dated folder; Ford, *A Time to Heal*, p. 151.

5. Irwin C. Hargrove and Samuel A. Morley, eds., *The President and the Council of Economic Advisors: Interviews with CEA Chairmen* (Boulder, Colo.: Westview Press, 1984), pp. 413–14; "A Conservative Who Can Compromise," *Time*, 15 June 1987, pp. 50–51; White House Communications Agency videotape, Ford press conference, 28 Aug. 1974, GFL, no. F42.

6. Roger Porter, *Presidential Decision Making: The Economic Policy Board* (Cambridge, Eng.: Cambridge University Press, 1980), p. 41.

7. L. William Seidman interview, 12 June 1985, Syers Papers, box 1.

8. Cole meeting notes, 20 Aug. 1974, Ford PP, Kenneth Cole Files, box 3, dated folder.

9. Barbara Kellerman, *The Political Presidency: Practice of Leadership* (New York: Oxford University Press, 1984), p. 160.

10. Herbert Stein, *Presidential Economics: The Making of Economic Policy from Roosevelt to Reagan and Beyond* (New York: Simon and Schuster, 1984), p. 213.

11. Robert Hartmann, *Palace Politics: An Insider's Account of the Ford Years* (New York: McGraw-Hill, 1980), p. 299.

12. Gerald R. Ford, interview with author, 1 Sept. 1988.

13. Porter, *Presidential Decision Making*, p. 103.

14. Fellner to Ford, 6 Dec. 1974, U.S. Council of Economic Advisors Records, GFL, Alan Greenspan Files, box 1, dated folder.

15. Porter, *Presidential Decision Making*, p. 104.

16. Kellerman, *Political Presidency*, p. 162.

17. Ron Nessen, *It Sure Looks Different from the Inside* (Chicago: Playboy Press, 1978), pp. 80–84.

18. *NYT*, 15 Jan. 1975, p. 12.

19. Bennett to Friedersdorf, 29 Jan. 1975, Ford PP, Max Friedersdorf Files, box 11, Economy, Jan. 1975 folder.

20. Nessen handwritten notes, 26 Mar. 1975, Nessen Papers, box 294, dated folder.

21. Nessen handwritten notes, 18 Mar. 1975, Nessen Papers, box 294, dated folder.

22. Ford, interview with author, 1 Sept. 1988, and William T. Kendall interview, 1985, Syers Papers, box 1.

23. Hedley Donovan, *Roosevelt to Reagan: A Reporter's Encounters with Nine Presidents* (New York: Harper and Row, 1985), p. 138; Robert J. Spitzer, *The Presidential Veto: Touchstone of the American Presidency* (Albany: State University of New York Press, 1988), p. 72; A. James Reichley, *Conservatives in an Age of Change: The Nixon and Ford Administrations* (Washington, D.C.: Brookings Institution, 1981), p. 332.

24. *Washington Star-News*, 20 Jan. 1975, p. 1.

25. Frank Zarb, interview with author, 7 Apr. 1989.

26. Zarb to Ford, 15 May 1975, Frank Zarb Papers, GFL, Memoranda to President File, box 1, dated folder.

27. Zarb to Rumsfeld and Connor, 10 July 1975, Zarb Papers, Memoranda to President File, box 1, dated folder.

28. Connor's meeting notes [handwritten], Ford PP, James Connor Files, Cabinet Meetings File, box 4.

29. Nessen handwritten notes, 13 Nov. 1975, Nessen Papers, box 296, dated folder.

30. Frank Zarb, interview with author, 7 Apr. 1989.

31. Ford, *A Time to Heal*, p. 341, and William E. Simon, *A Time for Truth* (New York: Berkley Books, 1978,) p. 88.

32. John J. Casserly, *The Ford White House: The Diary of a Speechwriter* (Boulder, Colo.: Associated University Press, 1977), p. 191.

33. Transcript of O'Neill speech, 7 Oct. 1975, in Ford PP, Friedersdorf Files, box 11, Economy, Feb. 1975–Mar. 1976 folder.

34. Meeting notes, 7 Oct. 1975, Ford PP, Robert K. Wolthuis Files, box 2, dated folder.

35. Meeting notes, 10 Dec. 1975, Ford PP, Wolthuis Files, box 2, dated folder.

36. Ford, *A Time to Heal*, pp. 338–39.

37. John W. Sloan, "Economic Policymaking in the Johnson and Ford Administrations," *Presidential Studies Quarterly* (Winter 1990): 113–14.

CHAPTER SIX. "BRUSH FIRES"

1. Michael Turner, *The Vice President as Policy Maker: Rockefeller in the Ford White House* (Westport, Conn.: Greenwood Press, 1982), p. 52.

2. Robert Hartmann, *Palace Politics: An Insider's Account of the Ford Years* (New York: McGraw-Hill, 1980), p. 306.

3. Reichley interview with James Cannon, Reichley Papers, box 1.

4. Comments of Richard Cheney in *The Ford Presidency: Twenty-two Intimate Perspectives of Gerald R. Ford*, ed. Kenneth Thompson (Lanham, Md.: University Press of America, 1988), p. 66.

5. Reichley interview with Nelson Rockefeller, Reichley Papers, box 2.

6. Cannon to Rumsfeld, 6 Oct. 1975, Cannon Papers, box 3, chief of staff folder.

7. Reichley interviews with Philip Buchen and Roderick Hills, Reichley Papers, box 1; Roger W. Caves, "An Historical Analysis of Federal Housing Policy from the Presidential Perspective: An Intergovernmental Focus," *Urban Studies* 26 (1989): 70–71; see also Irwin Ross, "Carla Hills Gives 'The Woman's Touch' a Brand-New Meaning," *Fortune*, Dec. 1975, pp. 122–23, and John C. Whitaker, *Striking a Balance: Environmental and Natural Resource Policy in the Nixon-Ford Years* (Washington, D.C.: American Enterprise Institution for Public Policy Research, 1976), p. 175.

8. John Robert Greene, *The Limits of Power: The Nixon and Ford Administrations* (Bloomington: Indiana University Press, 1992), p. 47.

9. Henry Hampton and Steve Fayer, *Voices of Freedom: An Oral History of the Civil Rights Movement from the 1950s through the 1980s* (New York: Bantam Books, 1990), p. 594.

10. A. James Reichley, *Conservatives in an Age of Change: The Nixon and Ford Administrations* (Washington, D.C.: Brookings Institution, 1981), pp. 276, 279.

11. Lester A. Sobel, ed., *Presidential Succession: Ford, Rockefeller, and the 25th Amendment* (New York: Facts on File, 1975), p. 44.

12. Reichley interview with Philip Buchen, Reichley Papers, box 1.

13. Victor H. Kramer, "The Case of Justice Stevens: How to Select, Nominate and Confirm a Justice to the U.S. Supreme Court," *Constitutional Commentary* 7 (Summer 1990): 326.

14. Reichley interview with Edward Levi, Reichley Papers, box 2.

15. Cole to Ford, 17 Oct. 1974, Ford PP, Cole Files, box 1, dated folder.

16. *NYT*, 13 Dec. 1975.

17. Rangel to Ford, 13 Dec. 1974; Buchen to Rangel, 14 Jan. 1975, Buchen Files, GFL, Box 9, Boston school busing folder.

18. Buchen to Nessen, 19 May 1976, Nessen Papers, White House Memoranda File, box 126, Buchen folder.

19. Ken Auletta, "Who's to Blame for the Fix We're In?" *New York*, 27 Oct. 27, 1975, p. 29.

20. Ron Chernow, *The House of Morgan: An American Banking Dynasty and the Rise of Modern Finance* (New York: Atlantic Monthly Press, 1990) p. 618; Gerald R. Ford, *A Time to Heal: The Autobiography of Gerald R. Ford* (New York: Harper and Row, 1979), p. 315; Robert W. Bailey, *The Crisis Regime: The New York City Financial Crisis* (Albany: State University of New York Press, 1984), pp. 3, 16; Donna Shalala and Carol Bellamy, "A State Saves a City: The New York Case," *Duke Law Journal* (1976): 1120.

21. Richard A. Loverd, "Presidential Decision Making during the 1975 New York Financial Crisis: A Conceptual Analysis" *Presidential Studies Quarterly* 21 (Spring 1991): 254–55.

22. Nessen handwritten notes, 13 May 1975, Nessen Papers, box 294, dated folder.

23. Chernow, *House of Morgan*, p. 620; Shalala and Bellamy, "A State Saves a City," pp. 1127–29; Loverd, "New York Financial Crisis," p. 258; Turner, *Vice President as Policy Maker*, p. 138.

24. Turner, *Vice President as Policy Maker*, p. 134.

25. Armbrister interview with Rockefeller, 21 Oct. 1977, Cannon Papers, box 35.

26. Turner, *Vice President as Policy Maker*, pp. 135–36.

27. Connor's meeting notes, Ford PP, Connor Files, Cabinet Meetings File, box 5.

28. Transcript of Rockefeller speech, 11 Oct. 1975, Ford PP, Staff Secretary, White House Special Files Unit, box 5, New York City, Oct. 1975 folder; John J. Casserly, *The Ford White House: The Diary of a Speechwriter* (Boulder: Colorado Associated University Press, 1977), p. 203.

29. Nessen handwritten notes, 24 Oct. 1975, Nessen Papers, box 295, dated folder.

30. "Issues and Answers," 2 Nov. 1975, RAC, videotape no. 78.

31. Meeting notes, 4 Nov. 1975, Ford PP, Wolthuis Files, box 2, dated folder.

32. Gardner to Ford, memorandum: "The New York Plan," 14 Nov. 1975, Ford PP, Richard Cheney Files, box 9, New York City crisis folder; Loverd, "New York Financial Crisis," p. 259.

33. *Washington Post*, 12 Nov. 1975, p. 1.

34. *NYT*, 18 Nov. 1975, p. A1.

35. Nessen handwritten notes, 28 Nov. 1975, Nessen Papers, box 296, dated folder.

36. *Washington Post*, 8 Dec. 1975.

37. Gerald R. Ford, interview with author, 1 Sept. 1988.

38. Rourke to Friedersdorf, 23 Oct. 1975, Ford PP, Marsh Files, Subject, box 22, NYC folder.

39. "The Tiger," *Time*, 17 Feb. 1975, p. 72.

40. Ford, *A Time to Heal*, p. 342.

41. Dunlop to Ford, 3 July 1975; Cannon meeting notes, 7 July 1975, Ford

PP, Cannon Files, box 48, dated folder; transcript of Dunlop testimony before the Subcommittee on Labor Management Relations, Committee on Education and Labor, 5 June 1975, Ford PP, Friedersdorf Files, box 11, common situs folder.

42. Newspaper clippings found in Ford PP, WHCF, Executive, BE 2-2, box 5.

43. Cannon to Ford, Dec. 1975, Ford PP, Cannon Files, box 8, common situs picketing folder.

44. Comments of Richard B. Cheney in Thompson, ed., *Ford Presidency*, p. 70; Anne Higgins to Ford, 6 Jan. 1977, Ford PP, Robert Hartmann Files, box 50 (copy in Nixon-Pardon GFL Vertical File).

45. Meeting notes, 10 Dec. 1975, Ford PP, Wolthuis Files, box 2, dated folder.

46. John Dunlop, telephone interview with author, 25 Aug. 1988.

47. *Ann Arbor News*, 14 Jan. 1975, p. 1.

48. Bob Woodward and Scott Armstrong, *The Brethren: Inside the Supreme Court* (New York: Simon and Schuster, 1979), pp. 357–95; Burger to Ford, 12 Nov. 1975; Douglas to Ford, 12 Nov. 1975; Ford to Douglas, 12 Nov. 1975, Ford PP, WHCF Executive, box 137, folder FG 51-A.

49. Memorandum, Levi to Ford, 10 Nov. 1975, Cheney Files, GFL, box 11, dated folder; Cheney to Connor, 9 Dec. 1975, Ford PP, Presidential Handwriting File, folder FG, Judicial Branch–Supreme Court; David O'Brien, "The Politics of Professionalism: President Gerald R. Ford's Appointment of Justice John Paul Stevens," *Presidential Studies Quarterly* 21 (Winter 1991): 114–15.

50. Woodward and Armstrong, *Brethren*, p. 401.

CHAPTER SEVEN. "A ROGUE ELEPHANT"

1. David W. Belin, *Final Disclosure: The Full Truth about the Assassination of President Kennedy* (New York: Charles Scribner's Sons, 1988), p. 76.

2. Ibid., p. 77.

3. William Colby, interview with author, 6 Apr. 1989; William Colby, *Honorable Men: My Life in the CIA* (New York: Simon and Schuster, 1978), pp. 337–38; John Ranelagh, *The Agency: The Rise and Decline of the CIA* (New York: Simon and Schuster, 1986), p. 554.

4. Belin, *Final Disclosure*, p. 91.

5. Karamessines to chief, CI Staff, 15 Aug. 1967; undated CIA communiqué, "Memorandum, Subject: MHCHAOS; Program Objectives" Special Operations Group, Counter Intelligence Staff, 1 June 1972; communication from Colby (order to terminate MHCHAOS), 5 March 1974, Ford PP, Cheney Files, box 5, Intelligence, Colby report [declassified].

6. William Colby, interview with author, 6 Apr. 1989.

7. James A. Wilderotter, interview with author, 7 Apr. 1989.

8. William Colby, interview with author, 6 Apr. 1989.

9. *NYT*, 24 Dec. 1974, p. 18.

10. Kissinger to Rumsfeld, 23 Dec. 1975, Ford PP, Cheney Files, GFL, box 5, Intelligence–General folder [declassified].

11. Rumsfeld to Kissinger, 23 Dec. 1974, Ford PP, Cheney Files, box 5, Intelligence folder, Colby report [declassified].

12. Colby to Ford, 24 Dec. 1974, Ford PP, Cheney Files, box 5, Intelligence folder, Colby report.

13. *Report to the President by the Commission on CIA Activities within the United States* (Washington, D.C.: U.S. Government Printing Office, 1975), pp. ix–x.

14. Loch Johnson, *A Season of Inquiry: The Senate Intelligence Investigation* (Lexington: University of Kentucky Press, 1985), p. 11.

15. Gerald R. Ford, *A Time to Heal: The Autobiography of Gerald R. Ford* (New York: Harper and Row, 1979), p. 230.

16. Paul C. Light, *Advice and Influence in the White House: Vice Presidential Power* (Baltimore: Johns Hopkins University Press, 1984), p. 185.

17. Belin, *Final Disclosure*, pp. 81–82.

18. Colby, *Honorable Men*, p. 400.

19. Tom Wicker, *On Press* (New York: Viking Press, 1978), pp. 188–96.

20. Buchen to Belin, 31 Mar. 1975, Ford PP, Buchen Files, subject, box 26, National Security chronological file folder.

21. Belin, *Final Disclosure*, pp. 103–29.

22. *Report to the President by the Commission on CIA Activities.*

23. "Meet the Press," 15 June 1975, Rockefeller Family Archives (RAC, VT no. 75).

24. Belin, *Final Disclosure*, pp. 163–64.

25. Crosby to Church, 20 Nov. 1975; Church to Crosby, 9 Jan. 1976, Frank Church Papers, Boise State University, series 2.6, box 1, folder 2.

26. Discussion comments of Michael Raoul-Duval, in Bernard J. Firestone and Alexej Ugrinsky, *Gerald R. Ford and the Politics of Post-Watergate America*, 2 vols. (Westport, Conn.: Greenwood Press, 1993), 2: 493.

27. Johnson, *Season of Inquiry*, pp. 72–75.

28. Church to Ford, 12 Mar. 1975, Ford PP, Cheney Files, subject, box 7, release to Church committee folder.

29. Buchen to Ford, 2 Apr. 1975, Ford PP, Cheney Files, subject, box 7, release to Church committee folder.

30. Johnson, *Season of Inquiry*, p. 39.

31. Meeting notes, 13 Oct. 1975, Duval Papers, box 11, dated folder [declassified].

32. Ford to Church, 31 Oct. 1975, Ford PP, Wolthuis Files, box 2, Church committee folder no. 1.

33. Johnson, *Season of Inquiry*, pp. 131–37.

34. Frank J. Smist, Jr., *Congress Oversees the United States Intelligence Community, 1947–1989* (Knoxville: University of Tennessee Press, 1990), pp. 77–79, and John Prados, *President's Secret Wars: CIA and Pentagon Covert Operations since World War II* (New York: William Morrow and Company, 1986), pp. 336–37.

35. Horan to Davis, 2 Apr. 1975, Ford PP, WHCF-Subject Files, EX SP 2-3-36 (1).

36. Prados, *President's Secret Wars*, pp. 340–41, and Jeffrey T. Richelson, *The U.S. Intelligence Community* (Cambridge, Mass.: Ballinger Publishing Company, 1985), p. 234.

37. Wayne S. Smith, "A Trap in Angola," *Foreign Policy* (Spring 1986): 72.

38. Prados, *President's Secret Wars*, p. 345.

39. Ibid., pp. 338–46; Robert S. Litwak, *Detente and the Nixon Doctrine: American Foreign Policy and the Pursuit of Stability, 1969–1976* (Cambridge, Eng.: Cambridge University Press, 1984), pp. 175–90.

40. Gerald Ford, "United States Foreign Intelligence Activities," Executive Order 11905, *Weekly Compilation of Presidential Documents* 12 (1976): pp. 234–43. An excellent summary of this Omnibus Order can be found in the papers of Michael Raoul-Duval in the overhead transparencies that he produced to explain the act to various constituencies (Raoul-Duval Papers, Intelligence Coordinating Group Files, AV 84-207B).

CHAPTER EIGHT. "REASSESSMENT"

1. Roderic H. Davison, *Turkey* (Englewood Cliffs, N.J.: Prentice-Hall, 1968), pp. 34, 62–63, 88–89, 151–53, 159–63; George Lenczowski, *American Presidents and the Middle East* (Durham, N.C.: Duke University Press, 1990), pp. 142–43; Roger Morris, *Uncertain Greatness: Henry Kissinger and American Foreign Policy* (New York: Harper and Row, 1977), pp. 271–76; Robert D. Schulzinger, *Henry Kissinger: Doctor of Diplomacy* (New York: Columbia University Press, 1989), pp. 175–76; Tad Szulc, *Then and Now: How the World Has Changed since World War II* (New York: William Morrow, 1990), p. 366.

2. Leo Cherne, comments in *The Ford Presidency: Twenty-two Intimate Perspectives of Gerald R. Ford*, ed. Kenneth Thompson (Lanham, Md.: University Press of America, 1988), p. 53.

3. Joseph Sisco, comments in ibid., p. 328.

4. Partial copy of Kissinger testimony before the Senate Foreign Relations Committee, 19 Sept. 1974, Ford PP, Wolthuis Files, box 2, Intelligence Investigations–Chile.

5. Schulzinger, *Kissinger: Diplomacy*, p. 181.

6. Sisco, comments in John Prados, *Keepers of the Keys: A History of the National Security Council from Truman to Bush* (New York: William Morrow, 1991), p. 354.

7. Walter Isaacson, *Henry Kissinger: A Biography* (New York: Simon and Schuster, 1992), p. 605.

8. Melvin Laird, "Is This Detente?" *Reader's Digest*, July 1975, p. 57.

9. Tad Szulc, "Pentagon Cool," *Washingtonian Magazine*, (Oct. 1974), p. 3.

10. Schulzinger, *Kissinger: Diplomacy*, p. 216.

11. Howard M. Sachar, *A History of the Jews in America* (New York: Alfred A. Knopf, 1992), p. 911.

12. Isaacson, *Kissinger: Biography*, p. 614.

13. Gerald R. Ford, *A Time to Heal; The Autobiography of Gerald R. Ford* (New York: Harper and Row, 1979), p. 138–39; Isaacson, *Kissinger: Biography*, p. 616.

14. "Principles of Agreement on Proposed Waiver of Jackson-Vanik Amendment," 17 Oct. 1974; Kissinger to Jackson, 18 Oct. 1974; Jackson to Kissinger, 18 Oct. 1974, Ford PP, Brent Scowcroft Name File, box 2, Jackson folder.

15. Ford, *A Time to Heal*, p. 139.

16. Harry Gelman, *The Brezhnev Politburo and the Decline of Detente* (Ithaca, N.Y.: Cornell University Press, 1984), p. 148.

17. John Newhouse, *War and Peace in the Nuclear Age* (New York: Alfred A. Knopf, 1989), p. 247, and Sachar, *Jews in America*, p. 919.

18. Ford, *A Time to Heal*, p. 214.

19. Newhouse, *War and Peace in the Nuclear Age*, p. 248.

20. Taken from meeting agenda (prepared by Scowcroft), 27 Nov. 1974, Ford PP, WHCF, box 32, folder FO 6-2 Executive.

21. Gerald R. Ford, interview with author, 1 Sept. 1988.

22. William B. Quandt, *Decade of Decisions: American Policy toward the Arab-Israeli Conflict, 1967–1976* (Berkeley: University of California Press, 1977), p. 258.

23. Isaacson, *Kissinger: Biography*, p. 631.

24. Ford, *A Time to Heal*, p. 183.

25. Quandt, *Decade of Decisions*, p. 257.

26. Ford, *A Time to Heal*, p. 247.

CHAPTER NINE. "THE RUNNING"

1. John Robert Greene, *The Limits of Power: The Nixon and Ford Administrations* (Bloomington: University of Indiana Press, 1992), p. 103.

2. George C. Herring, *America's Longest War: The United States and Vietnam, 1950–1975*, 2d ed. (New York, Alfred A. Knopf, 1986), p. 261.

3. Ford interview with Jerrold L. Schecter, 10 Feb. 1986, GFL, pp. 4–5. Letter quoted in its entirety in Nguyen Tien Hung and Jerrold Schecter, *The Palace File* (New York: Harper and Row, 1986), p. 240.

4. Hung and Schecter, *Palace File*, p. 241–42.

5. Thieu to Ford, 19 Sept. 1974, Ford PP, WHCF Executive, folder CO 165-2.

6. Springsteen to Scowcroft, 11 Oct. 1975, Ford PP, WHCF Executive, folder CO 165-2 [declassified]; Ford to Thieu, 24 Oct. 1974, Ford PP, WHCF Executive, folder CO 165-2.

7. Memcon, 13 Sept. 1974, Martin, Kissinger, Scowcroft, Ford, Kissinger-Scowcroft Files, Temporary Parallel File, box A1, dated folder [declassified].

8. Arnold R. Issacs, *Without Honor: Defeat in Vietnam and Cambodia* (New York: Vintage Books, 1982), chapter 8, passim, and William Shawcross, *Sideshow: Kissinger, Nixon, and the Destruction of Cambodia* (New York: Simon and Schuster, 1979), pp. 344–48, 355.

9. *NYT*, 29 Jan. 1975, p. 1; Ash to Ford, 14 Jan. 1975, Presidential Hand-

writing File, GFL, box 22, Foreign Affairs, Foreign Aid–South Vietnam folder [declassified].

10. Martin to Von Marbod, 17 Jan. 1975, NSC Convenience Files, GFL, box 6.

11. Kendall to Friedersdorf, 12 Mar. 1975, Ford PP, Friedersdorf Files, box 13, Indochina—January–March 1975 folder.

12. CODEL meeting with President Thieu, meeting transcript, 27 Feb. 1975; telegrams from American embassy, Saigon, 3 Mar. 1975, Ford PP, Wolthuis Files, box 5, Vietnam visit folder. Anecdotes on the visit of the delegation can be found in Hung and Schecter, *Palace File*, pp. 252–62.

13. Kim Willenson, ed. *The Bad War: An Oral History of the Vietnam War* (New York: New American Library, 1987), p. 316.

14. Hung and Schecter, *Palace File*, pp. 286–87.

15. Weyland to Ford, 4 Apr. 1975, Ford PP, WHCF Executive, box 59, folder CO-165-2; "Report to the President of the United States on the Situation in South Vietnam," Ford PP, Scowcroft Parallel File, box 1, Country File—Far East (Vietnam) folder [declassified]. Full report is in NSC Convenience Files, GFL, box 7, folder 012700173.

16. David Hume Kennerly, *Shooter* (New York: Newsweek Books, 1979), p. 174, and Gerald R. Ford, *A Time to Heal: The Autobiography of Gerald R. Ford* (New York: Harper and Row, 1979), p. 253.

17. Hung and Schecter, *Palace File*, p. 310.

18. Scowcroft meeting notes, 14 Apr. 1975, Kissinger-Scowcroft Files, Temporary Parallel File, GFL, box A1, memcons, dated folder [declassified].

19. John Prados, *Keepers of the Keys: A History of the National Security Council from Truman to Bush* (New York: William Morrow), p. 366.

20. Telegram, American embassy Phnom Penh to secretary of state, 6 Apr. 1975, WHCF, Subject Files, GFL, EX FO 3-2, 1 Apr. 1975–10 Apr. 1975 folder [declassified].

21. Walter Isaacson, *Kissinger: A Biography* (New York: Simon and Schuster, 1992), p. 639.

22. Nessen handwritten notes, 16 Apr. 1975, Nessen Papers, box 294, dated folder.

23. Willenson, ed., *Bad War*, pp. 309–10.

24. Ibid., p. 311.

25. Robert D. Schulzinger, *Henry Kissinger: Doctor of Diplomacy* (New York: Columbia University Press, 1989), p. 201.

26. Milton Friedman, interview with author, 22 July 1988.

27. Robert Hartmann, *Palace Politics: An Insider's Account of the Ford Years* (New York: McGraw-Hill, 1980), p. 323.

28. Nessen handwritten notes, 28 Apr. 1975, Nessen Papers, box 294, dated folder.

29. Editor's notes, in Willenson, ed., *Bad War*, p. 321.

30. Prados, *Keepers of the Keys*, p. 367.

31. Nessen handwritten notes, 29 Apr. Nessen Papers, box 294, dated folder.

32. Isaacson, *Kissinger: Biography*, p. 647.

33. Ron Nessen, *It Sure Looks Different from the Inside* (Chicago: Playboy Press, 1978), p. 112.

34. Ibid., p. 109.

CHAPTER TEN. "LET'S LOOK FEROCIOUS"

1. McCloskey to Brooke, 20 June 1975, Ford PP, Buchen Files, Subject, box 25, *Mayaguez* general folder.

2. Richard G. Head, F. W. Short, and R. C. McFarlane, *Crisis Resolution: Presidential Decision Making in the Mayaguez and Korean Confrontations* (Boulder, Colo.: Westview Press, 1978), p. 103.

3. James Nathan, "The *Mayaguez*, Presidential War, and Congressional Senescence," *Intellect* (Feb. 1976): 361.

4. Christopher Jon Lamb, *Belief Systems and Decision Making in the Mayaguez Crisis* (Gainesville: University of Florida Press, 1988), pp. 9, 81.

5. Richard E. Neustadt and Ernest R. May, *Thinking in Time: The Uses of History for Decision Makers* (New York: Free Press, 1986), p. 60.

6. Gerald R. Ford, *A Time to Heal: The Autobiography of Gerald R. Ford* (New York: Harper and Row, 1979), p. 276.

7. Head, Short, and McFarlane, *Crisis Resolution*, pp. 109–12.

8. David Hume Kennerly, telephone interview with author, 14 Sept. 1988.

9. "Possible Scenarios for Recovery of Ship and Crew" [top secret, undated], Ford PP, Buchen Files, Subject, box 25, *Mayaguez* general folder.

10. Head, Short, and McFarlane, *Crisis Resolution*, p. 113.

11. Memcon, telephone conversation, Scowcroft and Ford, 2:23 A.M., 13 May 1975, Ford PP, Scowcroft Parallel File, box 1, Office Files, Cambodia folder [declassified].

12. Ford, *A Time to Heal*, p. 277.

13. Marsh to Buchen ["Summary of the NSC Meeting"], 13 May 1975, Ford PP, Buchen Files, box 25, *Mayaguez* general folder [declassified].

14. Memcon, telephone conversation, Scowcroft and Ford, 8:10 P.M., 13 May 1975, Ford PP, Scowcroft Parallel File, box 1, Office Files, Cambodia folder [declassified].

15. Memcon, telephone conversation, Scowcroft and Wickham, 8:15 P.M., 13 May 1975, Ford PP, Scowcroft Parallel File, box 1, Office Files, Cambodia folder [declassified].

16. Memcon, telephone conversation, Scowcroft and Wickham, 9:48 P.M., 13 May 1975, Ford PP, Scowcroft Parallel File, box 1, Office Files, Cambodia folder [declassified].

17. Memcon, telephone conversation, Scowcroft and Ford, 9:50 P.M., 13 May 1975; Scowcroft to Wickham, 9:54 P.M., 13 May 1975, Ford PP, Scowcroft Parallel File, box 1, Office Files, Cambodia folder [declassified].

18. Head, Short, and McFarlane, *Crisis Resolution*, pp. 116–18.

19. Ibid., p. 131; Walter Isaacson, *Henry Kissinger: A Biography* (New York: Simon and Schuster, 1992), p. 650; Lamb, *Belief Systems*, p. 91.

20. Scowcroft notes of meeting with bipartisan congressional delegation, 14 May 1975, Ford PP, Scowcroft Parallel File, box 1, presidential memoranda, conversations folder [declassified].

21. Capt. Thomas D. DesBrisbay, "Fourteen Hours on Koh Tang" (USAF Southeast Asia Monograph Ser. 3, Washington, D.C.: U.S. Government Printing Office, 1975), p. 116; Head, Short, and McFarlane, *Crisis Resolution*, p. 132–33; Lamb, *Belief Systems*, pp. 21–31.

22. Lamb, *Belief Systems*, p. 93.

23. Ford, *A Time to Heal*, pp. 282, 284.

24. Lamb, *Belief Systems*, p. 98.

25. Ibid., p. 87.

26. Ron Nessen, *It Sure Looks Different from the Inside* (Chicago: Playboy Press, 1978), p. 129.

27. Ford, *A Time to Heal*, p. 284.

28. Friedersdorf to Ford, 16 May 1975, Ford PP, Buchen Files, Subject, box 25, *Mayaguez* general folder.

29. Meany to Ford, 18 June 1975, Scowcroft Files, Name File, box 3, Solzhenitsyn folder.

30. Helms and Thurmond to Ford, 23 June 1975, Scowcroft Files, Name File, box 3, Solzhenitsyn folder.

31. Marsh to Scowcroft, 23 June 1975, Scowcroft Files, Name File, box 3, Solzhenitsyn folder; Clift to Kissinger, 26 June 1975, Scowcroft Files, Name File, box 3, name folder. Kissinger schedule proposal for Ford, undated, Scowcroft Files, Name File, box 3, Solzhenitsyn folder.

32. Isaacson, *Kissinger: Biography*, p. 658.

33. Nessen handwritten notes, 2 July 1975, Nessen Papers, box 295, dated folder.

34. Ford, *A Time to Heal*, p. 298.

35. Kissinger to Ford, briefing paper, Ford PP, Scowcroft Parallel File, box 1, presidential and Kissinger trips, Helsinki folder [declassified] (emphasis Kissinger's).

36. Ford, *A Time to Heal*, p. 303–4, and John Newhouse, *War and Peace in the Nuclear Age* (New York: Alfred A. Knopf, 1989), p. 257.

37. Ford, *A Time to Heal*, p. 300.

38. Peter Golden, "Max Fisher, Diplomat," *Detroit Free Press Magazine*, 3 May 1992, pp. 12, 21.

39. Ford, *A Time to Heal*, p. 287.

40. Ibid., p. 247.

41. Isaacson, *Kissinger: Biography*, p. 635.

42. Ford, *A Time to Heal*, pp. 308–9; George Lenczowski, *American Presidents and the Middle East* (Durham, N.C.: Duke University Press, 1990), pp. 151–52; William B. Quandt, *Decade of Decisions: American Policy toward the Arab-Israeli Conflict, 1967–1976* (Berkeley: University of California Press, 1977), p. 275; Janet

and John Wallach, *Arafat: In the Eyes of the Beholder* (New York: Lyle Stuart, 1990), p. 348.

43. Meeting notes, 25 Sept. 1975, Ford PP, Wolthuis Files, box 2, dated folder.

CHAPTER ELEVEN. "I DIDN'T TAKE REAGAN SERIOUSLY"

1. Lou Cannon, *Reagan* (New York: G. P. Putnam's Sons, 1982), p. 199.

2. Garry Wills, *Innocents at Home: Reagan's America* (Garden City, N.Y.: Doubleday, 1987), pp. 328–29.

3. Gerald R. Ford, *A Time to Heal: The Autobiography of Gerald R. Ford* (New York: Harper and Row, 1979), p. 294.

4. *NYT*, 20 June 1975.

5. "Fred" to Jerry Jones, 20 June 1975, Ford PP, Jones Files, box 23, PFC folder no. 1.

6. Jones to Rumsfeld, 29 July 1975, Ford PP, Jones Files, box 23, PFC folder no. 1.

7. Callaway to Ford, "Weekly Report Number One," 15 July 1975, Ford PP, Cheney Files, box 14, dated folders.

8. Donald Rumsfeld, interview with author, 7 April 1989.

9. Gerald R. Ford, interview with author, 1 Sept. 1988.

10. Robert Hartmann, *Palace Politics: An Insider's Account of the Ford Years* (New York: McGraw-Hill, 1980), p. 303.

11. David Hume Kennerly, telephone interview with author, 14 Sept. 1988.

12. See, for one example, Rockefeller interview, 15 April 1976, WHO-TV, Des Moines, Iowa, RAC, video no. 91.

13. Armbrister interview with Rockefeller, 21 Oct. 1977, Cannon Papers, box 35.

14. Robert D. Schulzinger, *Henry Kissinger: Doctor of Diplomacy* (New York: Columbia University Press, 1989), p. 219.

15. Gary Paul Gates and Bob Schieffer, *The Acting President* (New York: E. P. Dutton, 1989), p. 59.

16. Transcript, "Meet the Press," 7 Dec. 1975, in Nessen Papers, Campaign Subject File, box 32, Callaway folder.

17. Ford, *A Time to Heal*, p. 333.

18. David Chagall, *The New Kingmakers* (New York: Harcourt Brace Jovanovich, 1981), p. 76.

19. Elizabeth Drew, *American Journal: The Events of 1976* (New York: Random House, 1976), p. 46.

20. Ronald Reagan, *An American Life: The Autobiography* (New York: Simon and Schuster, 1990), p. 201; David W. Moore, *The Super Pollsters: How They Measure and Manipulate Public Opinion in America* (New York: Four Walls Eight Windows, 1992), pp. 197–200.

21. Wayne Valis memo for the file, 10 Mar. 1976, Nessen Papers, Campaign Subject File, box 32, Campaign—general folder.

22. Cannon, *Reagan*, p. 213.

23. Chagall, *New Kingmakers*, p. 85.

24. Schulzinger, *Henry Kissinger: Diplomacy*, p. 226.

25. Ford to secretaries of state and defense (NSDM 302), 18 Aug. 1975, Ford PP, staff secretary: White House Special Files Unit, box 6, Panama Canal Treaty Negotiations, 1975 folder [declassified].

26. Roger S. Leeds, "The Panama Canal Treaty: Past and Present United States Interests," *Foreign Service Journal* 53 (March 1976): 6; news release, Department of State, Jan. 1975.

27. Paul B. Ryan, *The Panama Canal Controversy: U.S. Diplomacy and Defense Interests* (Stanford, Calif.: Hoover Institution Press, 1977), p. 123.

28. Transcript in Nessen Papers, Campaign Subject File, box 39, Reagan address folder.

29. Schulzinger, *Henry Kissinger: Diplomacy*, p. 228.

30. See *Ann Arbor News*, 5 May 1976, p. 49, and comments of Ron Nessen in *The Ford Presidency: Twenty-two Intimate Perspectives of Gerald R. Ford*, ed. Kenneth W. Thompson (Lanham, Md.: University Press of America, 1988), p. 188.

31. Doug Hill and Jeff Weingrad, *Saturday Night* (New York: Vintage Books, 1987), p. 188.

32. Gerald R. Ford, *Humor and the Presidency* (New York: Arbor House, 1987), pp. 47–48, and confidential interview with author.

33. Ford, *A Time to Heal*, p. 387.

34. Ibid., p. 382.

35. David Hume Kennerly, telephone interview with author, 14 Sept. 1988.

36. Kathleen Hall Jamieson, *Packaging the Presidency: A History and Criticism of Presidential Campaign Advertising* (New York: Oxford University Press, 1984), pp. 337–38, and Ron Nessen, *It Sure Looks Different from the Inside* (Chicago: Playboy Press, 1978), pp. 212–14.

37. Robert Fisk, *Pity the Nation: The Abduction of Lebanon* (New York: Atheneum Press, 1990), p. 84.

38. Fisk, *Pity the Nation*, p. 84; John Prados, *Keepers of the Keys: A History of the National Security Council from Truman to Bush* (New York: William Morrow, 1991), p. 373; Janet and John Wallach, *Arafat: In the Eyes of the Beholder* (New York: Lyle Stuart, 1990), p. 349.

39. Fisk, *Pity the Nation*, p. 84.

40. John Sears, telephone interview with author, 19 July 1988.

41. *Los Angeles Times*, 12 May 1976.

42. "Inside Congress," clipping in Nessen Papers, box 40, Schweicker folder.

43. Reichley interview with Richard Schweicker, Reichley Papers, box 2.

44. Jules Witcover, *Marathon: The Pursuit of the Presidency, 1972–1976* (New York: Viking Press, 1977), p. 462.

45. Marsh to Ford, 26 July 1976, Ford PP, Friedersdorf Files, box 3, campaign, May–July 1976 folder.

46. Garry Wills, *Lead Time: A Journalist's Education* (New York: Penguin Books, 1983), pp. 203, 208.

47. Ford, *A Time to Heal*, pp. 400–404; David Hume Kennerly, *Shooter* (New York: Newsweek Books, 1979), pp. 215–16; Nessen, *It Sure Looks Different from the Inside*, p. 238.

48. Ford, *A Time to Heal*, p. 404.

49. Armbrister interview with Rockefeller, 21 Oct. 1977, Cannon Papers, box 35.

50. Nessen handwritten notes, 15 Aug. 1976, Nessen Papers, box 297, dated folder.

51. Videotape, Ford acceptance address, White House Communications Agency, GFL, videotape F 658-F 659.

CHAPTER TWELVE. "THE NO-CAMPAIGN CAMPAIGN"

1. Walter LaFeber, *America, Russia and the Cold War*, 4th ed. (New York: John Wiley and Sons, 1980), p. 289.

2. Gerald R. Ford, *A Time to Heal: The Autobiography of Gerald R. Ford* (New York: Harper and Row, 1979), p. 378.

3. Elizabeth Drew, *American Journal; The Events of 1976* (New York: Random House, 1976), pp. 90–91.

4. Robert Shogan, *Promises to Keep: Carter's First 100 Days* (New York: Thomas Y. Crowell Company, 1977), p. 41.

5. Jimmy Carter, *Why Not the Best?* (Nashville, Tenn.: Broadman Press, 1975), p. 103.

6. Michael Raoul-Duval, interview with author, 8 Apr. 1989.

7. David Chagall, *The New Kingmakers* (New York: Harcourt Brace Jovanovich, 1981), p. 93, and Jules Witcover, *Marathon: The Pursuit of the Presidency, 1972–1976* (New York: Viking Press, 1977), p. 530.

8. Original copy in Ford PP, Dorothy Downton Files, box 1, campaign strategy folder. Quoted in Martin Schram, *Running for President, 1976: The Carter Campaign* (New York: Stein and Day, 1977), pp. 252–68; Ron Nessen, *It Sure Looks Different from the Inside* (Chicago: Playboy Press, 1978), pp. 244–45; and Witcover, *Marathon*, pp. 530–35.

9. Kathleen Hall Jamieson, *Packaging the Presidency: A History and Criticism of Presidential Campaign Advertising* (New York: Oxford University Press, 1984), pp. 346–47, and Malcolm MacDougall, *We Almost Made It* (New York: Crown Publishers, 1977), pp. 115–19.

10. L. Patrick Devlin interview with Doug Bailey, 7 Jan. 1977, in L. Patrick Devlin Papers, GFL. See also L. Patrick Devlin, "President Ford's Ad Man Reviews the 1976 Media Campaign [Interview with Doug Bailey]," *Indiana Speech Journal* 13 (Apr. 1978): 16.

11. Samuel E. Becker and Elmer W. Lower, "Broadcasting in Political Campaigns," in *The Great Debates: Carter vs. Ford, 1976*, ed. Sidney Kraus

(Bloomington: Indiana University Press, 1979), pp. 30–31, and Fred Bush speech to the Center for National Policy, 27 Feb. 1989, C-SPAN Videotape no. 6473.

12. Drew, *American Journal*, p. 398.

13. Undated memorandum, Nessen Papers, box 36, Campaign Subject File, Mondale folder.

14. Larry Speakes, interview with author, 8 Apr. 1989.

15. Witcover, *Marathon*, p. 615.

16. Ibid., p. 567.

17. Justice Department report, undated, Buchen Papers, box 22, Kelley general folder no. 1.

18. *New York Times*, 22 Sept. 1976, p. A25.

19. Saul Friedman, "Is Influence the Game of Ford's Golf Pals?" *Detroit Free Press*, 10 Oct. 1976.

20. *New York Times*, 5 June 1965, p. 62, 6 June 1965, p. 31, 7 June 1965, p. 73, and 30 June 1965, p. 74.

21. Newspaper clipping, "Journal of Commerce," 11 June 1976, in Ford PP, Buchen Files, box 53, President—Special Prosecutor Investigation folder no. 1; Leppert to Friedersdorf and Marsh, 20 Sept. 1976, Ford PP, Friedersdorf Files, box 3, campaign, Aug.–Sept. 1976 folder.

22. Ford, *A Time to Heal*, pp. 417–18; Ford PP, Buchen Files, box 53, Special Prosecutor Investigation, copies from Ford Congressional Papers.

23. Summary of first debate, Nessen Papers, box 35, debate folder.

24. Comments of Bob Orben in *The Ford Presidency: Twenty-two Intimate Perspectives of Gerald R. Ford*, ed. Kenneth Thompson (Lanham, Md.: University Press of America, 1988), p. 251.

25. Press release, 14 Oct. 1976, Ford PP, Buchen Files, box 54, Special Prosecutor Investigation—general folder; press release, 14 Oct. 1976, Ford PP, Buchen Files, box 54, Special Prosecutor Investigation—general folder; *Washington Post*, 1 Oct. 1976, p. 1; Evan Thomas, *The Man to See: Edward Bennett Williams* (New York: Simon and Schuster, 1991), p. 346.

26. United Press International report by William Citterell, in Nessen Papers, Campaign Subject File, box 31, Campaign—general.

27. *Ann Arbor News*, 5 Oct. 1976, p. 13.

28. Nessen, *It Sure Looks Different from the Inside*, p. 296.

29. Witcover, *Marathon*, p. 589.

30. On 20 March 1975, the *Los Angeles Times* reported that Carter had told a news conference that "the Ford defense budget for this year could be cut by about $15 billion without sacrificing national security" (in debate transcript in Nessen Papers, Campaign Subject File, box 36, debates, second folder).

31. NSC briefing book, in Ford PP, staff secretary, White House Special Files Unit, box 2, NSC briefing book folder no. 1.

32. Videotape, rehearsal for second debate, White House Communications Agency, GFL, videotape AV 92-12-148 (emphasis mine).

33. Stuart Spencer, on "Campaigning for the Presidency," PBS, 7 Jan. 1992.

34. Transcript in Nessen Papers, Campaign Subject File, box 36, debates, second folder.

35. Chagall, *New Kingmakers*, p. 114.

36. Ibid., p. 118.

37. Ibid., p. 120.

38. Jimmy Carter, *Keeping Faith: Memoirs of a President* (New York: Bantam Books, 1982), p. 27.

39. Jonathan Moore and Janet Fraser, eds., *Campaign for President: The Managers Look at '76* (Cambridge, Mass.: Belinger Publishing Company, 1977), p. 5.

CHAPTER THIRTEEN. "IF I'M REMEMBERED"

1. "The Big 200th Bash," *Time*, 5 July 1976, p. 8.

2. Bernard J. Firestone and Alexej Ugrinsky, *Gerald R. Ford and the Politics of Post-Watergate America*, 2 vols. (Westport, Conn.: Greenwood Press, 1993), 2: 671.

3. Alan M. Webber, "Gerald R. Ford: The Statesman as CEO," *Harvard Business Review* (Sept.–Oct. 1987): 77.

4. Gerald R. Ford, *A Time to Heal: The Autobiography of Gerald R. Ford* (New York: Harper and Row, 1979), pp. 263–64.

5. Adlai Stevenson III, interview with author, 30 Mar. 1987.

6. Reichley interview with Robert Goldwyn, Reichley Papers, box 1.

7. Hugh Sidey and Fred Ward, *Portrait of a President* (New York: Harper and Row, 1975), p. 36.

8. Gerald R. Ford, interview with author, 1 Sept. 1988.

BIBLIOGRAPHICAL ESSAY

The Gerald R. Ford Library (hereafter GFL), located on the campus of the University of Michigan in Ann Arbor, leads the presidential library system in the opening of new material, and as the information is made available to the public, the scholarly assessment of Ford's presidency has grown exponentially. Although the Ford administration continues to be given a comparatively small amount of space in survey treatments on virtually every subject, the number of significant scholarly works dealing with the Ford years that appeared in the 1980s makes possible an adequate bibliographical treatment of the subject. What follows is not a complete list of available sources nor a complete list of the material used in the writing of this book. Rather, it is an introduction to the wealth of material available to Ford researchers, with comments on which analyses might serve as valuable starting points.

BIBLIOGRAPHIES AND REFERENCE MATERIAL

The only full bibliographic treatment of Ford's life and presidency is John Robert Greene, *Gerald R. Ford: A Bibliography* (Westport, Conn.: Greenwood Press, 1994). The work is annotated and includes a chronology. See also George J. Lankevich, ed., *Gerald R. Ford: Chronology, Documents, and Bibliographical Aids* (Dobbs Ferry, N.Y.: Oceana Publications, 1977). A helpful guide to the sources is found in the Ford chapter in Kenneth E. Davison, ed., *The American Presidency: A Guide to Information Sources* (Detroit: Gale Research Company, 1983). Other helpful listings of Ford material are found in *The American Presidency: A Historical Bibliography* (Santa Barbara, Calif.: ABC-Clio Information Services, 1984); the section on Ford in Fenton S. Martin and Robert U. Goehlert, *American Presidents: A Bibliography* (Washington, D.C.: Congressional Quarterly, 1987); Fenton

S. Martin and Robert U. Goehlert, *The American Presidency: A Bibliography* (Washington, D.C.: Congressional Quarterly, 1987); and Fenton S. Martin and Robert U. Goehlert, *The Presidency: A Research Guide* (Santa Barbara, Calif.: ABC-Clio Information Services, 1985). Myron J. Smith, Jr., ed., *Watergate: An Annotated Bibliography of Sources in English, 1972–1982* (Metuchen, N.J.: Scarecrow Press, 1983), is also helpful.

PRIMARY MATERIAL

The archival record available at the Gerald R. Ford Library, opened in 1981 on the campus of the University of Michigan, is both impressive and significant. Most of Ford's prepresidential, congressional, vice-presidential, and presidential files, the files of his White House staff members, and several other donated sets of personal papers are available to qualified researchers. Those interested in a specific subject should begin with the relevant files from the White House Central Files (WHCF), the permanent filing unit within the White House complex. Although most White House staff members maintained their private office files, they were encouraged to use the WHCF system. Most of the substantive material is found in the Subject Files, which includes a highly cross-referenced filing system. The WHCF provides a broad view of the administration, but the White House Special Files is a more select collection. Made up of material taken from the WHCF by a staff secretary, the Special Files includes much of the sensitive and controversial records of the administration, including a large file of material marked "The President Has Seen."

Yet it is in the files and papers of the White House staff that the best archival record of the Ford administration can be found. The most important collection on the whole of the Ford presidency are the files of Philip R. Buchen. As Ford's counsel, Buchen received copies of most White House paperwork, including much of the National Security material not found elsewhere. Buchen's files are the best source for the pardon, the Marine Engineers Beneficial Association (MEBA) probe, and the Patman investigation, and are particularly strong on amnesty and the disposition of the Nixon papers. Also helpful for an overview of the administration are the Jerry Jones files. As White House staff secretary, Jones received copies of memorandums on virtually every routine matter. His files also contain several folders of exceptional presidential meeting minutes and a great deal of singular memorandums from staff members. See also the files of James M. Cannon, John G. Carlson, Richard B. Cheney, Kenneth R. Cole, Jr., James E. Connor, Dorothy Downton, Jay T. French, Max L. Friedersdorf, Alexander M. Haig, Henry Kissinger and Brent Scowcroft (Name File and Temporary Parallel File), John O. Marsh, Kenneth Rush, William Timmons, and Robert K. Wolthuis; the records of the U.S. Council of Economic Advisors; the papers of Benton Becker, Dean Burch, Howard "Bo" Callaway, Leo Cherne, Charles E. Goodell, Robert Teeter, and Frank G. Zarb; and the files and papers of Robert Hartmann and Ronald Nessen.

Of the special collections at the GFL, the assortment of interviews by scholars and writers are by far the most helpful. The James H. C. Hyde, Jr., and Stephen J. Wayne Oral History Collection includes twenty-four taped interviews with members of the White House staff, the Bureau of the Budget, and the Office of Management and Budget (OMB). The papers of A. James Reichley contain summaries of interviews conducted during his research for *Conservatives in an Era of Change* (discussed below). The Audio-Visual Department of the GFL also holds a complete collection of the weekly news summaries produced during the Ford tenure by the White House Communications Agency, a complete set of Ford's nationally televised speeches, some 280,000 negatives of pictures shot by the White House Photographer's Office during the Ford tenure as vice president and president, and some 30,000 other photos.

Helpful manuscript sources in other archives include Hugh Carey Gubernatorial Records, New York State Archives, Albany, N.Y.; Frank Church Papers, Boise State University, Idaho; Frank Nelson Elliott Papers, Michigan State University, Historical Collections and Archives; Samuel J. Ervin, Jr., Papers, Southern Historical Collection, University of North Carolina, Chapel Hill; Hubert H. Humphrey Papers. Minnesota Historical Society; and the Richard M. Nixon Presidential Papers, WHCF: Subject File, Richard M. Nixon Presidential Materials Project, National Archives.

For the public record of the Ford years, consult Richard M. Nixon, *Public Papers of the Presidents of the United States: Richard Nixon, 1969–1974*, 6 vols. (Washington, D.C.: U.S. Government Printing Office, 1975), and Gerald R. Ford, *Public Papers of the Presidents of the United States: Gerald R. Ford, 1974–1976*, 6 vols. (Washington, D.C.: U.S. Government Printing Office, 1975–79). See also Michael V. Doyle, ed., *Gerald R. Ford: Selected Speeches* (Arlington, Va.: R. W. Beatty, 1973), and Janet Podell and Steven Anzovin, eds., *Speeches of the American Presidents* (New York: H. W. Wilson Company, 1988). A helpful collection of interviews with and seminar interaction among Ford administration principals can be found in Kenneth W. Thompson, ed., *The Ford Presidency: Twenty-Two Intimate Perspectives of Gerald R. Ford* (Lanham, Md.: University Press of America, 1988).

In many ways, Robert Hartmann, *Palace Politics: An Insider's Account of the Ford Years* (New York: McGraw-Hill, 1980), is the most important book yet available on the Ford years—surpassing even Ford's own memoirs in insight and readability. Two other memoirs of import come from within the administration. Ron Nessen, *It Sure Looks Different from the Inside* (Chicago: Playboy Press, 1978), is much less a book on the press than a memoir of the entire administration. Nessen admits—and his book documents—how he became an advocate for Ford rather than an objective conduit between the president and the press. White House photographer David Hume Kennerly dealt with Ford's career through 1979 in *Shooter* (New York: Newsweek Books, 1979). Written as irreverently as his reputation would suggest, the book shows Kennerly's closeness to the First Family and makes clear his disdain for Kissinger and Rumsfeld. Less helpful memoirs are John R. Coyne, Jr., *Fall In and Cheer: A Thoughtful, Often Irreverent View of American Politics* (Garden City, N.Y.: Doubleday and Company, 1979); John J. Casserly, *The Ford White House: The Diary of a Speechwriter* (Boulder: Colorado Associated University Press, 1977); Alexander M. Haig, Jr., *Inner Circles: How America Changed the World* (New York: Warner Books, 1992); and Richard M. Nixon, *The Memoirs of Richard Nixon* (New York: Grosset and Dunlap, 1978). Reference is made below to other memoirs where appropriate to subject matter.

Gerald Ford has himself been a rather prolific writer, producing no less than three books, five contributed book chapters, seven articles for professional journals, and twelve articles for magazines. Ford's first book, *Portrait of the Assassin* (New York: Simon and Schuster, 1965), was written with John R. Stiles, a Grand Rapids friend who had served as Ford's 1948 campaign manager. The book is a defense of the conclusions of the Warren Commission, reportedly using classified FBI material that the commission had agreed to keep secret. His second book, *A Time to Heal: The Autobiography of Gerald R. Ford* (New York: Harper and Row, 1979), was researched and ghosted by Trevor Armbrister of *Reader's Digest*. Even for the self-effacing genre of presidential memoirs, *A Time to Heal* is a disappointment. Though often revealing, Ford chose a straight chronological organization, and the book suffers as a result—overly long chapters and a choppy narrative (the disjointed treatment of the economy suffers the most from this style) make it a confusing read. His most recent book, *Humor and the Presidency* (New York: Arbor House, 1987), offers a short history of political humor, beginning with Thomas Nast.

Of Ford's other writings, his several magazine and professional journal articles are the most important. In "Who Can Save the G.O.P.?" *Fortune* (January 1965), pp. 140–41, the young minority leader advanced the unpopular argument that the GOP could no longer afford to link its fortunes to the southern Democrats—no "coalition"—and must learn to stand on its own. In "Impeachment: A Mace for the Federal Judiciary," *Notre Dame Lawyer* 46 (Summer 1974): 669–77, Ford stresses the idea that impeachment is a "political process." In his "Attorney General Edward H. Levi," *University of Chicago Law Review* 52 (Spring 1985): 284–89, Ford summarizes the process behind his appointment of Levi and of John Paul Stevens to the Supreme Court.

SECONDARY MATERIAL

There is as yet no complete scholarly biography of Gerald R. Ford. The best study is James Cannon, *Time and Chance: Gerald Ford's Appointment with History* (New York: Harper Collins, 1994). Cannon served as Ford's director of the Domestic Council, yet the book, based largely on research in the GFL and Ford's previously unreleased diaries, offers a solid view of Ford's career up to the pardon. The rest of Ford's tenure is briefly summarized, and Cannon is unfailingly positive toward his subject. Nevertheless, it is the best view of Ford's personal and political development yet available.

All other biographical works leave a great deal to be desired. Dave LeRoy, *Gerald Ford: The Untold Story* (Arlington, Va.: Beatty, 1974), was hurriedly printed in a vanity venue and includes nothing "untold"; it does include, however, several good, previously unpublished photos of Ford. Bud Vestal, *Jerry*

Ford, Up Close: An Investigative Biography (New York: Coward, McCann and Geoghegan, 1974), is hardly investigative and rather a surface treatment, written immediately after Ford's nomination as vice president. Jerald terHorst began his *Gerald Ford and the Future of the Presidency* (New York: Third Press, 1974), while he was a reporter for the *Detroit News*. As a result of his aborted tenure as Ford's press secretary, however, the work was cut short and covers only the first days of the administration. Jan Aaron, *Gerald Ford: President of Destiny* (New York: Fleet Press, 1975), is a campaign biography (the White House Staff provided the photographs), but the work is still one of some substance as it includes a great deal of helpful detail on Ford's early life. Richard Reeves, *A Ford, Not a Lincoln* (New York: Harcourt Brace Jovanovich, 1975), is the most critical of Ford's biographers, centering his book on a discussion of Ford's lack of intellectual grit. Clark R. Mollenhoff, *The Man Who Pardoned Nixon* (New York: St. Martin's Press, 1976), focuses on the pardon, and as evidenced by his subtitle—*A Documented Account of Gerald Ford's Presidential Retreat from Credibility*—is as critical of Ford as Reeves. A later biography of Ford, Edward L. and Frederick H. Schapsmeier, *Gerald R. Ford's Date with Destiny: A Political Biography* (New York: Peter Lang, 1989), lacks balance—the authors include only two brief chapters on the presidency of Ford.

The best study of Ford's early political career is William A. Syers, "The Political Beginnings of Gerald R. Ford: Anti-Bossism, Internationalism, and the Congressional Campaign of 1948," *Presidential Studies Quarterly* 20 (Winter 1990): 127–42. *President Ford: The Man and His Record* (Washington D.C.: Congressional Quarterly, 1974), and S. C. McElroy, *Ralph Nader Congress Project: Citizens Look at Congress, Gerald R. Ford* (Old Tappan, N.J.: Grossman Publishers, 1972), provide good summaries of Ford's voting record. The best view of Ford's role on the Warren Commission can be found in Henry Hurt, *Reasonable Doubt* (New York: Holt, Rinehart and Winston, 1985); see also Jack Harrison Pollack, *Earl Warren: The Judge Who Changed America* (Englewood Cliffs, N.J.: Prentice-Hall, 1979). On Ford's move into House leadership, see Robert Peabody, "The Ford-Halleck Minority Leadership Contest" (Issues in Practical Politics, Case No. 40; New York: McGraw Hill, 1966). John Ehrlichman, *Witness to Power: The Nixon Years* (New York: Pocket Books, 1982), is helpful for an understanding of the relationship between Ford and the Nixon White House. On the Douglas impeachment, see "Role of Vice-President Designate Gerald R. Ford in the Attempt to Impeach Associate Supreme Court Justice William O. Douglas" (Library of Congress: Legislative Reference Service, 1973). On the Patman imvestigation, consult John Dean, *Blind Ambition: The White House Years* (New York: Simon and Schuster, 1976); Marjorie Boyd, "The Watergate Story: Why Congress Didn't Investigate until After the Election," *Washington Monthly*, April 1973, pp. 37–45; and Clark R. Mollenhoff, *Game Plan for Disaster: An Ombudsman's Report on the Nixon Years* (New York: W. W. Norton, 1976).

The basic source for Ford's confirmation as vice president is his published testimony before the House and Senate. See U.S. Congress, Senate, Committee on the Rules and Administration, 93d Congress, *Nomination of Gerald R. Ford of Michigan to be President of the United States* (Washington, D.C.: U.S. Government

Printing Office, 1973). For a discussion of the several challenges to Ford's credibility made during those hearings, see Arnold A. Hutschnecker, *The Drive for Power* (New York: M. Evans and Company, 1974); Robert N. Winter-Berger, *The Washington Pay-Off* (New York: Dell, 1972); and Robert N. Winter-Berger, *The Gerald Ford Letters* (Secaucus, N.J.: Lyle Stuart, 1974). A good chronology of events can be found in Lester A. Sobel, ed., *Presidential Succession: Ford, Rockefeller, and the 25th Amendment* (New York: Facts on File, 1975).

An excellent study of an office that is only beginning to attract the interest of serious scholars is Joel K. Goldstein, *The Modern American Vice Presidency: The Transformation of a Political Institution* (Princeton, N.J.: Princeton University Press, 1982). Paul C. Light, *Advice and Influence in the White House: Vice Presidential Power* (Baltimore: Johns Hopkins University Press, 1984), is also helpful. Marie D. Natoli, *American Prince, American Pauper: The Contemporary Vice Presidency in Perspective* (Westport, Conn.: Greenwood Press, 1985), offers only a surface treatment of Ford. For an anecdotal account of Ford's vice-presidency, see Elizabeth Drew, *Washington Journal: The Events of 1973-1974* (New York: Random House, 1975).

James M. Naughton, "The Change in Presidents: Plans Began Months Ago," *New York Times*, 26 Aug. 1974, pp. 1ff., is an important article that should be consulted first on the transition to the Ford presidency. Using Buchen as a key source, Naughton is the first author to piece together the story of the several different transition teams. This article should be followed by Buchen's own contribution to James P. Pfiffner and R. Gordon Hoxie, eds., *The Presidency in Transition* (New York: Center for the Study of the Presidency, 1989), "The Making of an Unscheduled Presidential Transition." Nancy B. Smith, "The Transition from President Nixon to President Ford," also in Pfiffner and Hoxie, uses bits of new material from the GFL but improves little on Naughton's and Buchen's treatment. Robert Sam Anson, *Exile: The Unquiet Oblivion of Richard M. Nixon* (New York: Simon and Schuster, 1984), offers the most engaging treatment of the drama of the transition period. See also Theodore H. White, *Breach of Faith: The Fall of Richard Nixon* (New York: Atheneum, 1975), and Bob Woodward and Carl Bernstein, *The Final Days* (New York: Simon and Schuster, 1976).

The two scholarly monographs that discuss the full scope of the Ford presidency do so in volumes that treat the Nixon and Ford presidencies as a whole. A. James Reichley, *Conservatives in an Age of Change: The Nixon and Ford Administrations* (Washington, D.C.: Brookings Institution, 1981), was the first one-volume treatment of the two administrations. A member of Ford's staff, Reichley concludes that Ford was generally conservative in domestic affairs and had "no grasp" of foreign affairs (p. 337). John Robert Greene, *The Limits of Power: The Nixon and Ford Administrations* (Bloomington: Indiana University Press, 1992), sees Ford to have been working from within the framework of a presidency more limited in terms of its influence than at any other time in its history. Other scholarly works assessing the Ford presidency include Roger B.. Porter, "Gerald R. Ford: The Healing Presidency," in *Leadership in the Modern Presidency*, ed. Fred I. Greenstein (Cambridge: Harvard University Press, 1988); Richard B. Morris, ed., *Encyclopedia of American History*, 6th ed. (New York: Harper and

Row, 1982), "Domestic Policy: The Ford Years, 1974–1977," pp. 545–55, and "Foreign Policy: The Ford-Kissinger Years, 1974–1977," pp. 566–69; and Philip Shabecoff, "Appraising Presidential Power: The Ford Presidency," in *The Presidency Appraised*, ed. Thomas E. Cronin and Rexford G. Tugwell, 2d ed. (New York: Praeger, 1977).

Two other general works on the Ford years were written by journalists specializing in the presidency. The day after Ford was sworn in, Jack Rosenthal of the *New York Times* asked Jerry terHorst if a reporter could shadow Ford for a week. Ford agreed, except for "my daily meetings with Henry." The result was John Hersey, *The President* (New York: Knopf, 1975). Hersey followed Ford from Monday 10 March to Saturday 15 March 1975. Writing in a chatty style that allows the reader to meet some of the major players, Hersey shows a pro-Hartmann/anti-Rumsfeld bias. Hersey's book was extracted in "The President," *New York Times Magazine* (20 Apr. 1975). *Time* magazine correspondent Hugh Sidey and photographer Fred Ward collaborated for the useful *Portrait of a President* (New York: Harper and Row, 1975). Ward's photos are an excellent introduction, and Sidey's commentary is entertaining. On the whole, Sidey is more sympathetic to the administration in these pages than he was in his *Time* column.

One other general source deserves separate mention. In April 1989 Hofstra University held a national conference on the presidency of Gerald R. Ford. Addressed several times by Ford, the conference was an impressive collection of scholarly assessment and personal reflection by the principals in the Ford administration. Several of the papers, speeches, and discussant commentary shared with the conference have been published in Bernard J. Firestone and Alexej Ugrinsky, *Gerald R. Ford and the Politics of Post-Watergate America*, 2 vols. (Westport, Conn.: Greenwood Press, 1993).

Stephen J. Wayne, *The Legislative Presidency* (New York: Harper and Row, 1978), is a readable institutional portrait, offering good detail on the setup of the White House staff, the Domestic Coucil, and congressional relations; his "Running the White House: The Ford Experience," *Presidential Studies Quarterly* (Spring–Summer 1977): 95–101, is less helpful. Based on a handful of interviews and anecdotal evidence, Wayne's article is less an objective study than a critical editorial about the limitations of Ford's staff. Several other studies of Ford's staffing problems are Edward D. Feigenbaum, "Staffing, Organization, and Decision-Making in the Ford and Carter White Houses," *Presidential Studies Quarterly* 10 (Summer 1980): 364–77, and R. Gordon Hoxie, "Staffing the Ford and Carter Presidencies," in *Organizing and Staffing the Presidency*, ed. Bradley D. Nash (New York: Center for the Study of the Presidency, 1980). The best piece on the Ford cabinet is a chapter by Shirley Anne Warshaw, "Cabinet Government in the Modern Presidency," in Pfiffner and Hoxie, eds., *The Presidency in Transition*.

Several of Ford's key White House advisers attended a conference where they spoke on their experience, but the published result of this appearance is disappointing. Herbert J. Storing, ed., *The Ford White House* (Lanham, Md.: University Press of America, 1986), offers the transcript of a 23 April 1977 program at the University of Virginia's Miller Center, which included on the panel James

Cavanaugh, Richard Cheney, James Connor, Richard Goldwyn, James Lynn, Donald Rumsfeld, and Brent Scowcroft. The book, however, is frustrating because of the many typographical errors as well as the editorial omission of comments by participants who later decided that they did not want to be quoted on a specific point.

On the chief of staff, Michael Medved, *The Shadow Presidents: The Secret History of the Chief Executives and their Top Aides* (New York: Times Books, 1979), is problematic. Reviewing the office to the Lincoln administration, Medved offers a chapter on each chief of staff—except Haig and Rumsfeld. The chapter on Cheney is helpful, however. Cheney and Rumsfeld participated on a 1986 panel discussing the role of the chief of staff. A transcript of that interview was published as Samuel Kernell and Samuel L. Popkin, *Chief of Staff: Twenty-Five Years of Managing the Presidency* (Berkeley: University of California Press, 1986).

Contemporary biographical sketches of Ford's key advisers include "A Conservative Who Can Compromise [Alan Greenspan]," *Time*, 15 June 1987, pp. 50–51; Gage William Chapel, "Speech Writing in the Ford Administration: An Interview with Speech Writer Robert Orben, *Exetasis*, 15 June 1976, pp. 16–17; Don Hill, "The President's Man from the Shenandoah Valley [Jack Marsh]," *Virginia-Pilot*, 1 Sept. 1974; Lloyd Shearer, "Don Rumsfeld: He's President Ford's Number One Man," *Parade*, 2 Feb. 1975, pp. 4–5ff.; "The Gentle Crippled Man that Jerry Ford Trusts [Philip Buchen]," *People Weekly*, 30 Sept. 1974, pp. 4–7; and "The President's Eyes and Ears [Hartmann]," *Time*, 2 Sept. 1974, p. 13.

It is useful to begin a study of Ford's pardon of Richard Nixon by consulting those constitutional scholars who deal with the question of the extent of the executive pardoning power. These works include Patrick R. Cowlishaw, "The Conditional Presidential Pardon," *Stanford Law Review* (Nov. 1975): 149–77; W. H. Humbert, *The Pardoning Power of the President*, (Washington, D.C.: American Council on Public Affairs, 1941); and Samuel Williston, "Does a Pardon Blot Out Guilt?" *Harvard Law Review* 28 (May 1915): 647–63. The operative Supreme Court cases under discussion by the White House in September 1974 are ex parte Garland (1866) and *Burdick v. U.S.* (1915). The majority opinion in both cases was clear: a pardon *does* "blot out guilt."

The seminal work on the pardon is Seymour Hersh, "The Pardon: Nixon, Ford, Haig and the Transfer of Power," *Atlantic*, Aug. 1983, pp. 55–78. Hersh traces Ford's ties to Nixon, the Patman Committee and the August 1974 discussions between Ford and Haig. The big revelation in the article is that on 7 September 1974 Nixon called Ford and threatened to claim a deal if Ford did not pardon him right away. An exception to this point was taken by a Republican member of the House Judiciary Committee in Robert McClory, "A Rebuttal: Was the Fix in between Ford and Nixon?" *National Review*, 14 Oct. 1983, pp. 1264–72.

Robert Sam Anson, *Exile: The Unquiet Oblivion of Richard M. Nixon* (New York: Simon and Schuster, 1984), offers the most detailed and interesting look at the story of the negotiations behind the pardon. Stanley I. Kutler, *The Wars of Watergate: The Last Crisis of Richard Nixon* (New York: Alfred A. Knopf, 1990), offers a full chapter on the pardon, based on wide-ranging interviews and a good use of the available archival record. In his *Inner Circles: How America Changed the*

World (New York: Warner Books, 1992), Alexander Haig gives his view of the August 1 meetings for the first time and makes the completely unbelievable argument that he played no role in the pardon. Richard M. Nixon, *In the Arena: A Memoir of Victory, Defeat and Renewal* (New York: Simon and Schuster, 1990), offers an interesting vignette on why he *chose* to accept the pardon.

Memoirs of members of the Watergate Special Prosecution Force help to flesh out the negotiations between Buchen and Special Prosecutor Leon Jaworski. These works include Richard Ben-Veniste and George Frampton, Jr., *Stonewall: The Real Story of the Watergate Prosecution* (New York: Simon and Schuster, 1977); James Doyle, *Not Above the Law: The Battles of Watergate Prosecutors Cox and Jaworski* (New York: William Morrow and Company, 1977); and Leon Jaworski, *The Right and the Power* (New York: Pocket Books, 1977).

The second chapter of Hedrick Smith's fascinating *Power Game: How Washington Works* (New York: Random House, 1988) sets the historical background for the congressional upheavals of the period and offers a wonderful prism through which to view the entirety of the Ford presidency. A helpful summary of the congressional elections of 1974 and the goals of the "Watergate Babies" is John E. Yang, "How the Watergate Class of '74 Played Kings of the Hill," *Washington Post National Weekly Edition*, 22–28 June 1992, pp. 12–13. On specific issues of the congressional retrieval of power that directly affected the Ford tenure, see Kenneth M. Holland, "The War Powers Resolution: An Infringement on the President's Constitutional and Prerogative Powers," Harold C. Relyea, "Reconsidering the National Emergencies Act: Its Evolution, Implementation, and Deficiencies," in *The Presidency and National Security Policy*, ed. R. Gordon Hoxie (New York: Center for the Study of the Presidency, 1984), and Robert F. Turner, *The War Powers Resolution: Its Implementation in Theory and Practice* (Philadelphia: Foreign Policy Research Institution, 1983).

There is no truly adequate study of Ford's relationship with Capitol Hill. The issue is touched upon briefly in Paul C. Light, *The President's Agenda: A Domestic Policy Choice from Kennedy to Reagan* (Baltimore: Johns Hopkins University Press, 1982); Robert J. Spitzer, *The Presidential Veto: Touchstone of the American Presidency* (Albany: State University of New York Press, 1988); and Wayne, *The Legislative Presidency*. Yet the best analysis of this issue is found in the amusing anecdotes offered in Tip O'Neill, *Man of the House* (New York: Random House, 1987).

During the Ford administration, the criticism of the president tended to follow the lead of two journalists. The more influential of these, discussed in chapter 4 of this book, was Richard Reeves, "Jerry Ford and His Flying Circus: A Presidential Diary," *New York*, 25 Nov. 1974, pp. 42–46. An important primary souce in the development of the Ford image, Reeves's article was better known for the cover and title-page picture, which portrays Ford as Bozo the Clown. A more in-depth study was offered by Garry Wills, "He's Not So Dumb," *New York Review of Books*, 16 Oct. 1975, pp. 18–26. In this review of books on Ford by Sidey, Hersey, terHorst, and Reeves, Wills charges that the authors all *missed* Ford—either by pandering to the presidency or by downplaying the fact that the "good old Jerry image blunts criticism" (p, 22). Even when journalists attempted to praise Ford, they did so in a backhanded sort of way. See Saul Friedman, "In Praise of Honest Ignorance: A Kind Word for Jerry Ford," *Harper's*, Aug. 1974, pp. 16–26.

In the area of the Ford image, scholars have produced the poorest work on the Ford presidency. Several recent scholarly works on presidential image-making have followed Reeves's lead and treat Ford with condescension. Robert Underhill's study of the public pronouncements of the modern presidents, *The Bully Pulpit: From Franklin Roosevelt to Ronald Reagan* (New York: Vantage Press, 1987), is weakly researched, general in its conclusions, and particularly insufficient on Ford. William C. Spraegens, ed., *Popular Images of American Presidents* (New York: Greenwood Press, 1988), is also disappointingly thin. Gerald Gardner, *All the President's Wits: The Power of Presidential Humor* (New York: Beechtree Books, 1986), uses a particularly patronizing tone toward Ford as he likens him to Chance the gardener in the movie *Being There* (p. 109). An exception to these works is John Anthony Maltese, *Spin Control: The White House Office of Communications and the Management of Presidential News* (Chapel Hill: University of North Carolina Press, 1992); on the attempts made by Ford's advisers to alter his generally unfavorable image, Maltese is superb.

A balanced scholarly study of Ford's press relations has yet to be written. Mark J. Rozell, *The Press and the Ford Presidency* (Ann Arbor: University of Michigan Press, 1992), analyzes the reaction of only the print media, inexplicably ignoring the television criticism that was so disastrous for Ford. Joseph C. Spear, *Presidents and the Press: The Nixon Legacy* (Cambridge: Massachusetts Institute of Technology Press, 1984), is confusingly organized but shot full of good anecdotes on Ford. Charles Press and Kenneth Verberg, *American Politicians and Journalists* (Glenview, Ill.: Scott, Foresman and Company, 1988), is weakly written and offers little of substance on Ford.

The merits of Ron Nessen's *It Sure Looks Different from the Inside* have already been discussed. The several other memoirs of press correspondents during the Ford years must be read with caution—they are all usually pro-Kissinger in tone and written in a manner that seems to thank Kissinger for the access to which they have been accorded. See Nancy Dickerson, *Among Those Present: A Reporter's View of Twenty-Five Years in Washington* (New York: Random House, 1976); Hedley Donovan, *Roosevelt to Reagan: A Reporter's Encounters with Nine Presidents* (New York: Harper and Row, 1985); and John Herbers, *No Thank You, Mr. President* (New York: Norton, 1976).

Ford made his feelings on his treatment by the press clear at the 18 January 1989 forum, "The Presidency and the Press," held at the Gannett Center of Columbia University. A summary of that seminar can be found in Andrew Radolf, "Trivial Images and the Presidency: Former Presidents Carter and Ford Assess the Press," *Editor and Publisher* (28 Jan. 1989): 7–8.

A serious biography of Betty Ford is also long overdue. The only one presently available, Bruce Cassiday, *Betty Ford: Woman of Courage* (New York: Dale Brooks, 1978), makes no great attempt at scholarship but is readable and interestingly written. Mrs. Ford's own two volumes of memoirs, *The Times of My Life* (New York: Harper and Row, 1978), and *Betty: A Glad Awakening* (Garden City,

N.Y.: Doubleday and Company, 1987), are stiffly written and prone to preaching. The memoir of Mrs. Ford's press secretary, Sheila Raab Weidenfeld, *First Lady's Lady: With the Fords at the White House* (New York: G. P. Putnam's Sons, 1979), has come under fire from virtually every quarter, most notably from its two main targets—Mrs. Ford and Ron Nessen—and must be read with extreme caution.

Of the growing literature on the First Lady, Myra Gutlin, *The President's Partner: The First Lady in the Twentieth Century* (New York: Greenwood Press, 1989), is the most useful for a study of the influence of Betty Ford. Basing her analysis on an interview with Mrs. Ford as well as on secondary sources, Gutlin places Mrs. Ford in the same category ("advocate") as Eleanor Roosevelt, Lady Bird Johnson, Rosalyn Carter, and Nancy Reagan. Also helpful are Paul F. Boller, Jr., *Presidential Wives: An Anecdotal History* (New York: Oxford University Press, 1988); Peter Hay, *All the President's Ladies: Anecdotes of the Women behind the Men in the White House* (New York: Viking Press, 1988); Eliot Fremont Smith, "Reporting (Gasp!) What Betty Ford Said," *Columbia Journalism Review* (Nov.-Dec. 1975): 15–17; and Leesa Tobin, "Betty Ford: A Woman for Women," *Presidential Studies Quarterly* 20 (Fall 1990): 761–67.

Jay David, *The Young Fords* (New York: Award Books, 1975), is an informally written view of the Ford family, with a chapter devoted to each child. Also helpful are Barbara Kellerman, *All the President's Kin* (New York: Free Press, 1981), and Sadra L. Quinn and Sanford Kanter, *America's Royalty: All the President's Children* (Westport, Conn.: Greenwood Press, 1983).

Government reports offer the best insight into Ford's first foray into domestic affairs—his program to offer clemency to Vietnam era draft offenders. Begin with the study commissioned by the Pentagon to analyze the effects of the program—Department of Defense, Office of the Deputy Chief of Staff for Personnel, Department of the Army, *After Action Report: Implementation of President's Clemency Program*, 2 vols. (Oct. 1975). D. Bruce Bell and Beverly W. Bell, "Desertion and Antiwar Protest: Findings from the Ford Clemency Program," *Armed Forces and Society* 3 (Spring 1977): 433–43, gives a good profile of those affected by the program, and the executive summary at the beginning of *Presidential Clemency Board: Report to the President* (Washington, D.C.: U.S. Government Printing Office, 1975) is a superb synopsis of the entirety of the process. Lawrence Baskir and William A. Strauss, *Chance and Circumstance: The Draft, the War, and the Vietnam Generation* (New York: Vintage Books, 1978), offers the most mature analysis of the issue. This book is extracted in "The Wounded Generation," *American Heritage*, Apr./May 1978, pp. 23–29. Also helpful is Myra MacPherson, *Long Time Passing: Vietnam and the Haunted Generation* (New York: New American Library, 1984).

Studies on the economic situation have produced the best analysis of any area of domestic policy under Ford. Lester A. Sobel, ed., *Ford and the Economy* (New York: Facts on File, 1976), offers a wealth of statistical material. Ford's reports to the Congress, *Economic Report of the President: February, 1975; January, 1976; January, 1977*, 3 vols. (Washington, D.C.: U.S. Government Printing Office, 1975–77), also offers much helpful material but makes for difficult reading for the novice. A better starting point is a readable five-page summary of Ford's economic policy in Herbert Stein, *Presidential Economics: The Making of Economic Policy from Roosevelt to Reagan and Beyond* (New York: Simon and Schuster, 1984). Roger B. Porter, *Presidential Decision Making: The Economic Policy Board* (Cambridge: Harvard University Press, 1980), is the best book on Ford's economic policy and was used profitably for this work. Although engagingly written and of scholarly substance, Porter's book is quite defensive, however. John W. Sloan, "Economic Policymaking in the Johnson and Ford Administrations," *Presidential Studies Quarterly* (Winter 1990): 111-25, offers a good explanation of the relationship between these presidents and their chief economic advisers. Irwin C. Hargrove and Samuel A. Morley, eds., *The President and the Council of Economic Advisors: Interviews with CEA Chairmen* (Boulder, Colo.: Westview Press, 1984), includes the transcript of an excellent interview with Greenspan. Ford's budget policy is explained in some detail in David S. Ippolito, *Uncertain Legacies: Federal Budget Policy from Roosevelt through Reagan* (Charlottesville: University of Virginia Press, 1990). The memoirs of William E. Simon, *A Time for Truth* (New York: Berkley Books, 1978), fills in some gaps but on the whole is tremendously self-promoting.

The energy crisis of the mid-1970s is in sore need of a detailed scholarly assessment. David Howard Davis, "Energy Policy in the Ford Administration," in *The Politics of Policy Making in America: Five Case Studies*, ed. David A. Caputo (San Francisco: W. H. Freeman and Company, 1977), offers a worthy though brief survey of the subject. There are also interesting bits found in Daniel Yergin, *The Prize: The Epic Quest for Oil, Money, and Power* (New York: Simon and Schuster, 1991).

Virtually nothing has been written on Ford's approach to social policy. The best summary of the Boston busing crisis is found in episode seven of the acclaimed television series *Eyes on the Prize II: The Keys to the Kingdom, 1974–1980* (PBS Television, 1989). The episode concentrates more on 1974 than it does on 1975, but the detail of the rest of the story is provided in the outstanding study by Henry Hampton and Steve Fayer, *Voices of Freedom: An Oral History of the Civil Rights Movement from the 1950s through the 1980s* (New York: Bantam Books, 1990).

On other issues of domestic and social policy, see Roger W. Caves, "An Historical Analysis of Federal Housing Policy from the Presidential Perspective: An Intergovernmental Focus," *Urban Studies* 26 (1989): 59–76; David O'Brien, "The Politics of Professionalism: President Gerald R. Ford's Appointment of Justice John Paul Stevens," *Presidential Studies Quarterly* 21 (Winter 1991): 114–15; Flora Davis, *Moving the Mountain: The Women's Movement in America since 1960* (New York: Simon and Schuster, 1991); Paul MacAvoy and John Snow, eds., *Ford Administration Papers on Regulatory Reform*, 8 vols. (Washington, D.C.: American Enterprise Institute for Public Policy Research, 1977); Ardith Maney, *Still Hungry after All These Years: Food Assistance Policy from Kennedy to Reagan* (Westport, Conn.: Greenwood Press, 1989); H. Guyford Stever, "Science Advice: Out of and Back into the White House," *Technology and Society* 2 (1980): 61–75; and John C. Whitaker, *Striking a Balance: Environmental and Natural Resource*

Policy in the Nixon-Ford Years (Washington, D.C.: American Enterprise Institute for Public Policy Research, 1976).

The best book on the subject of the vice-presidency of Nelson A. Rockefeller is Michael Turner, *The Vice President as Policy Maker: Rockefeller in the Ford White House* (Westport, Conn.: Greenwood Press, 1982). Turner's book should be followed by Paul C. Light's thoughtful "Vice-Presidential Influence under Rockefeller and Mondale," *Political Science Quarterly* 98 (Winter 1983–84): 617–40.

The starting place for any discussion of the Central Intelligence Agency is John Ranalagh, *The Agency: The Rise and Decline of the CIA* (New York: Simon and Schuster, 1986), an excellent survey backed by strong detail. It should be followed by John Prados, *President's Secret Wars: CIA and Pentagon Covert Operations since World War II* (New York: William Morrow and Company, 1986), particularly recommended for the novice interested in the CIA's involvement in foreign conflict. Prados also offers a summary of the three major congressional investigations during the Ford years. Jeffrey T. Richelson, *The U.S. Intelligence Community* (Cambridge, Mass.: Ballinger Publishing Company, 1985), is less gracefully written than either of the books by Ranelagh or Prados, but it offers necessary background on the organization of American intelligence operations. Glenn P. Hastedt and R. Gordon Hoxie, "The Intelligence Community and American Foreign Policy: The Reagan and Carter Administrations," in *The Presidency and National Security Policy*, ed. R. Gordon Hoxie (New York: Center for the Study of the Presidency, 1984), offers good background to the issue in its opening comments. James Bamford, *The Puzzle Palace: A Report on NSA, America's Most Secret Agency* (Boston: Houghton Mifflin, 1982), is the standard work on its subject. Less helpful are Loch Johnson, *America's Secret Power: The CIA in a Democratic Society* (New York: Oxford University Press, 1989); John M. Orman, *Presidential Secrecy and Deception: Beyond the Power to Persuade* (Westport, Conn.: Greenwood Press, 1980); and David Wise, *The American Police State: The Government against the People* (New York: Vintage Books, 1978).

On the Rockefeller, Church, and Pike investigations, begin with Frank J. Smist, Jr.'s, worthy *Congress Oversees the United States Intelligence Community, 1947–1989* (Knoxville: University of Tennessee Press, 1990), with the caution that the author seems to be pandering to many of his interview sources, most notably Frank Church. Smist's survey should be immediately followed with three memoirs of participants in the investigations. David W. Belin, *Final Disclosure: The Full Truth about the Assassination of President Kennedy* (New York: Charles Scribner's Sons, 1988), is a self-serving but fascinating and detailed memoir by the chief counsel of the Rockefeller Commission. Belin's work is particularly noteworth for his willingness to criticize the commission when necessary; Loch Johnson, *A Season of Inquiry: The Senate Intelligence Investigation* (Lexington: University of Kentucky Press, 1985), does not offer the same balance for the Church committee. Johnson was an aide to Frank Church during the life of the committee, and his book is an unabashed tribute to the committee and a hero-worshiping testimonial to Frank Church. William Colby, *Honorable Men: My Life in the CIA* (New York: Simon and Schuster, 1978), is the most dispassionate of the three memoirs. Also on Colby see David Wise, "Colby of CIA—

CIA of Colby," *New York Times Magazine*, 1 July 1973, pp. 9ff. Ford's leaking of the details of the assassination plots to the *New York Times* is related in Tom Wicker, *On Press* (New York: Viking Press, 1978). The *Report to the President by the Commission on CIA Activities within the United States* (Washington, D.C.: U.S. Government Printing Office, 1975) is both readable and surprisingly brief.

Martin Shefter, *Political Crisis/Fiscal Crisis: The Collapse and Revival of New York City* (New York: Basic Books, 1985), is the place to begin a study of the New York City fiscal crisis. Robert W. Bailey, *The Crisis Regime: The New York City Financial Crisis* (Albany: State University of New York Press, 1984), offers an examination that analyzes the different agencies and studies germane to the city's crisis regime of 1975–76. Richard A. Loverd, "Presidential Decision Making during the 1975 New York Financial Crisis: A Conceptual Analysis," *Presidential Studies Quarterly* 21 (Spring 1991): 251–67, is oversimplistic and not particularly well-written, yet it is helpful for its detail on the steps taken by the state after Ford turned them down. Donna Shalala and Carol Bellamy, "A State Saves a City: The New York Case," *Duke Law Journal* (1976): 1119–32, offers a good explanation of the genesis of the Municipal Assistance Corporation (MAC).

Robert S. Litwak, *Detente and the Nixon Doctrine: American Foreign Policy and the Pursuit of Stability, 1969–1976* (Cambridge, Eng.: Cambridge University Press, 1984), has become a classic thematic interpretation. The duality between "detente" and "devolution" is key to Litwak's difficult yet important work. He also offers excellent capsule treatments of SALT (without a lot of detail on the negotiations), the fall of Vietnam, and Angola. While concentrating on SALT, William C. Hyland, *Mortal Rivals: Superpower Relations from Nixon to Reagan* (New York: Random House, 1987), offers a useful broad overview of foreign policies in the post-Watergate period. To supplement the dearth of foreign policy material in the GFL, consult the documents in Richard P. Stebbins and Ellaine P. Adam, eds., *American Foreign Relations: 1974–1976: A Documentary Record*, 3 vols. (New York University Press, 1977–78).

Robert D. Schulzinger, *Henry Kissinger: Doctor of Diplomacy* (New York: Columbia University Press, 1989), is the best one-volume study of its subject; it is also the best single piece available on Ford's foreign policy. Balanced, judiciously written, using both the Nixon and the Ford papers, Schulzinger's three excellent chapters are the best written on Ford's foreign policy. It should be followed by John Prados, *Keepers of the Keys: A History of the National Security Council from Truman to Bush* (New York: William Morrow, 1991). Broader in scope than his title would suggest, Prados's one chapter on Ford ("A Ford, Not a Lincoln") offers an excellent survey of Ford's foreign policy that is not limited to the actions and decisions of the National Security Council. Walter Isaacson, *Henry Kissinger: A Biography* (New York: Simon and Schuster, 1992), is both readable and quotable; however, Isaacson makes nowhere near as wide a use of the archival record as does Schulzinger. Douglas Kinnard, "James R. Schlesinger as Secretary of Defense," *Naval War College Review* 32 (1979): 22–34, offers a helpful, if glowing, assessment of its subject.

Roderic H. Davison, *Turkey* (Englewood Cliffs, N.J.: Prentice-Hall, 1968), offers strong historical background for the Cyprus-Greece crisis. Roger Morris,

Uncertain Greatness: Henry Kissinger and American Foreign Policy (New York: Harper and Row, 1977), supplements this backgound with a good political history of the September 1974 congressional imposition of the embargo on Turkey. Mohamed El-Khaus and Barry Cohen, eds., *NSSM 39: The Kissinger Study of Southern Africa* (Westport, Conn.: Lawrence Hill and Company, 1976), is a 1969 document with an excellent opening summary that sets a perfect stage for Ford's Angolan and Mozambiquan policy. On the details of the Angolan Civil War, begin with Wayne S. Smith, "A Trap in Angola," *Foreign Policy* (Spring 1986): 61–74. Arthur Jay Klinghoffer, *The Angolan War: A Study of Soviet Policy in the Third World* (Boulder, Colo.: Westview Press, 1980), is a useful discussion that concludes that Angola was an arena for the fighting-out of concerns largely not their own. See also Tad Szulc, *Fidel: A Critical Portrait* (New York: William Morrow, 1986), and Stephen R. Weissman, "CIA Covert Action in Zaire and Angola: Patterns and Consequences," *Political Science Quarterly* 94 (1979): 263–86.

Any of the above-mentioned general works offers an acceptable beginning for a study of U.S.-Soviet relations. For an excellent survey of administration policy from the Soviet point of view, consult Robin Edmonds, *Soviet Foreign Policy: The Brezhnev Years* (New York: Oxford University Press, 1983). See also Harry Gelman, *The Brezhnev Politburo and the Decline of Detente* (Ithaca, N.Y.: Cornell University Press, 1984). For an important comtemporary view of the decline of détente, consult the surprisingly anti-Soviet thesis advanced by former Secretary of Defense Melvin Laird in "Is This Detente?" *Reader's Digest*, July 1975, pp. 54–57. An important scholarly assessment of this development through the Reagan administration is John Lewis Gaddis, "The Rise, Fall, and Failure of Detente," *Foreign Affairs* (Winter 1983): 354–73. Paula Stern, *Water's Edge: Domestic Politics and the Making of American Foreign Policy* (Westport, Conn.: Greenwood Press, 1979), offers a solid chapter on Ford's role in the decline of the détente mentality and is a good place to begin on Soviet emigration and the Jackson-Vanik amendment. Howard M. Sachar, *A History of the Jews in America* (New York: Alfred A. Knopf, 1992), also offers a good synopsis of the history of Jackson-Vanik but misses Ford's political motivation in dealing with the issue. Not so Roger B. Porter, *The U.S.-U.S.S.R. Grain Agreement* (New York: Cambridge University Press, 1984), which discusses an important outgrowth of Nixon's move toward détente and Ford's politically attuned reaction to the situation. Begin a study of SALT II with John Newhouse, *War and Peace in the Nuclear Age* (New York: Alfred A. Knopf, 1989). In the companion book of the PBS series of the same name, Newhouse offers a superb chapter of understandable background on the treaty negotiations.

William B. Quandt, *Decade of Decisions: American Policy toward the Arab-Israeli Conflict, 1967–1976* (Berkeley: University of California Press, 1977) is an excellent survey of its subject and was used with profit in my attempt to sketch out the complexities of Middle Eastern politics and Ford's reassessment of them. Also helpful was George Lenczowski, *American Presidents and the Middle East* (Durham, N.C.: Duke University Press, 1990). Peter Golden, "Max Fisher, Diplomat," *Detroit Free Press Magazine*, 3 May 1992, pp. 6–7ff., clearly outlines the importance of the role played by the Detroit businessman in negotiating with the Israelis. Robert Fisk, *Pity the Nation: The Abduction of Lebanon* (New York: Atheneum Press, 1990), is best on the withdrawal of Americans from that nation and concludes that Ford's actions were purely an election-year stunt. See also Matti Golan, *The Secret Conversations of Henry Kissinger* (New York: Quadrangle/*New York Times* Book Company, 1976), and Janet and John Wallach, *Arafat: In the Eyes of the Beholder* (New York: Lyle Stuart, 1990).

David L. Anderson's chapter, "Gerald R. Ford and the President's War in Vietnam," in *Shadow on the White House: Presidents and the Vietnam War, 1945–1975,* ed. Anderson (Lawrence: University Press of Kansas, 1993), is a useful starting point for the subject and makes excellent use of the available archival material. A more detailed survey is offered by Arnold R. Issacs in the well-written *Without Honor: Defeat in Vietnam and Cambodia* (New York: Vintage Books, 1982). Other good primers include George C. Herring, *America's Longest War: The United States and Vietnam, 1950–1975,* 2d ed. (New York, Alfred A. Knopf, 1986). The standard work on the fate of Cambodia remains William Shawcross, *Sideshow: Kissinger, Nixon, and the Destruction of Cambodia* (New York: Simon and Schuster, 1979).

P. Edward Haley, *Congress and the Fall of South Vietnam and Cambodia* (East Brunswick, N.J.: Associated University Presses, 1983), offers a clearly written account of how Congress dealt with the Ford administration's aid requests. William Appleman Williams, Thomas McCormick, Lloyd Gardner, and Walter LaFeber, eds., *America in Vietnam: A Documentary History* (Garden City, N.Y.: Doubleday, 1985), includes transcripts of a significant portion of that congressional debate. The last eight chapters of Nguyen Tien Hung and Jerrold Schecter's surprisingly balanced *Palace File* (New York: Harper and Row, 1986) pieces together a fascinating insiders' viewpoint of the fall of South Vietnam, based on the secret correspondence between Nixon, Ford, and Thieu. Frank Snepp, *Decent Interval: An Insider's Account of Saigon's Indecent End* (New York: Random House, 1977), offers a work criticizing the embassy for not heeding intelligence reports that the city was going to be overrun.

Several oral histories have contributed a great deal to our understanding of "The Running." They include Larry Englemann, *Tears before the Rain: An Oral History of the Fall of South Vietnam* (New York: Oxford University Press, 1990), and Kim Willenson, ed., *The Bad War: An Oral History of the Vietnam War* (New York: New American Library, 1987). Ellis Cose, *A Nation of Strangers: Prejudice, Politics, and the Populating of America* (New York: William Morrow, 1992), offers a good chapter ("A Legacy of Vietnam") on the problem of the Vietnamese refugees.

Several excellent books have been written on the rescue of the *Mayaguez*. *Time* magazine's Roy Rowan produced an "instant history" of the event (the White House provided him with pictures), *The Four Days of Mayaguez* (New York: W. W. Norton, 1975). Despite the rush to publish, the book is of some substance; Rowan's interviews with each of the crew members led to his writing an adventure story that is better on the actual capture of the ship and the crew's recollections of that moment than it is on the inner-sanctum White House decisionmaking. For that purpose, Rowan's book is supplanted by Richard G. Head,

F. W. Short, and R. C. McFarlane, *Crisis Resolution: Presidential Decision Making in the Mayaguez and Korean Confrontations* (Boulder, Colo.: Westview Press, 1978), which outlines the crisis-management process in the White House Situation Room. Christopher Jon Lamb, *Belief Systems and Decision Making in the Mayaguez Crisis* (Gainesville: University of Florida Press, 1988), is an excellent critique, arguing that instead of being a rescue mission, the operation was punitive. Lamb's book is excerpted in his "Belief Systems and Decision Making in the Mayaguez Crisis," *Presidential Studies Quarterly* 99 (Winter 1984–85): 681–702. Capt. Thomas D. DesBrisbay, "Fourteen Hours on Koh Tang" (USAF Southeast Asia Monograph Series 3, Washington, D.C.: U.S. Government Printing Office, 1975), is the established primary source for the Marine assault on the island.

There are many scholarly studies that dissect this well-documented moment in crisis management. Those observers who view it as a success include Richard E. Neustadt and Ernest R. May, *Thinking in Time: The Uses of History for Decision Makers* (New York: Free Press, 1986), and Michael J. Hamm, "The *Pueblo* and *Mayaguez* Incidents: A Study of Flexible Response and Decision Making," *Asian Survey* 17 (June 1977): 545–55. Those scholars who conclude that the White House was less than forthcoming about its plans and its motives include Dan F. Hahn, "Corrupt Rhetoric: President Ford and the *Mayaguez* Affair," in *Essays in Presidential Rhetoric*, ed. Theodore Windt (Dubuque, Iowa: Kendall-Hunt Publishing Company, 1983); James Nathan, "The *Mayaguez*, Presidential War, and Congressional Senescence," *Intellect* (February 1976): 360–62; and Robert Zutz, "The Recapture of the SS *Mayaguez*: Failure of the Consultation Clause of the War Powers Resolution," *New York University Journal of International Law and Politics* 8 (1976): 457–78.

The introduction to Vojtech Mastny, ed., *Helsinki, Human Rights, and European Security: Analysis and Documentation* (Durham, N.C.: Duke University Press, 1986), is the best short survey of the Conference on Security and Cooperation in Europe (CSCE) available. John J. Maresca, *To Helsinki: The Conference on Security and Cooperation in Europe, 1973–1975* (Durham, N.C.: Duke University Press, 1985), offers the view of a participant in the negotiations. Warren Zimmerman, "Making Moscow Pay the Price for Rights Abuses," *New York Times*, 1 August 1986, p. A27, includes a brief synopsis of the Helsinki Conference and serves as a helpful summary. For an excellent summary of Ford's Eastern European policy post-Helsinki as well as a cogent explanation of the Sonnenfeldt Doctrine, see Leo Ribuffo, "Is Poland a Soviet Satellite? Gerald Ford, the Sonnenfeldt Doctrine, and the Election of 1976," *Diplomatic History* 14 (Summer 1990): 385–403.

On other issues of foreign policy see Millicent Anne Gates, *The Dragon and the Snake: An Account of the Turmoil in China, 1976–1977* (Philadelphia: University of Pennsylvania Press, 1986); Jiuji Kasai, *The New U.S.-Japan Era* (Tokyo: Japan-American Cultural Society, 1976); Daniel P. Moynihan, *A Dangerous Place: Defending America at the UN* (New York: Berkley Books, 1975); Robert D. Putnam, *Hanging Together: The Seven Power Summits* (Cambridge: Harvard University Press, 1984); Paul B. Ryan, *The Panama Canal Controversy: U.S. Diplomacy and Defense Interests* (Stanford, Calif.: Hoover Institution Press, 1977); and Robert G.

Sutter, *China-Watch: Toward Sino-American Reconciliation* (Baltimore: Johns Hopkins University Press, 1978).

An invaluable reference source for a study of the 1976 presidential election is U.S. Congress, House, Committee on House Administration, *The Presidential Campaign, 1976*, 2 vols. (Washington, D.C.: U.S. Government Printing Office, 1978–79). Impeccably indexed, this collection of speeches by both candidates is arranged by subject. Volume 1 deals with Carter; volume 2 with Ford; volume 3 offers a complete transcript of the three presidential debates and the vice-presidential one. The best primer on the election is David Chagall, *The New Kingmakers* (New York: Harcourt Brace Jovanovich, 1981); his chapter, "How Carter Won," is a strong summary of both Ford's and Carter's campaigns. Robert Shogan, *None of the Above: Why Presidents Fail—and What Can Be Done about It* (New York: New American Library, 1982), offers a prescient view of the role that the candidates' characters played in their election fortunes.

On the whole, the primaries held much more fascination for journalists writing on the 1976 election than did the fall campaign. Jules Witcover, *Marathon: The Pursuit of the Presidency, 1972–1976* (New York: Viking Press, 1977), is well written and interesting, but he includes 542 pages on the prefall campaign and only 114 pages on the fall campaign. Elizabeth Drew, *American Journal: The Events of 1976* (New York: Random House, 1976), offers fascinating anecdotes but again less than one-quarter of the book deals with the fall campaign. Theodore H. White, *America in Search of Itself: The Making of the President, 1956–1980* (New York: Harper and Row, 1982), is much less satisfying than any of his earlier works; however, his analysis on the impact of inflation on the campaign is excellent. Other studies of the campaign include Alexander P. Lamis, *The Two-Party South* (New York: Oxford University Press, 1984); David Howell et al., *Gentlemanly Attitudes: Jerry Ford and the Campaign of '76* (Washington, D.C.: HKJV Publications, 1980); David W. Moore, *The Super Pollsters: How They Measure and Manipulate Public Opinion in America* (New York: Four Walls Eight Windows, 1992); and Jonathan Moore and Janet Fraser, eds., *Campaign for President: The Managers Look at '76* (Cambridge, Mass: Belinger Publishing Company, 1977).

Ronald Reagan does not appear to be interested in reliving the 1976 campaign. In *An American Life: The Autobiography* (New York: Simon and Schuster, 1990), he includes all of three pages on the entirety of the 1976 election; his *Speaking My Mind: Selected Speeches* (New York: Simon & Schuster, 1989) includes no speeches from 1976. Turn instead to Lou Cannon, *Reagan* (New York: G. P. Putnam's Sons, 1982), and to Gary Paul Gates and Bob Schieffer, *The Acting President* (New York: E. P. Dutton, 1989), for excellent analyses of the role of John Sears in the Reagan candidacy. In his chapter "The Sears Interregnum," Garry Wills, *Innocents at Home: Reagan's America* (Garden City, N.Y.: Doubleday, 1987), blames Sears, and particularly the Schweiker decision, for Reagan's defeat. Also helpful on Reagan's developing ideology is F. Clifton White, *Why Reagan Won: A Narrative History of the Conservative Movement, 1964–1980* (Chicago: Regnery Gateway, 1981). Two excellent memoirs that shed light on both sides of the primary race are Harry S. Dent, *The Prodigal South Returns to Power* (New York: John Wiley and Sons, 1977), and Peter Hannaford, *The Reagans: A*

Political Portrait (New York: Coward and McCann, 1983). On specific issues in the primaries, see Lansing Lamott, "Ready on the Right—Bo Callaway Commences Firing in the 1976 Campaign," *People Weekly*, 11 August 1975, pp. 14–15, and Farley Yang, "Turning a Runaway into a Race: The Role of Foreign Policy Issues in the 1976 Republican Primaries," *Michigan Journal of Political Science* 7 (Fall 1986): 108–28. Bob Dole gives his view on being chosen as Ford's running mate in Bob and Elizabeth Dole, *The Doles: Unlimited Partners* (New York: Simon and Schuster, 1988). A better analysis of the Dole campaign, however, comes from his press secretary, Larry Speakes, *Speaking Out: The Reagan Presidency from Inside the White House* (New York: Avon Books, 1988). On the financing of Ford's campaigns, the definitive work is Herbert E. Alexander, *Financing the 1976 Election* (Washington, D.C.: Congressional Quarterly Press, 1979).

A full study of the literature of the Carter campaign has been included in the bibliographical essay found in Burton I. Kaufman, *The Presidency of James Earl Carter* (Lawrence: University of Kansas Press, 1993). My study also profited from Robert Shogan, *Promises to Keep: Carter's First 100 Days* (New York: Thomas Y. Crowell Company, 1977), and Martin Schram, *Running for President, 1976: The Carter Campaign* (New York: Stein and Day, 1977).

Malcolm MacDougall, *We Almost Made It* (New York: Crown Publishers, 1977), is the only published primary source dealing exclusively with the Ford campaign and his advertising. A more scholarly assessment of Ford's advertising is found in the standard work in the field, Kathleen Hall Jamieson, *Packaging the Presidency: A History and Criticism of Presidential Campaign Advertising* (New York: Oxford University Press, 1984). See also L. Patrick Devlin, "Contrasts in Presidential Campaign Commercials of 1976," *Central States Speech Journal* 28 (1977): 238–49; L. Patrick Devlin, "President Ford's Ad Man Reviews the 1976 Media Campaign [Interview with Doug Bailey]," *Indiana Speech Journal* 13 (Apr. 1978): 14–28; and Vic Gold, *PR as in President* (Garden City, N.Y.: Doubleday, 1977). The most prescient analysis of the role of the press in the campaign can be found in Tom Wicker, *On Press*.

Not surprisingly, the televised Ford-Carter debates have received the lion's share of scholarly analysis written about the campaign. Begin with the short summary of the debates found in Edward Hinck, *Enacting the Presidency: Political Argument, Presidential Debates and Presidential Character* (Westport, Conn.: Praeger, 1993). For more detail, consult the strong collection of articles, usually written by participants, in Sidney Kraus, ed., *The Great Debates: Carter vs. Ford, 1976* (Bloomington: Indiana University Press, 1979). Of the many scholarly assessments, particularly of the climactic second debate on foreign policy, the most thought-provoking are Goodwyn Berquist and Kevin Sauter's chapters in *Rhetorical Studies of National Political Debates: 1960–1988*, ed. Robert V. Friedenberg (Westport, Conn.: Praeger, 1990); Lloyd F. Bitzer and Theodore Rueter, *Carter vs. Ford: The Counterfeit Debates of 1976* (Madison: University of Wisconsin Press, 1980); Lev E. Dobriansky, "The Unforgettable Ford Gaffe," *Ukranian Quarterly* 3 (1977): 366–77; and Robert K. Tiemens, "Television's Portrayal of the 1976 Presidential Debates: An Analysis of Visual Content," *Communications Monographs* 45 (1978): 362–70.

Those interested in keeping pace with the rapidly growing literature on the Ford administration should consult the *Gerald R. Ford Foundation Newsletter*, published quarterly by the GFL in conjunction with the Gerald R. Ford Foundation, Grand Rapids, Michigan.

INDEX

Holtzman, Elizabeth, 183; and Hungate Committee, 57–58
Hoover, Herbert, 4
House of Representatives, U.S., 121; Appropriations Committee, 3, 68, 91; Armed Services Committee, and the CIA, 102; Banking and Currency Committee (Patman Committee), 9–11, 182; Black Caucus, 55, 89; Democratic Caucus, 58; and détente with USSR, 122; Judiciary Committee, 88; Judiciary Committee, and Ford's confirmation as vice-president, 10, 12–13; Judiciary Committee, and impeachment of Nixon, 14–15; Judiciary Committee, and Rockefeller's confirmation as vice president, 31; Judiciary Committee, Subcommittee on Criminal Justice (Hungate Committee), 45, 56–58, 101; Republican Conference (Caucus), 5; Select Committee on Intelligence, 112; Ways and Means Committee, 76
Housing policy, of Ford, 77, 85
Humor and the Presidency (Ford), 167
Humphrey, Hubert, 6
Hungate, William L., 56
Hungate Committee. *See* House of Representatives, Judiciary Committee, Subcommittee on Criminal Justice
Hussein, King of Jordan, 127

Inauguration: of Ford as president, 16–17, 34; of Ford as vice president, 13
India, 88, 90
Indonesia, and capture of the *Mayaguez*, 144
Inflation. *See* Economic policy
Inflation summit (September 1974), 61, 71
Intelligence Coordinating Group (ICG), 111
Intelligence operations. *See* CIA
Intelligence Oversight Board (IOB), 115
Intercontinental Ballistic Missiles (ICBMs), and SALT II, 124, 125
Interior, Department of, 70; and Economic Policy Board, 69
Internal Revenue Service, and Nixon papers, 51
Israel: and Ford administration "reassessment" of Middle East policy, 128–29, 144, 153–55; and Lebanese civil war, 168–69; and Nixon administration, 126–27; and Sinai I Accord, 127; and Sinai II Accord, 128–29, 153–55; and Yom Kippur War, 68, 126

Jackson, Henry: and détente, 121–23; and election of 1976, 122; Ford on, 123; and Helsinki Summit, 153; and Jackson-Vanik amendment, 122–23; and oil tariff, 77, 101; and SALT, 124, 125–26; and Vietnam War, 122
Jackson-Kennedy bill (February 1974, on oil tariffs), 77, 78, 101
Jackson-Vanik amendment, 122–23, 152
Jacobs, Andrew, 7
Jarriel, Tom, 63
Javits, Jacob, 123, 137
Jaworski, Leon, 47, 57; and pardon of Nixon, 51–52
Jews: and the Holocaust, 139; and Jackson-Vanik amendment, 122–23; and Stevenson amendment, 123
Johnson, Lyndon, 20, 22, 23, 102; and civil rights, 86; and common situs picketing, 96; and election of 1964, 5; on Ford, 6, 61; and investigation of the CIA, 106; and Operation CHAOS, 104; and Panama Canal, 164; and seizure of the *Pueblo*, 144; and Vietnam War, 122, 165; and Warren Commission, appointment of Ford to, 5
Joint Chiefs of Staff (JCS), 101, 108, 148
Jones, Jerry, 26–27, 159
Jonkman, Bartel, 3
Jordan, James, 168
Jordan, 127, 168. *See also* Sinai I Accord; Sinai II Accord
Juilliard School of Music, 69
Jupiter missiles, and Turkey, 118
Justice, Department of, 183; and Boston busing crisis, 88–90; and clemency program for Vietnam era draft evaders, 40–42; and Patman Committee investigation, 11

Katzenbach, Nicholas De B., 106
Kelley, Clarence: charged with impropriety, 179–80; and MEBA probe, 181. *See also* FBI
Kennedy, Edward M.: and Boston busing crisis, 87; and oil tariff, 77, 101
Kennedy, Jacqueline, 34
Kennedy, John, 5, 65, 70, 121; assassination of, 5, 34, 108; and CIA assassination plots, 103–4, 108; and civil rights, 86; and common situs picketing, 96; debates with Nixon, 181; and election of 1960, 4, 181
Kennedy, Robert F., and CIA assassination plots, 108

Whyte, William: charged with impropriety (1976), 180; and second transition team to Ford presidency, 25–26
Wicker, Tom, 107
Wickham, Gen. John A., and *Mayaguez*, 145, 147
Widnall, William R., 10
Will, George, 31, 108
Williams, Edward Bennett, 182
Wills, Garry, 172
Wilson, and capture of the *Mayaguez*, 149
Wilson, Woodrow, 175
Wirth, Timothy, 58
Witcover, Jules, 179
Women's issues, 33–34, 99
Woodcock, Leonard, 3
Woodward, Bob, 61, 63

World War II, 20, 38, 103, 111, 152, 184, 192; and American balance of powers, 53; and Ford, 2–3

Yale University, 2
Yalta Conference (1945), 120, 126, 153
Yom Kippur War (1973), 20, 68, 113, 120, 126. *See also* Egypt; Israel
Young Turks (Republican party), 5, 25, 41
Yugoslavia, 166

Zaire, and Angolan Civil War, 113
Zarb, Frank, 70, 74, 78, 79; background of, 70; on oil decontrol, 77
Ziegler, Ronald, 50–51, 64. *See also* Press, and Nixon